Cutie and the BEAST

story & art by
YUHI AZUMI

Contents

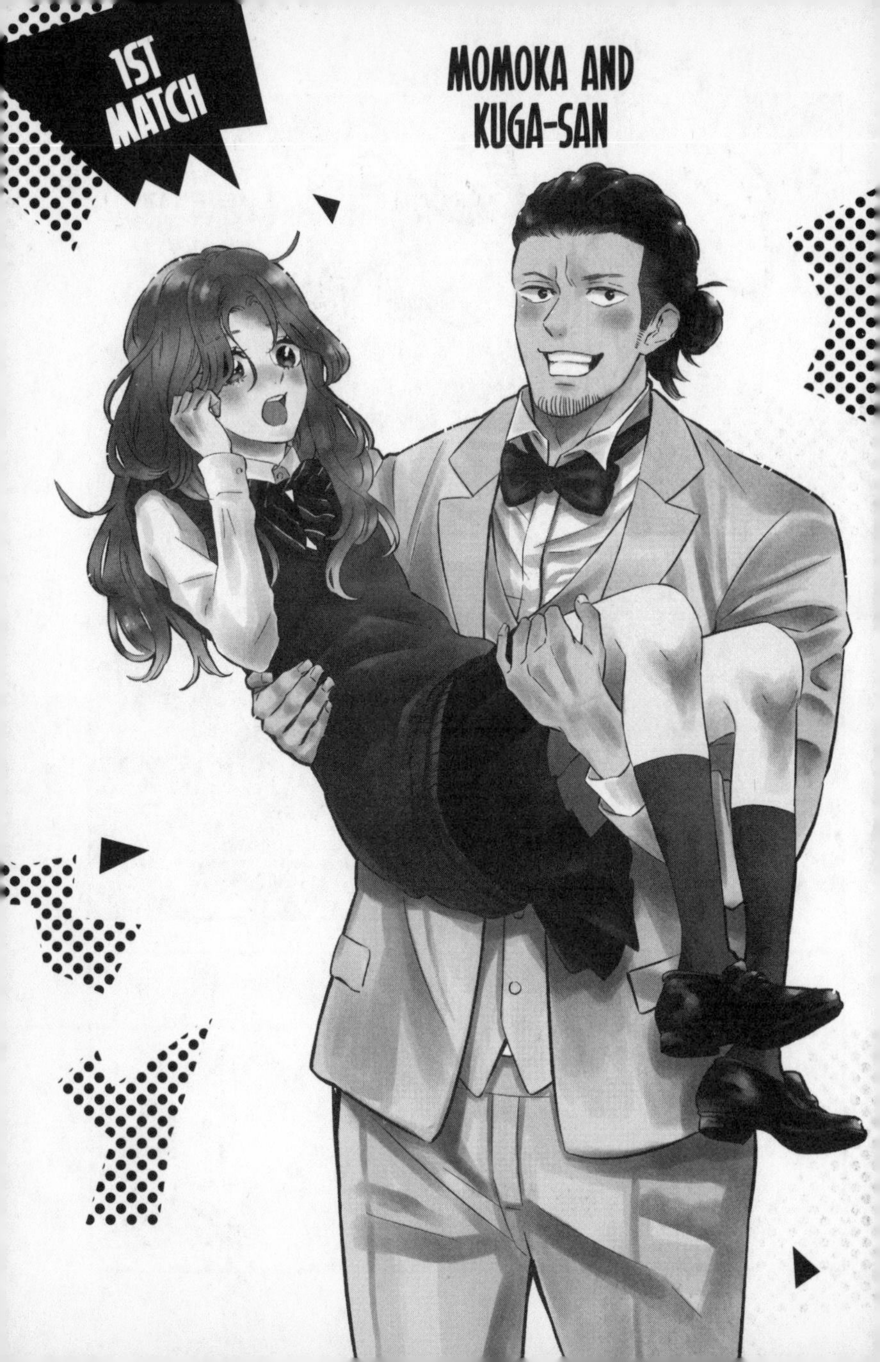
1ST MATCH
MOMOKA AND KUGA-SAN

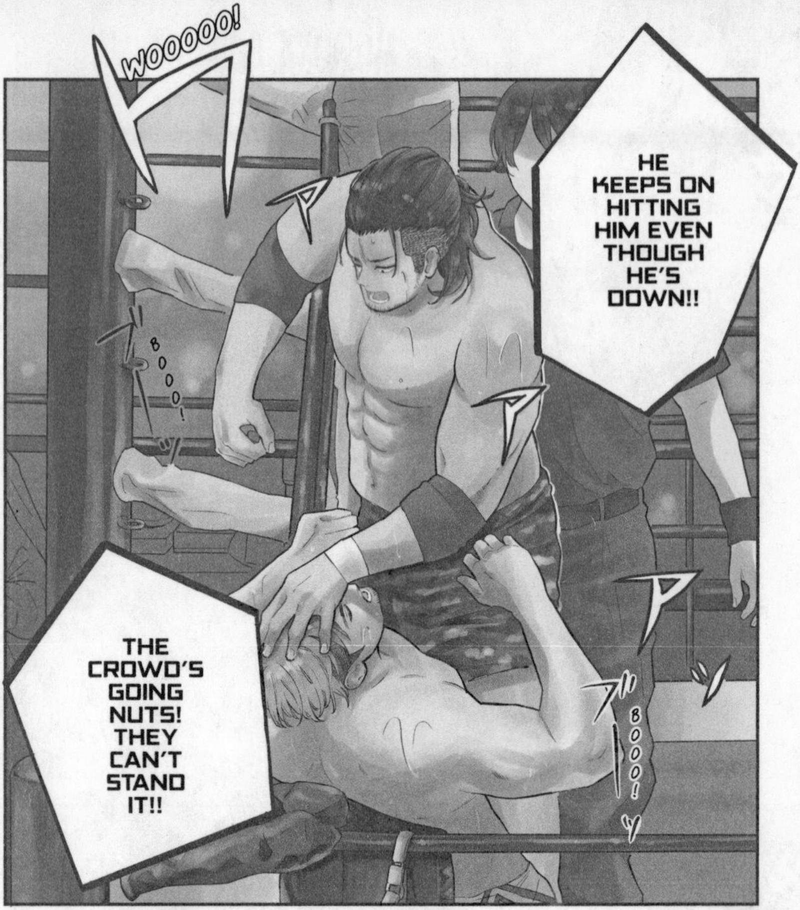
HE KEEPS ON HITTING HIM EVEN THOUGH HE'S DOWN!!
WOOOOO!
BOOOO!
THE CROWD'S GOING NUTS! THEY CAN'T STAND IT!!
BOOOO!

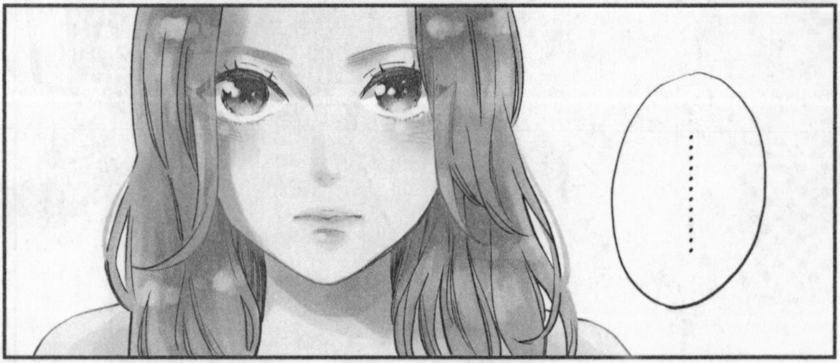
……

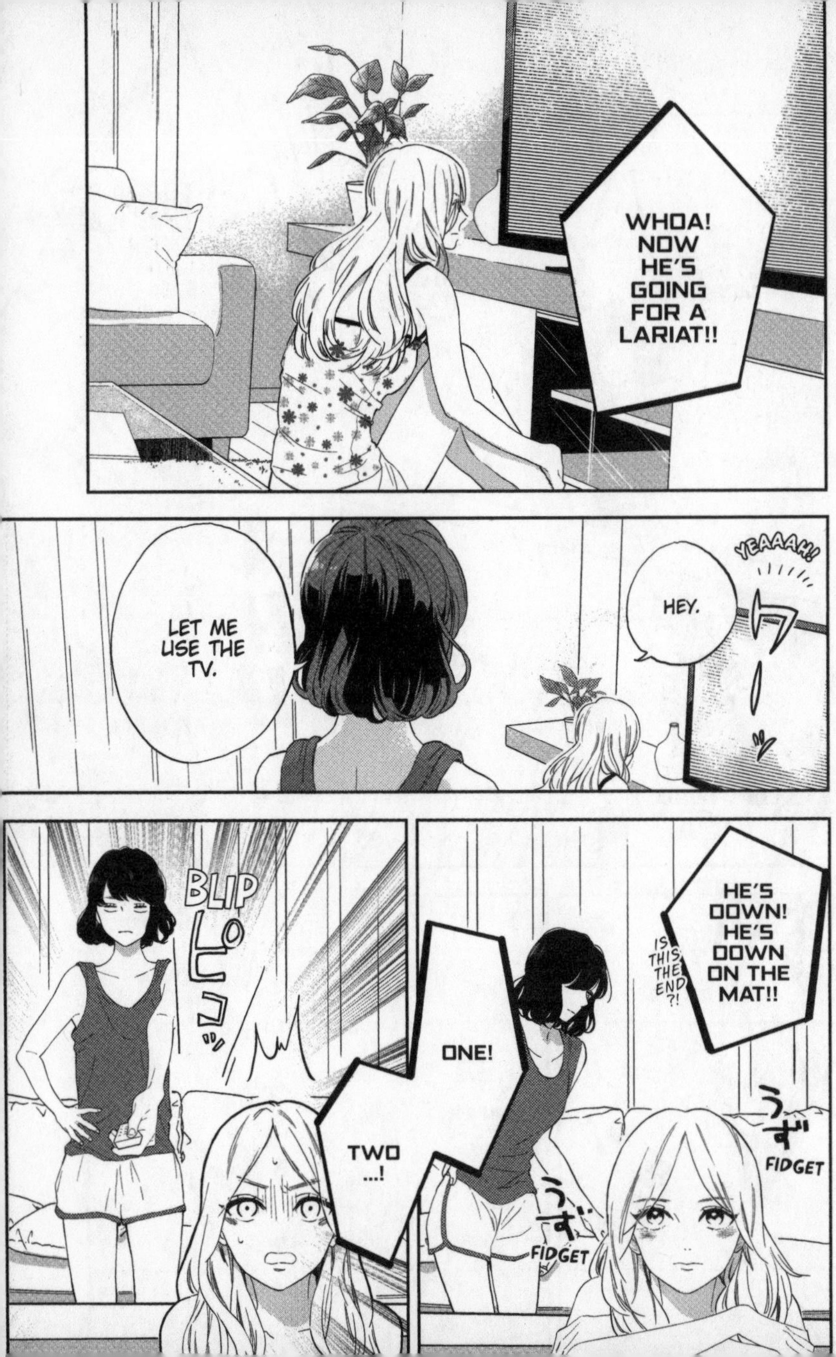
WHOA! NOW HE'S GOING FOR A LARIAT!!
YEAAAH!
ワー
HEY.
LET ME USE THE TV.
HE'S DOWN! HE'S DOWN ON THE MAT!!
IS THIS THE END?!
うず
FIDGET
うず
FIDGET
ONE!
TWO ...!
BLIP
ピコッ

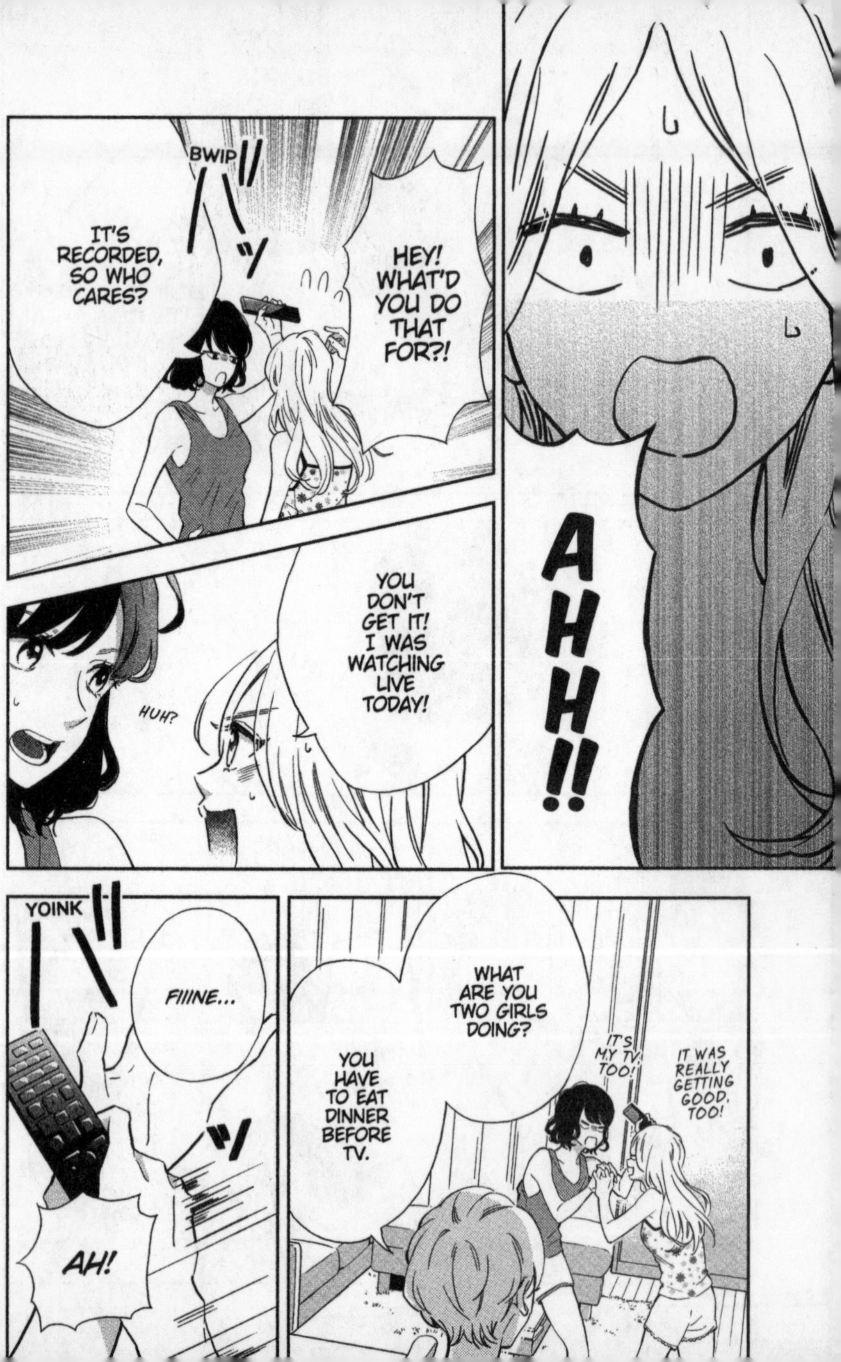
AHHH!!
BWIP
HEY! WHAT'D YOU DO THAT FOR?!
IT'S RECORDED, SO WHO CARES?
YOU DON'T GET IT! I WAS WATCHING LIVE TODAY!
HUH?
IT WAS REALLY GETTING GOOD, TOO!
IT'S MY TV TOO!
WHAT ARE YOU TWO GIRLS DOING?
YOU HAVE TO EAT DINNER BEFORE TV.
FIIINE...
YOINK
AH!

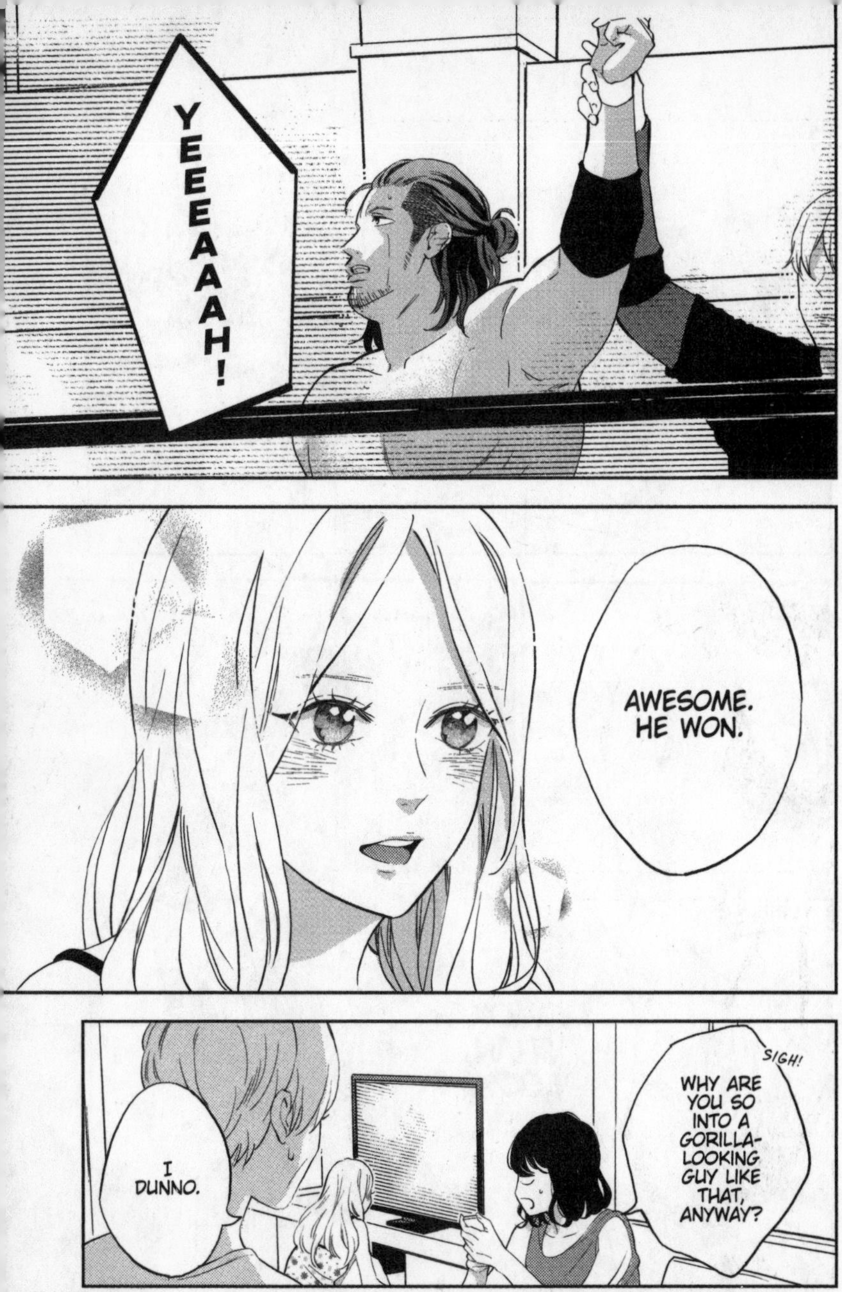
YEEEAAAH!
AWESOME. HE WON.
SIGH!
WHY ARE YOU SO INTO A GORILLA-LOOKING GUY LIKE THAT, ANYWAY?
I DUNNO.

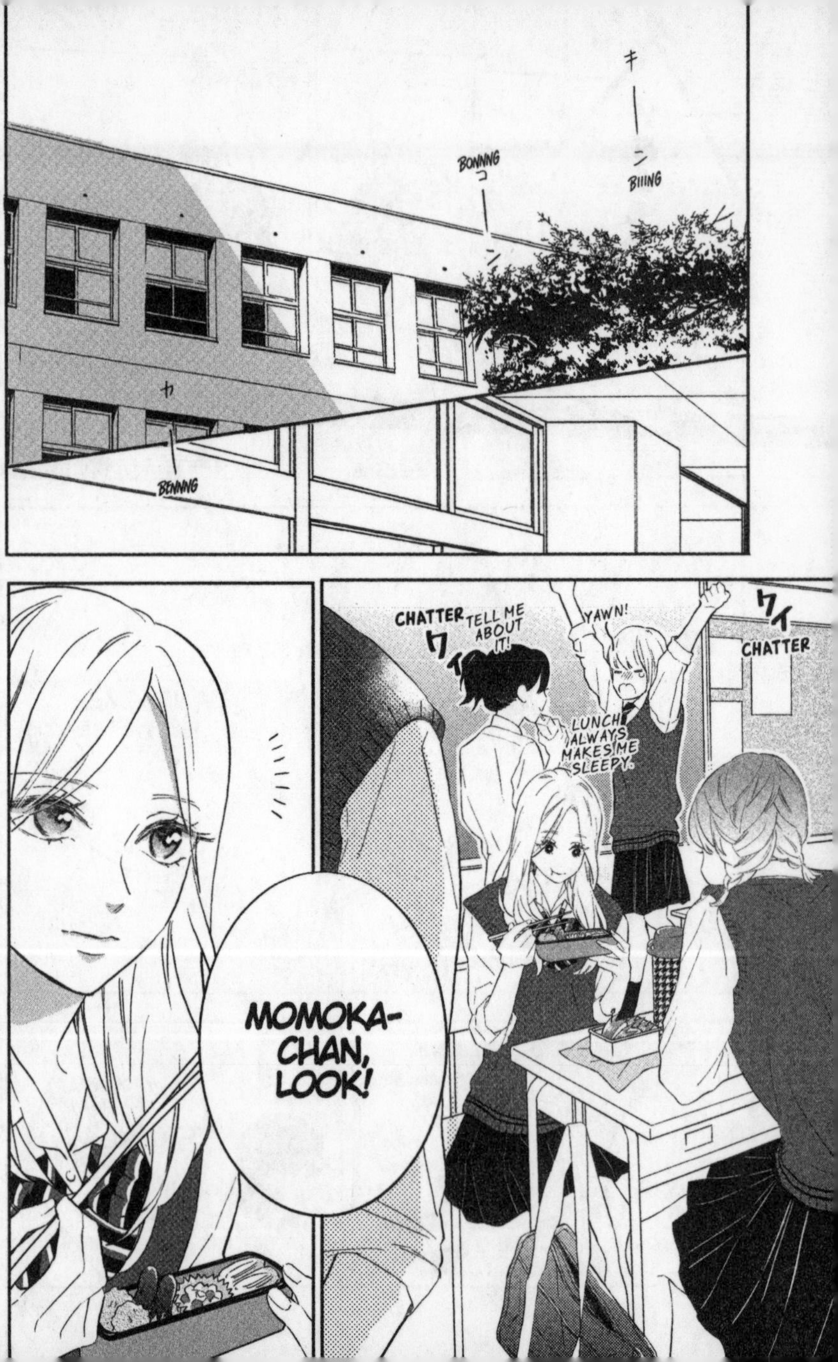
キーン
BIIING
コーン
BONNNG
カーン
BENNNG
ワイ
CHATTER
YAWN!
LUNCH ALWAYS MAKES ME SLEEPY.
TELL ME ABOUT IT!
CHATTER
ワイ
MOMOKA-CHAN, LOOK!

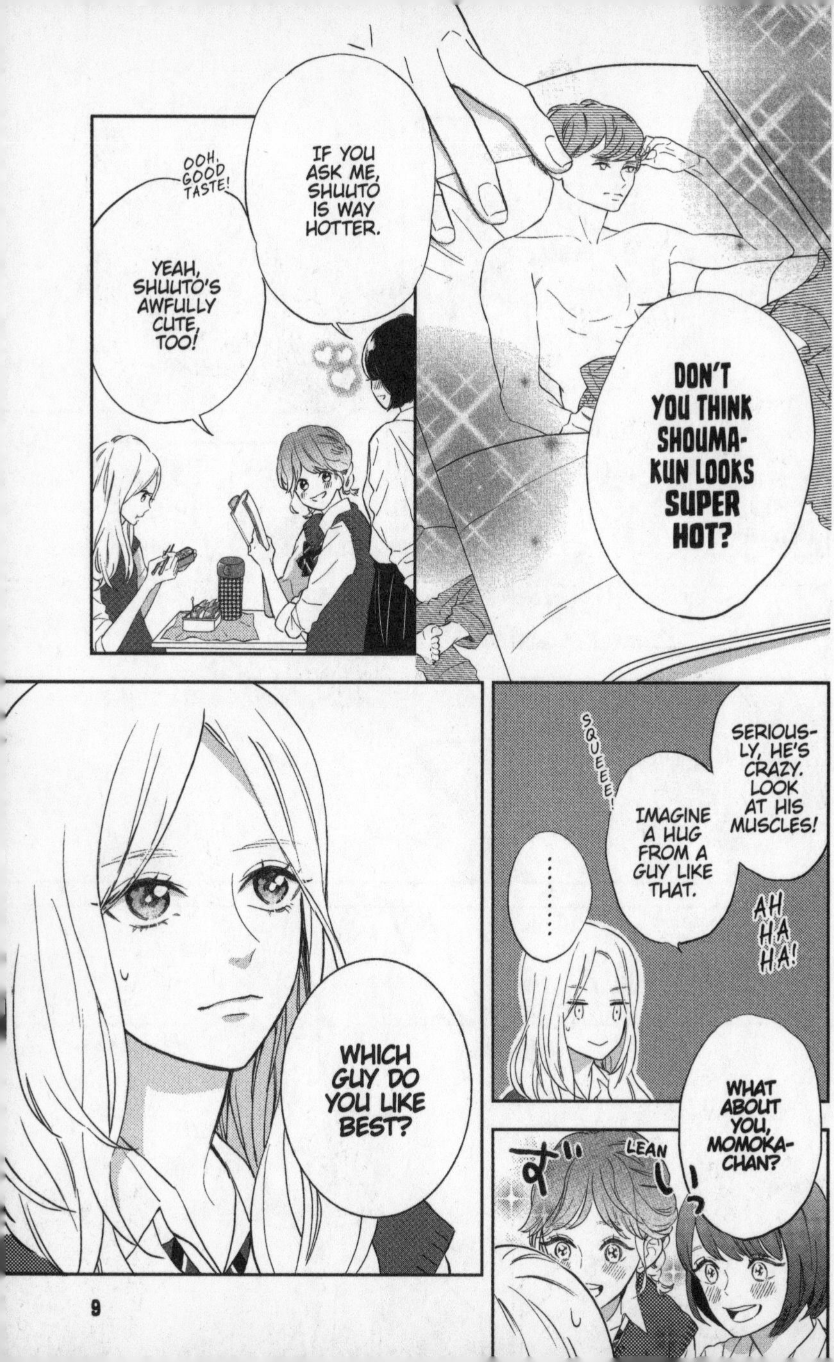
DON'T YOU THINK SHOUMA-KUN LOOKS SUPER HOT?
IF YOU ASK ME, SHUUTO IS WAY HOTTER.
OOH, GOOD TASTE!
YEAH, SHUUTO'S AWFULLY CUTE, TOO!
SERIOUS-LY, HE'S CRAZY. LOOK AT HIS MUSCLES!
SQUEEEE!
IMAGINE A HUG FROM A GUY LIKE THAT.
AH HA HA!
......
WHAT ABOUT YOU, MOMOKA-CHAN?
LEAN
すいっ
WHICH GUY DO YOU LIKE BEST?

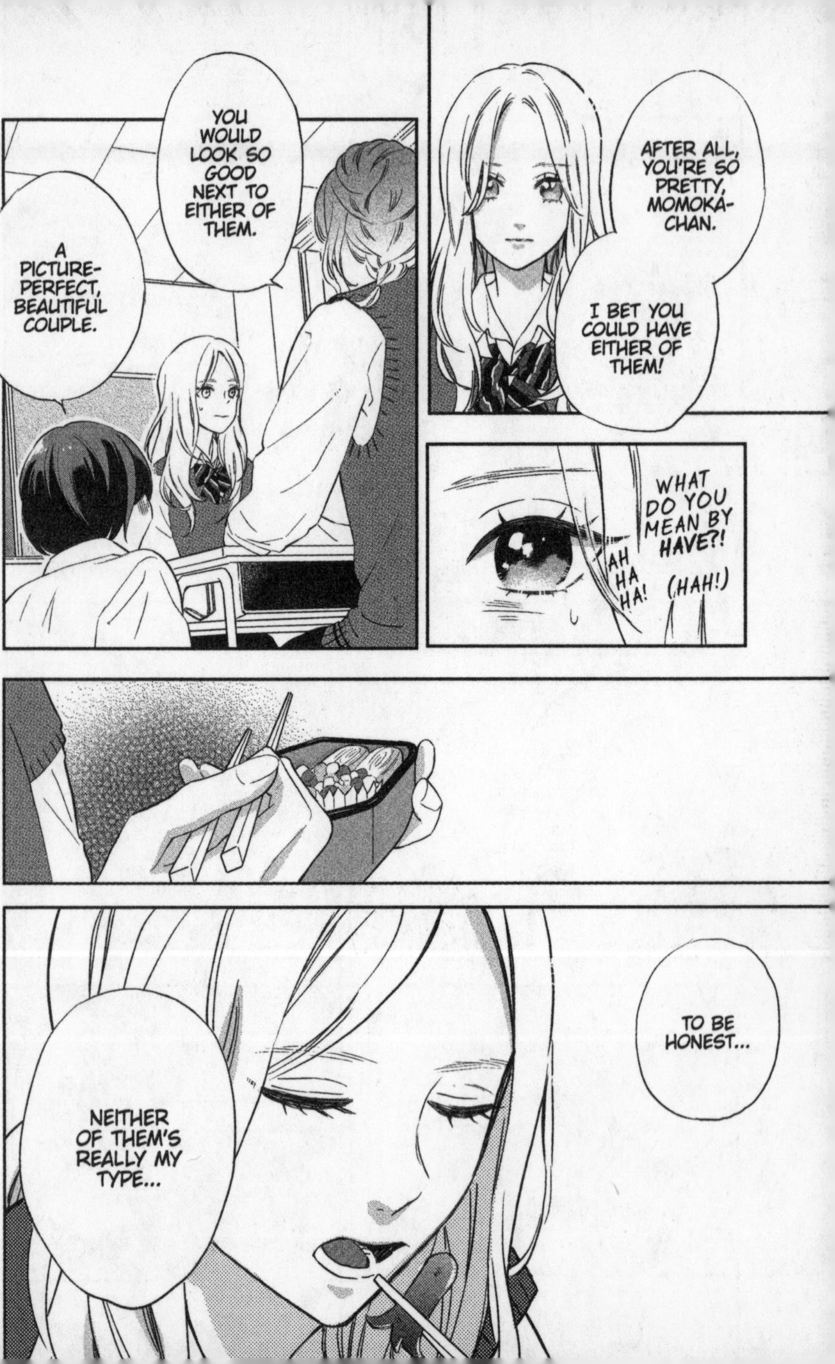
AFTER ALL, YOU'RE SO PRETTY, MOMOKA-CHAN.
I BET YOU COULD HAVE EITHER OF THEM!
WHAT DO YOU MEAN BY HAVE?!
(HAH!)
AH HA HA!
YOU WOULD LOOK SO GOOD NEXT TO EITHER OF THEM.
A PICTURE-PERFECT, BEAUTIFUL COUPLE.
TO BE HONEST...
NEITHER OF THEM'S REALLY MY TYPE...

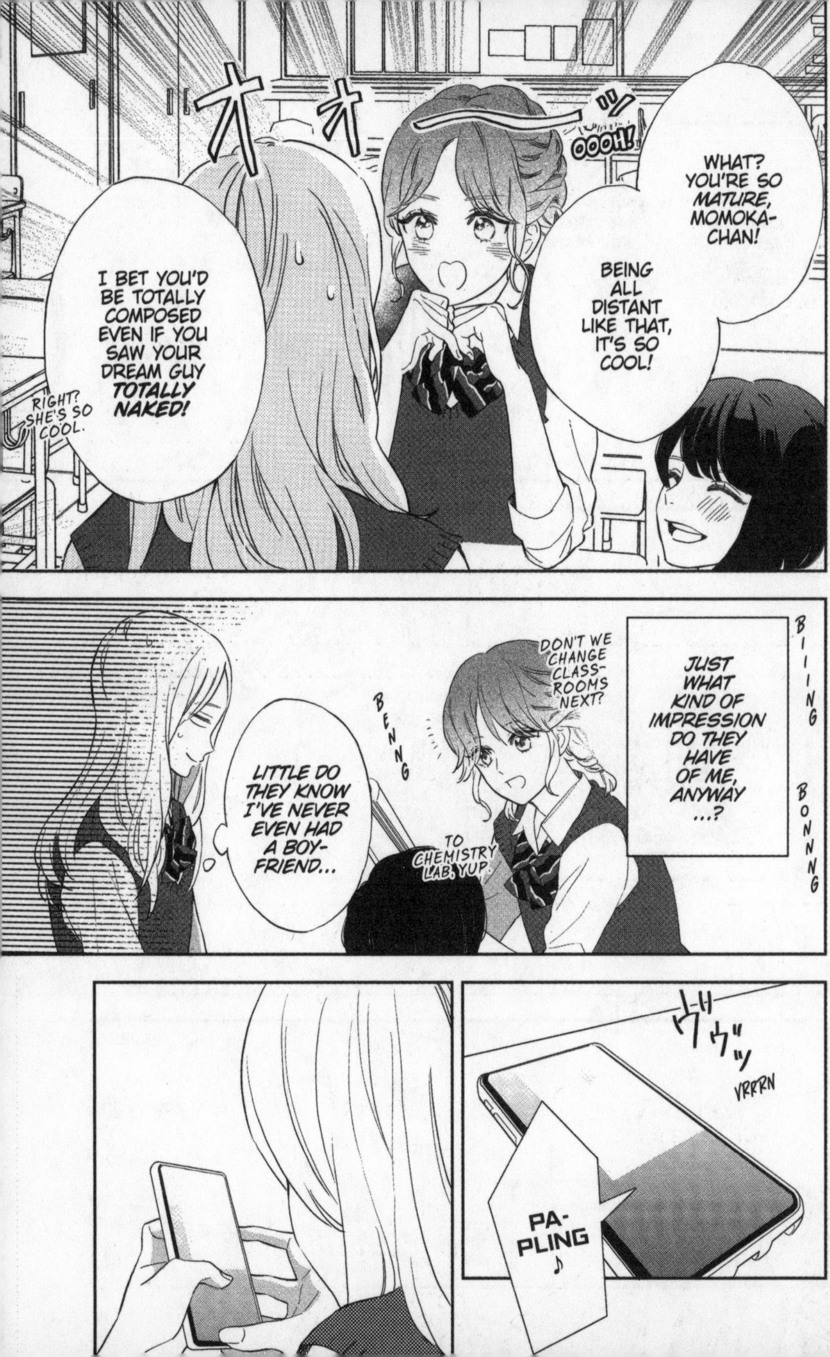
オオーッ
OOOH!
WHAT? YOU'RE SO *MATURE,* MOMOKA-CHAN!
BEING ALL DISTANT LIKE THAT, IT'S SO COOL!
I BET YOU'D BE TOTALLY COMPOSED EVEN IF YOU SAW YOUR DREAM GUY **TOTALLY NAKED!**
RIGHT? SHE'S SO COOL.
BIIING
BONNNG
JUST WHAT KIND OF IMPRESSION DO THEY HAVE OF ME, ANYWAY ...?
DON'T WE CHANGE CLASS-ROOMS NEXT?
BENNG
TO CHEMISTRY LAB, YUP.
LITTLE DO THEY KNOW I'VE NEVER EVEN HAD A BOY-FRIEND...
ヴヴッ
VRRRN
PA-PLING ♪

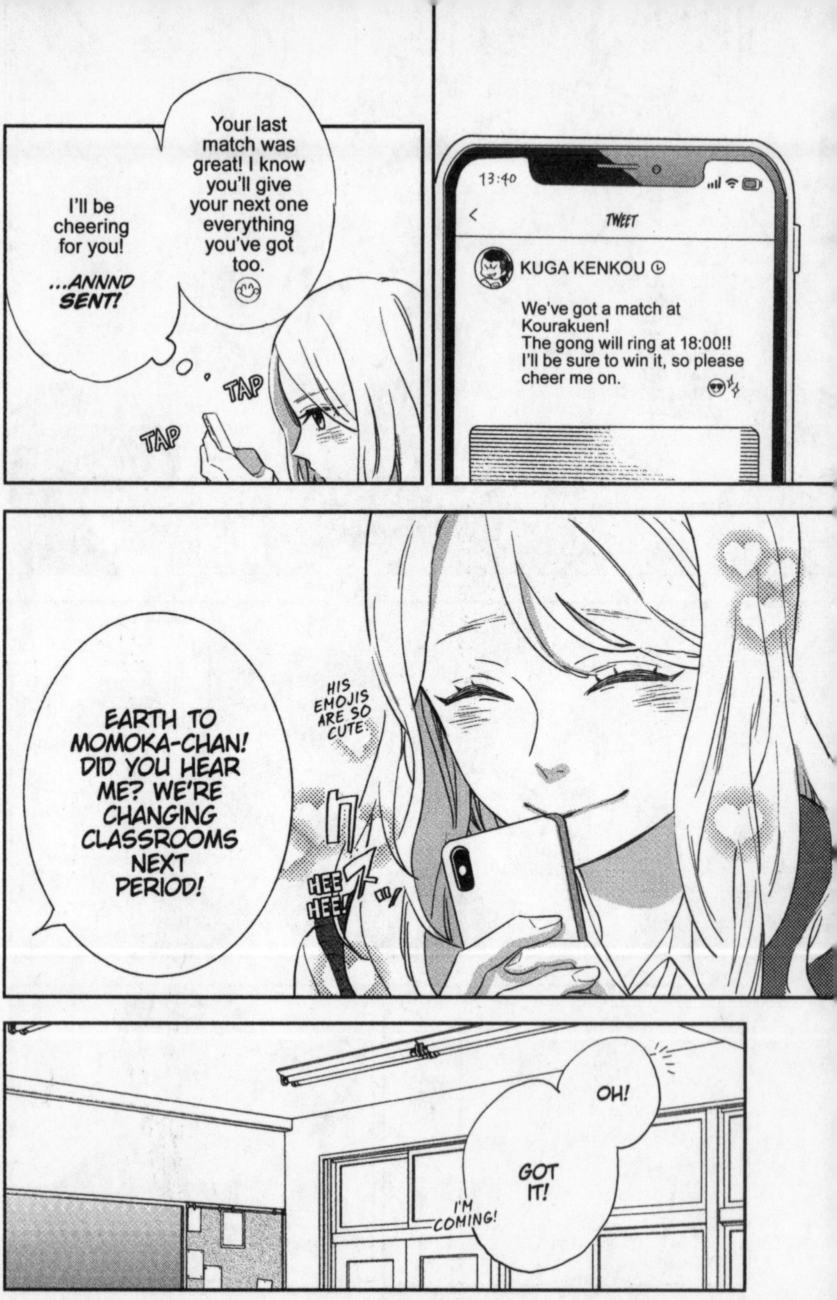
13:40
TWEET
KUGA KENKOU
We've got a match at Kourakuen!
The gong will ring at 18:00!!
I'll be sure to win it, so please cheer me on.
Your last match was great! I know you'll give your next one everything you've got too.
I'll be cheering for you!
...ANNND SENT!
TAP
TAP
HIS EMOJIS ARE SO CUTE.
HEE HEE!
EARTH TO MOMOKA-CHAN! DID YOU HEAR ME? WE'RE CHANGING CLASSROOMS NEXT PERIOD!
OH!
GOT IT!
I'M COMING!

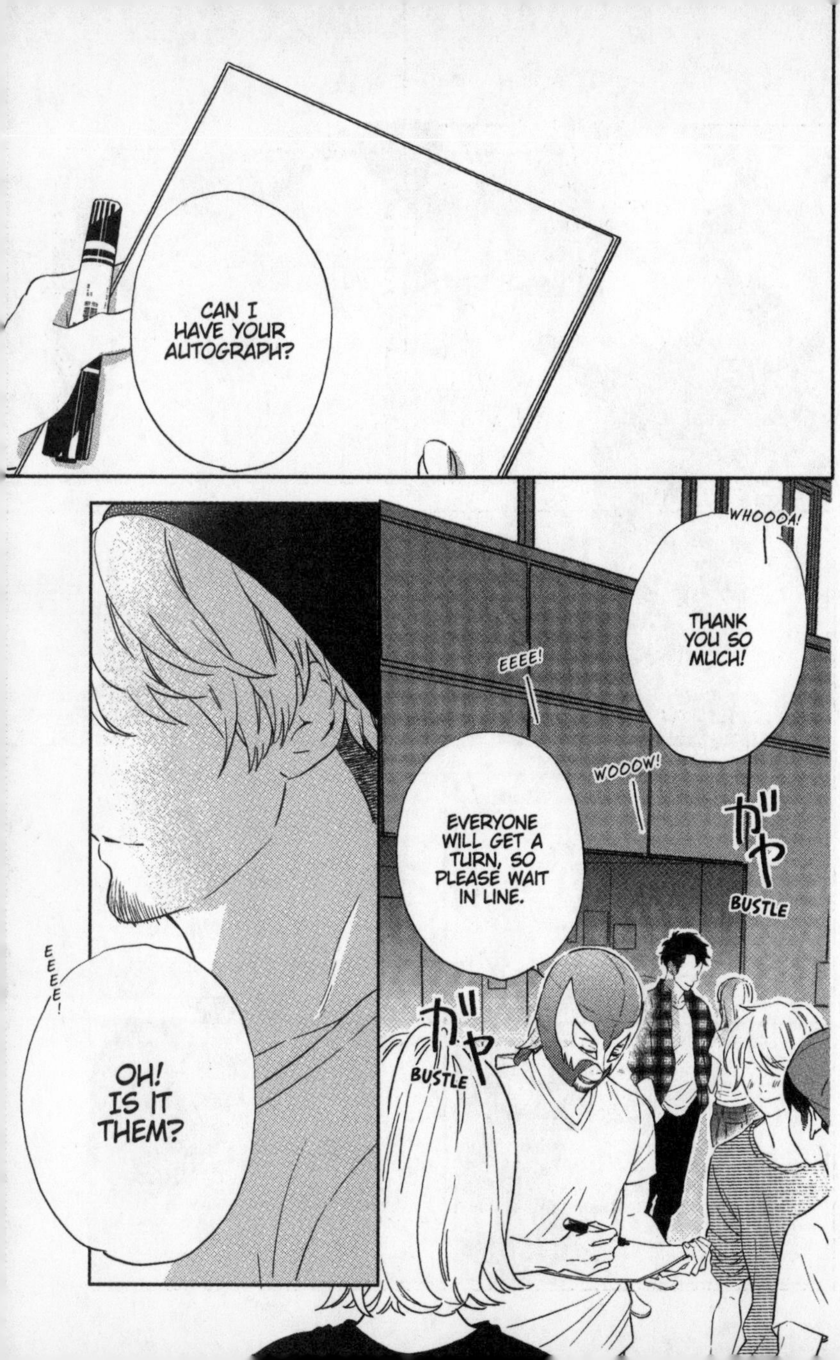
CAN I HAVE YOUR AUTOGRAPH?
WHOOOA!
THANK YOU SO MUCH!
EEEE!
WOOOW!
ガヤ
BUSTLE
EVERYONE WILL GET A TURN, SO PLEASE WAIT IN LINE.
ガヤ
BUSTLE
EEEE!
OH! IS IT THEM?

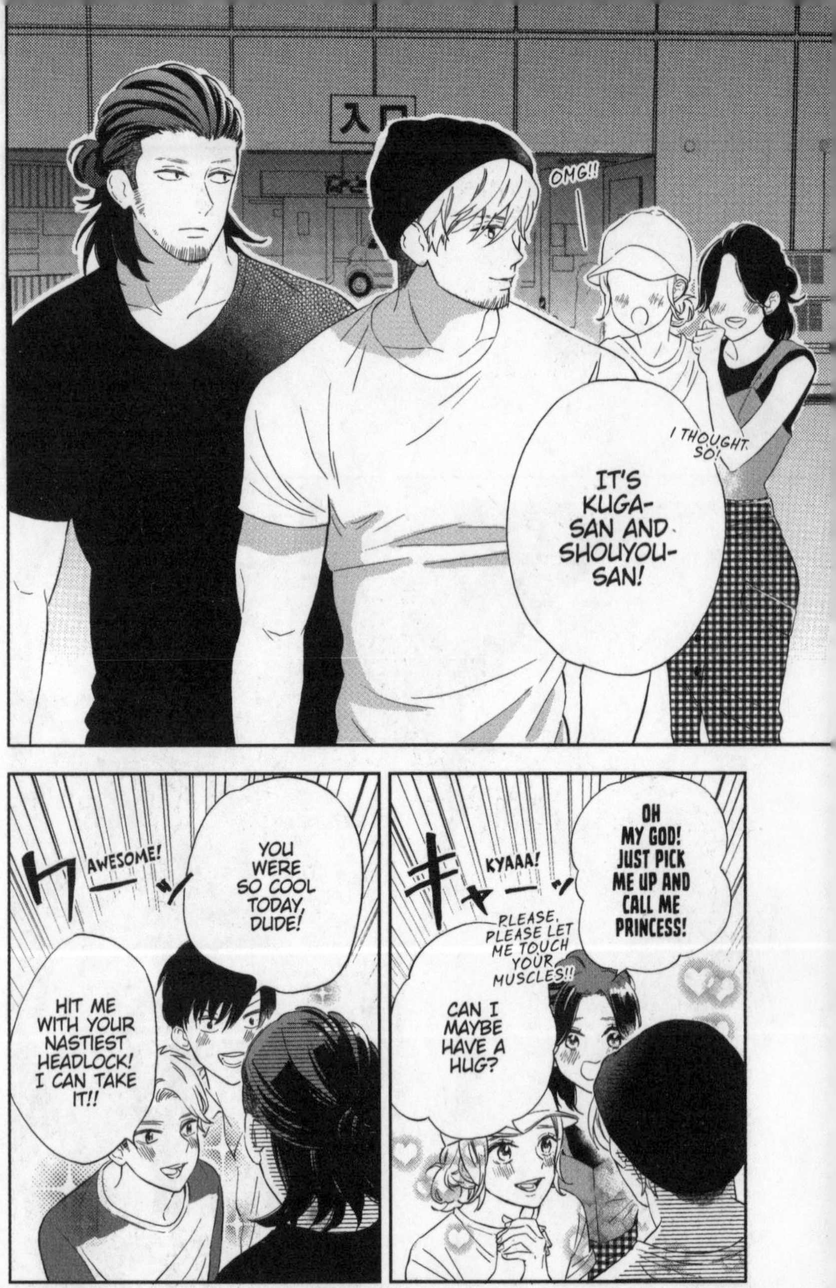
入口
OMG!!
I THOUGHT SO!
IT'S KUGA-SAN AND SHOUYOU-SAN!
OH MY GOD! JUST PICK ME UP AND CALL ME PRINCESS!
KYAAA!
PLEASE, PLEASE LET ME TOUCH YOUR MUSCLES!!
CAN I MAYBE HAVE A HUG?
YOU WERE SO COOL TODAY, DUDE!
AWESOME!
HIT ME WITH YOUR NASTIEST HEADLOCK! I CAN TAKE IT!!

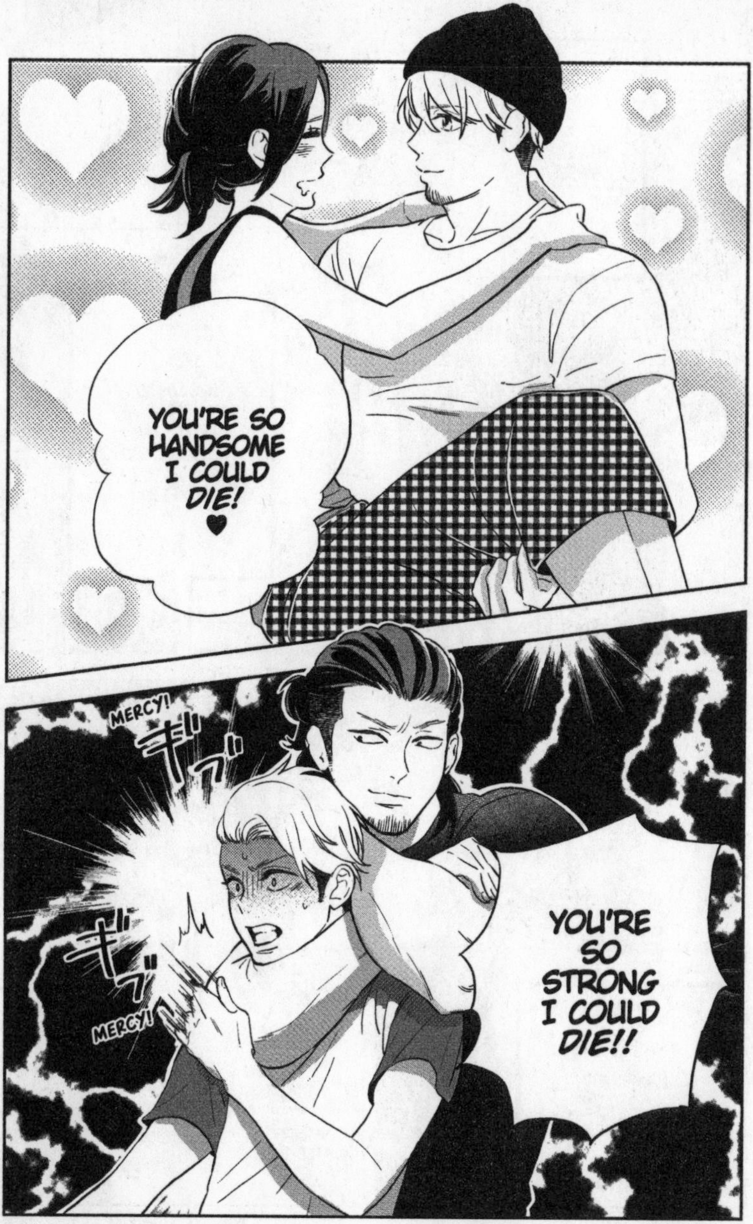
YOU'RE SO HANDSOME I COULD DIE! ♥
YOU'RE SO STRONG I COULD DIE!!
MERCY!
MERCY!

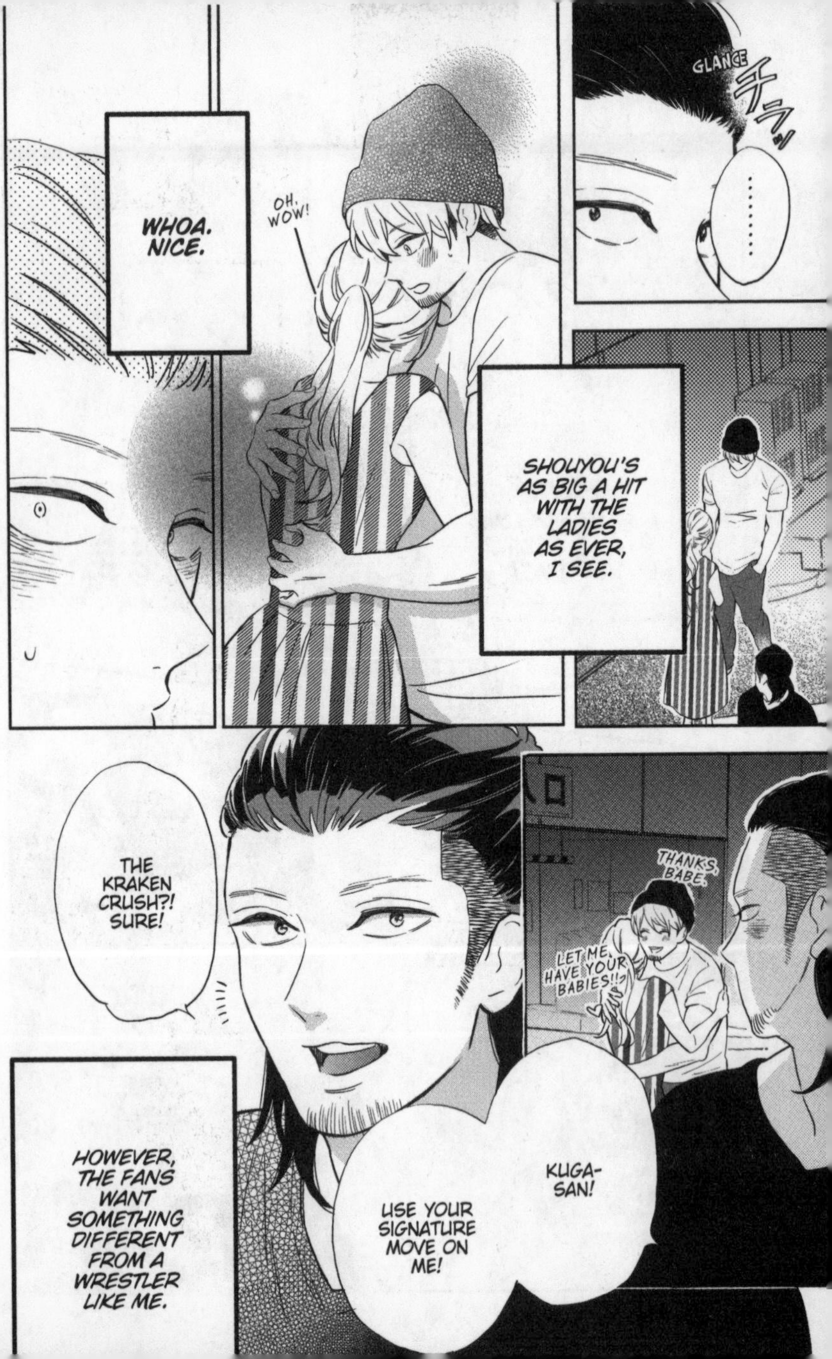
GLANCE
チラッ
......
SHOUYOU'S AS BIG A HIT WITH THE LADIES AS EVER, I SEE.
OH, WOW!
WHOA. NICE.
THANKS, BABE.
LET ME HAVE YOUR BABIES!!
KUGA-SAN!
USE YOUR SIGNATURE MOVE ON ME!
THE KRAKEN CRUSH?! SURE!
HOWEVER, THE FANS WANT SOMETHING DIFFERENT FROM A WRESTLER LIKE ME.

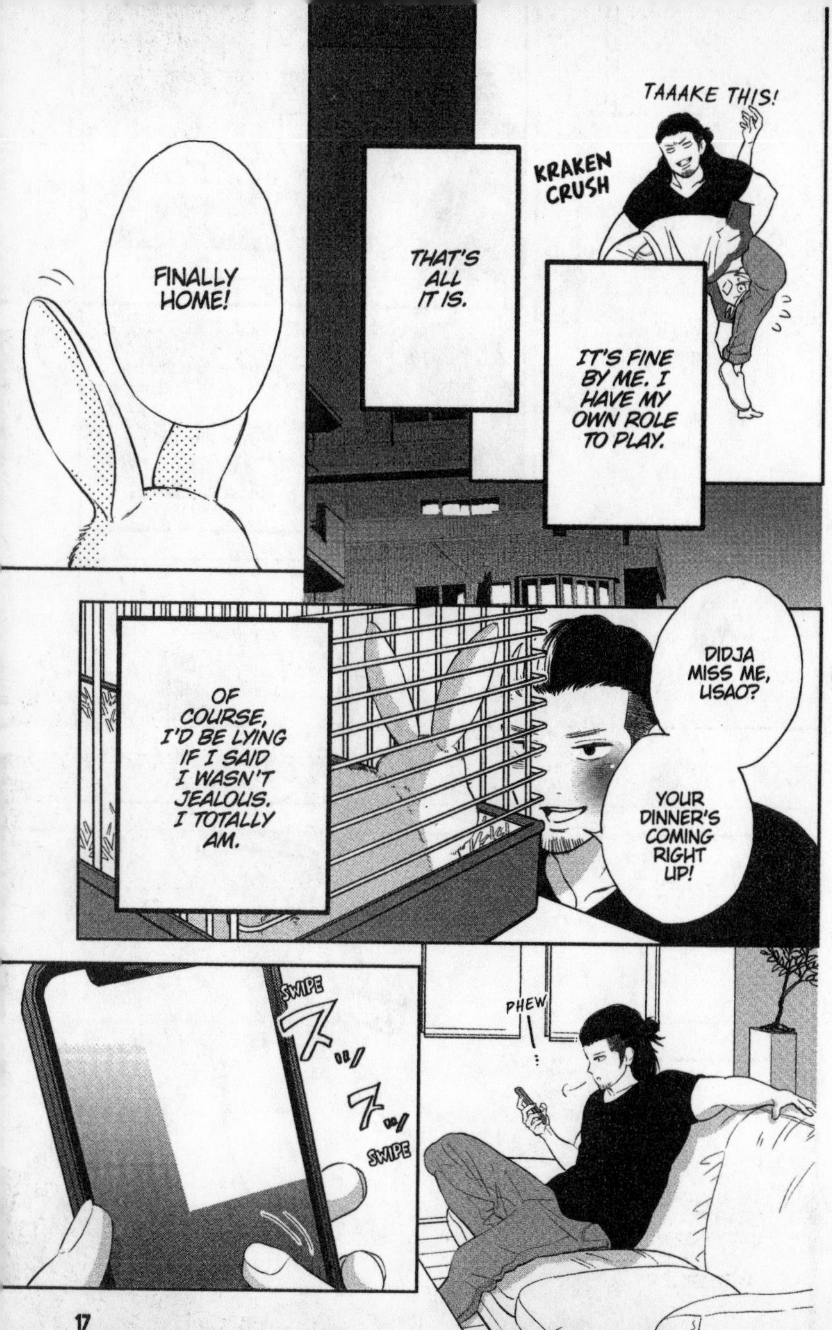
TAAAKE THIS!
KRAKEN CRUSH
IT'S FINE BY ME. I HAVE MY OWN ROLE TO PLAY.
THAT'S ALL IT IS.
FINALLY HOME!
DIDJA MISS ME, USAO?
YOUR DINNER'S COMING RIGHT UP!
OF COURSE, I'D BE LYING IF I SAID I WASN'T JEALOUS. I TOTALLY AM.
PHEW
SWIPE
SWIPE

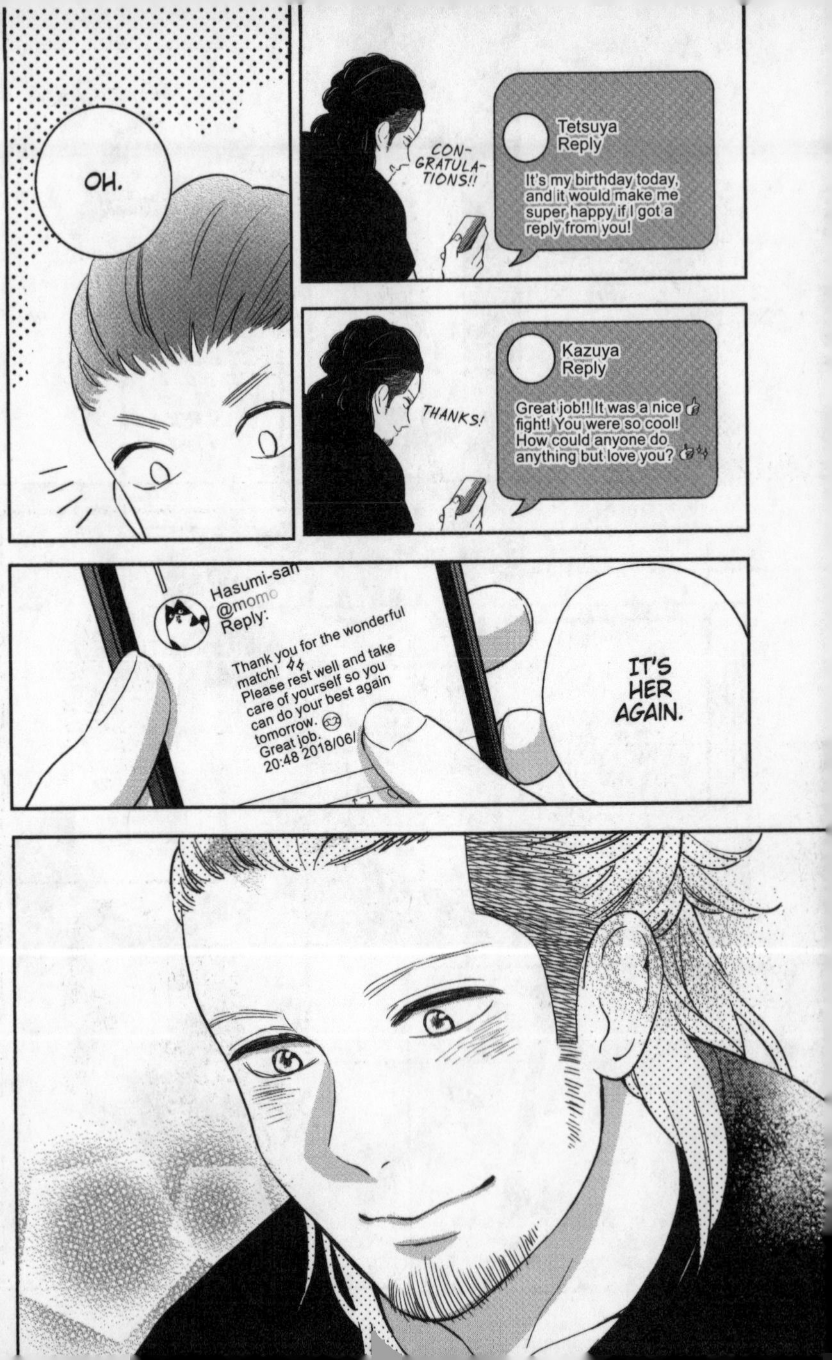
Tetsuya
Reply
It's my birthday today, and it would make me super happy if I got a reply from you!
CON-GRATULA-TIONS!!
Kazuya
Reply
Great job!! It was a nice fight! You were so cool! How could anyone do anything but love you?
THANKS!
OH.
IT'S HER AGAIN.
Hasumi-san
@momo
Reply:
Thank you for the wonderful match! Please rest well and take care of yourself so you can do your best again tomorrow. Great job.
20:48 2018/06/

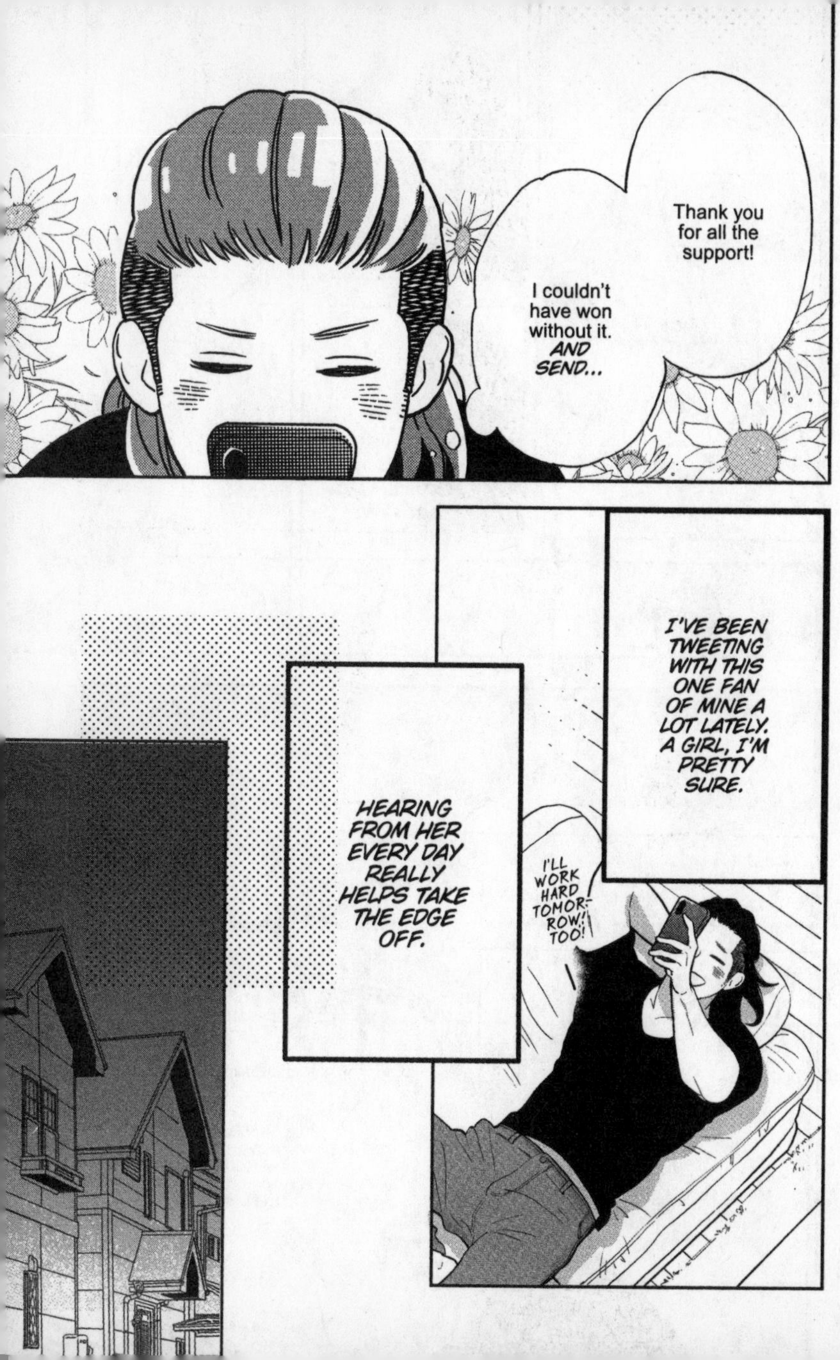
Thank you for all the support!
I couldn't have won without it.
AND SEND...
I'VE BEEN TWEETING WITH THIS ONE FAN OF MINE A LOT LATELY. A GIRL, I'M PRETTY SURE.
I'LL WORK HARD TOMOR-ROW, TOO!
HEARING FROM HER EVERY DAY REALLY HELPS TAKE THE EDGE OFF.

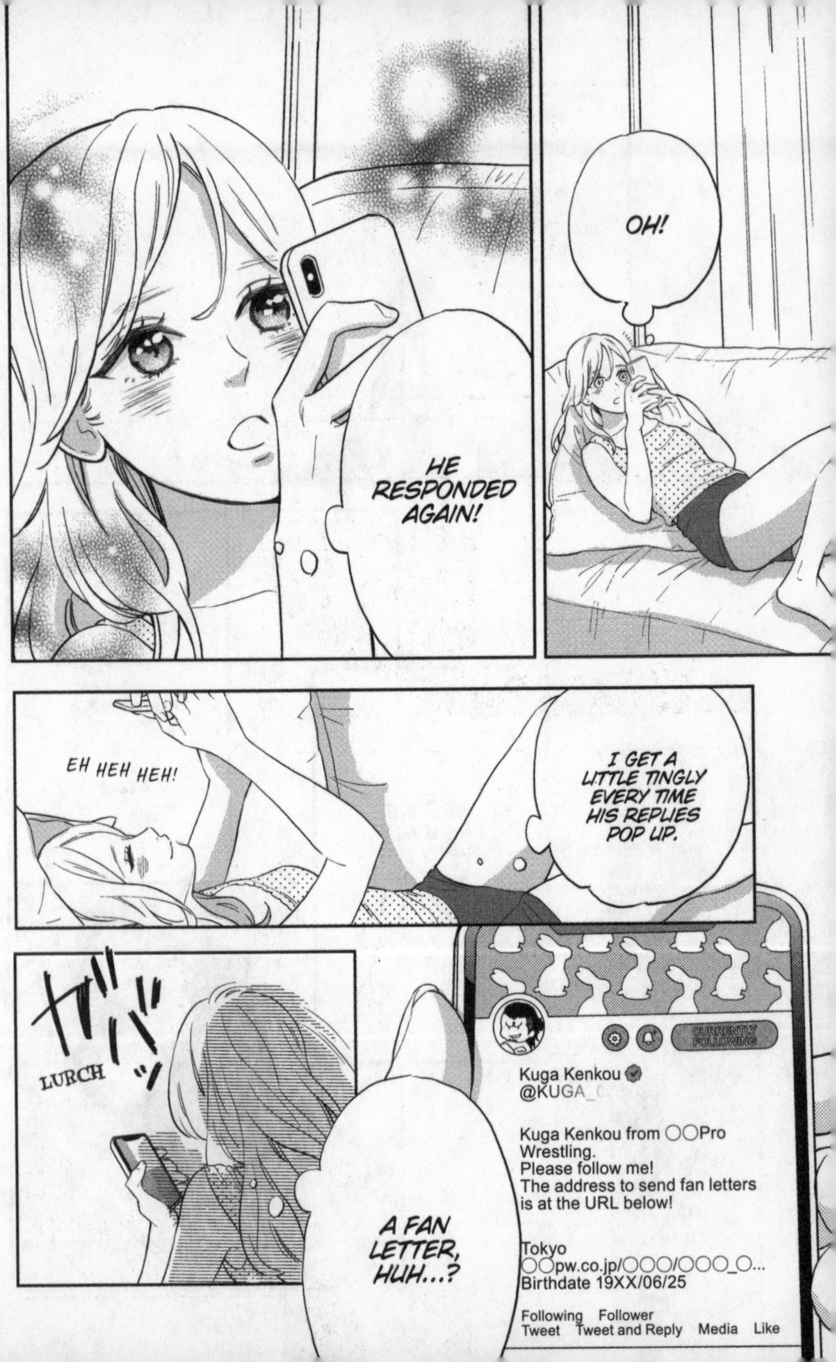
OH!
HE RESPONDED AGAIN!
I GET A LITTLE TINGLY EVERY TIME HIS REPLIES POP UP.
EH HEH HEH!
CURRENTLY FOLLOWING
Kuga Kenkou
@KUGA_
Kuga Kenkou from ◯◯Pro Wrestling.
Please follow me!
The address to send fan letters is at the URL below!
Tokyo
◯◯pw.co.jp/◯◯◯/◯◯◯_◯...
Birthdate 19XX/06/25
Following Follower
Tweet Tweet and Reply Media Like
A FAN LETTER, HUH...?
ガバッ
LURCH

I MIGHT BE ABLE TO EXPRESS MYSELF BETTER WITH A LETTER.

· · · · · · · ·

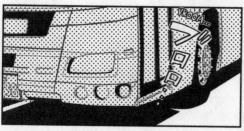

VROOM...

ZZZ.

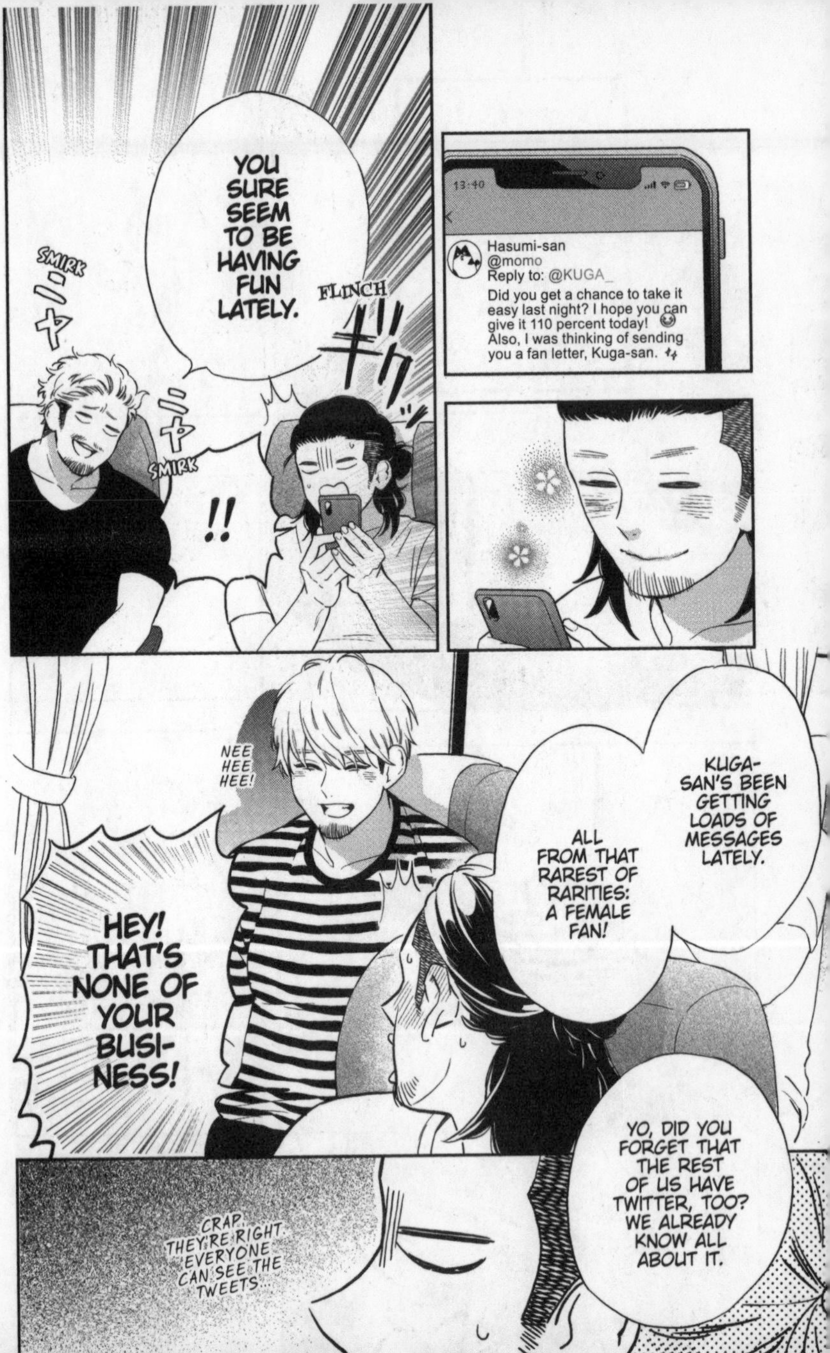
13:40
Hasumi-san
@momo
Reply to: @KUGA_
Did you get a chance to take it easy last night? I hope you can give it 110 percent today!
Also, I was thinking of sending you a fan letter, Kuga-san.
YOU SURE SEEM TO BE HAVING FUN LATELY.
FLINCH
SMIRK
SMIRK
!!
KUGA-SAN'S BEEN GETTING LOADS OF MESSAGES LATELY.
ALL FROM THAT RAREST OF RARITIES: A FEMALE FAN!
NEE HEE HEE!
HEY! THAT'S NONE OF YOUR BUSI-NESS!
YO, DID YOU FORGET THAT THE REST OF US HAVE TWITTER, TOO? WE ALREADY KNOW ALL ABOUT IT.
CRAP. THEY'RE RIGHT. EVERYONE CAN SEE THE TWEETS...

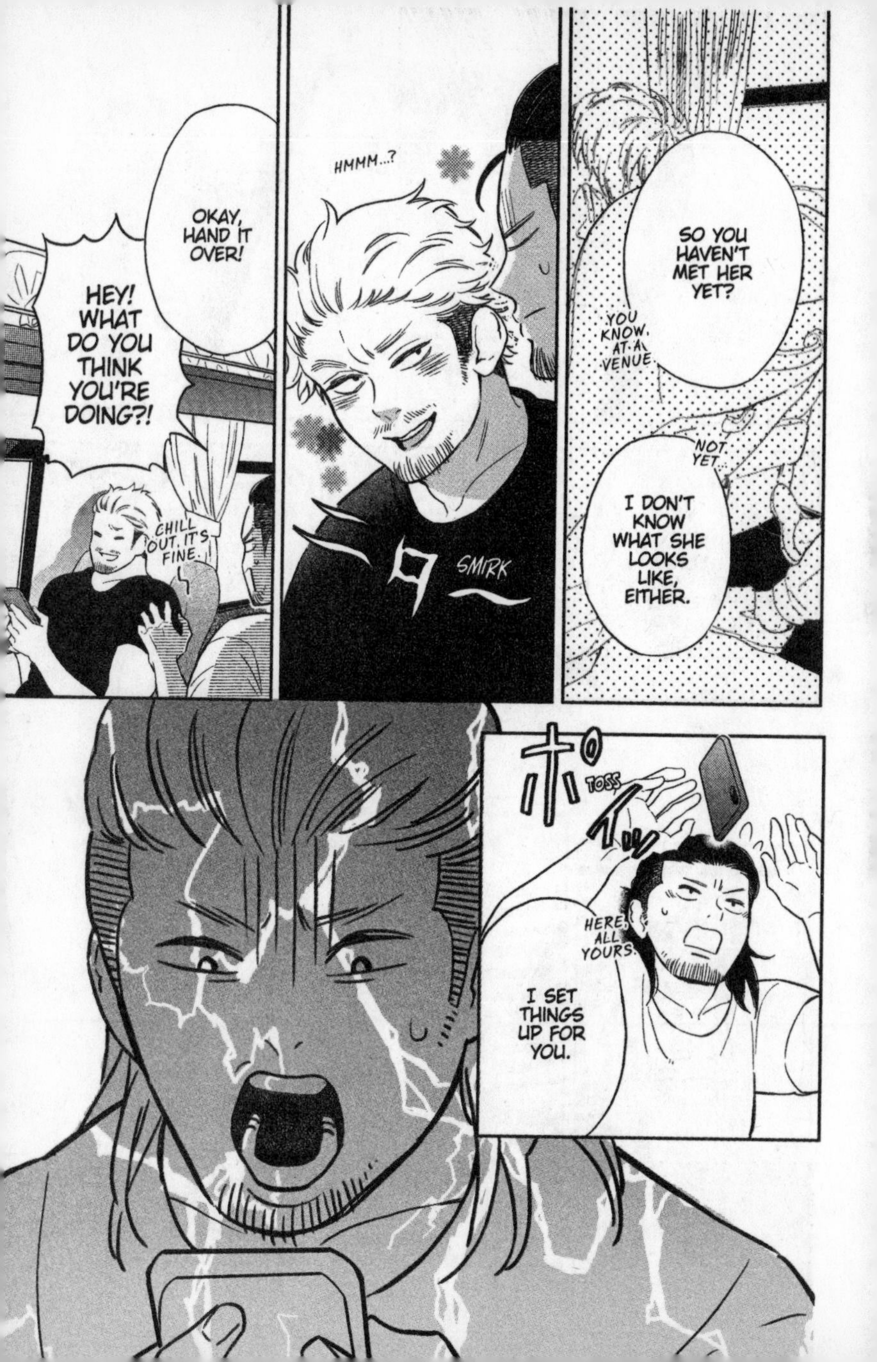
SO YOU HAVEN'T MET HER YET?
YOU KNOW, AT A VENUE.
NOT YET...
I DON'T KNOW WHAT SHE LOOKS LIKE, EITHER.
HMMM...?
SMIRK
OKAY, HAND IT OVER!
HEY! WHAT DO YOU THINK YOU'RE DOING?!
CHILL OUT. IT'S FINE.
ポイ
TOSS
HERE, ALL YOURS.
I SET THINGS UP FOR YOU.

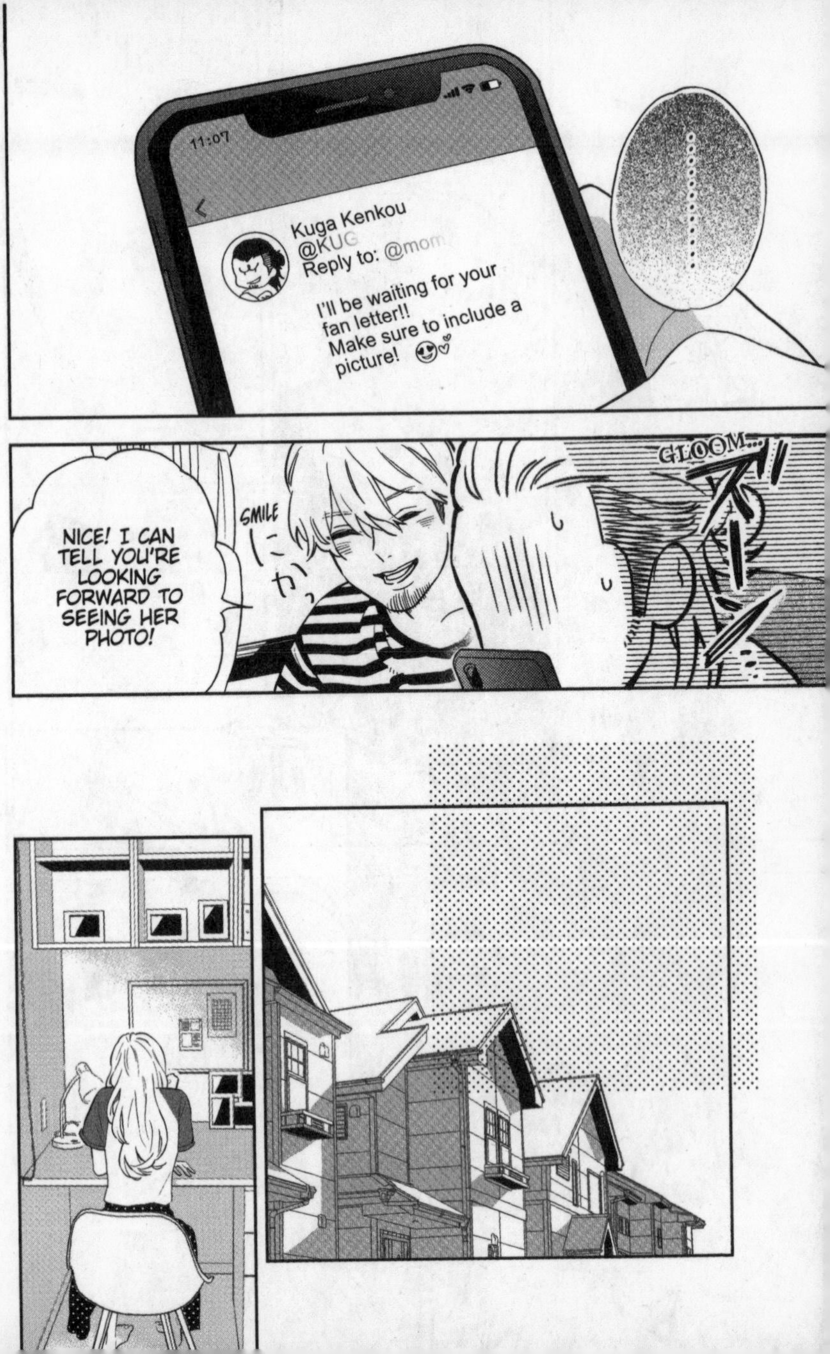
11:07
Kuga Kenkou
@KUG
Reply to: @mom
I'll be waiting for your fan letter!! Make sure to include a picture!
GLOOM...
SMILE
NICE! I CAN TELL YOU'RE LOOKING FORWARD TO SEEING HER PHOTO!

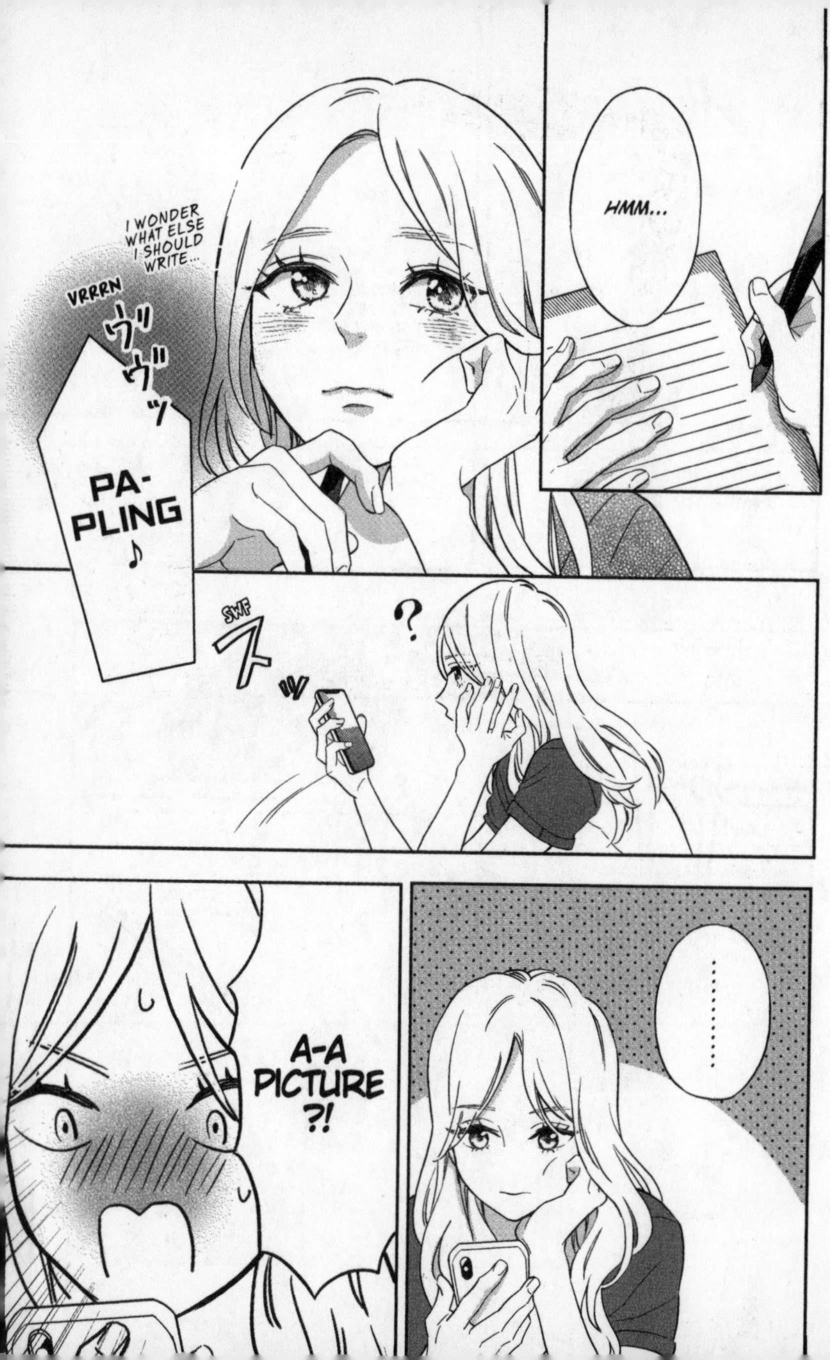
HMM...
I WONDER WHAT ELSE I SHOULD WRITE...
VRRRN
ヴヴッ
PA-PLING ♪
?
SWF
スッ
......
A-A PICTURE ?!

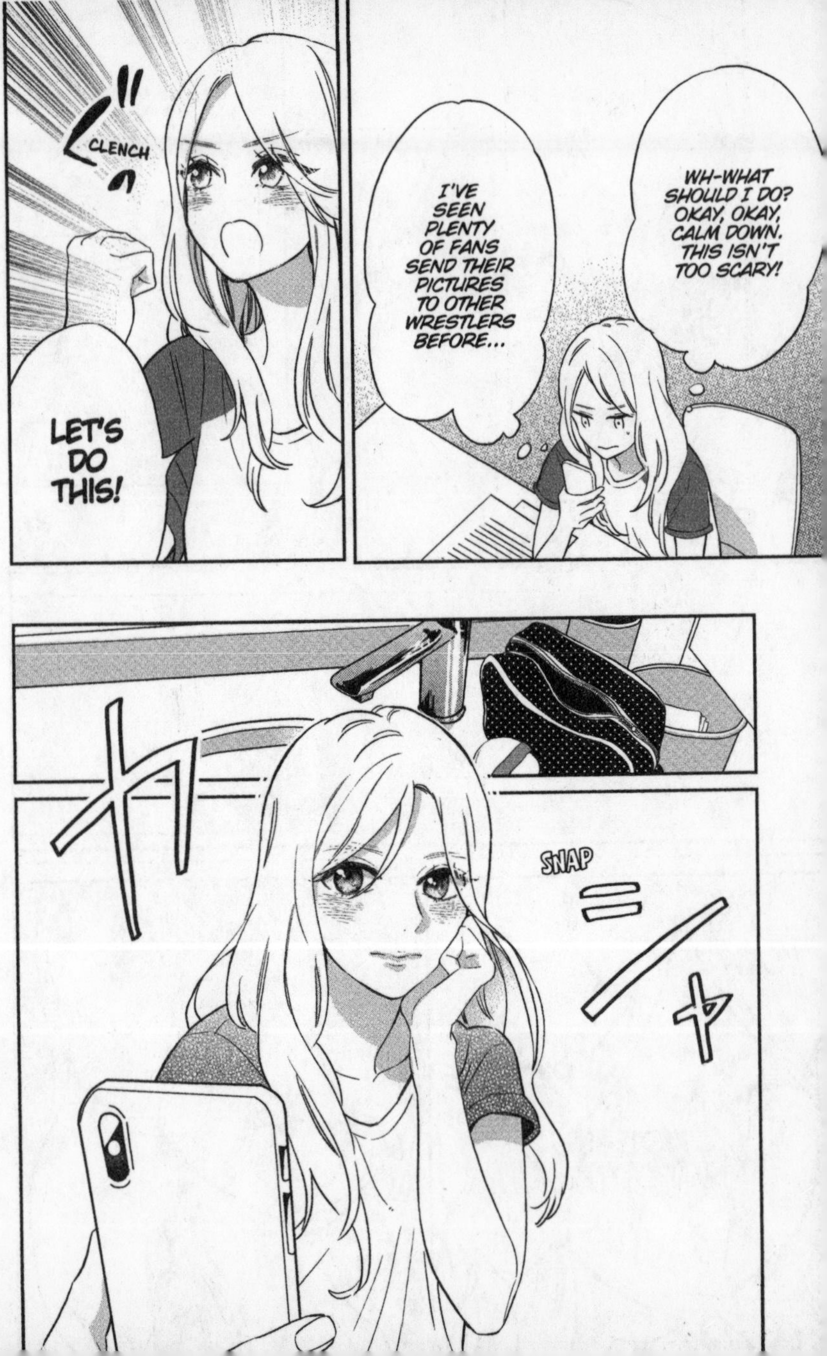
WH-WHAT SHOULD I DO? OKAY, OKAY, CALM DOWN. THIS ISN'T TOO SCARY!
I'VE SEEN PLENTY OF FANS SEND THEIR PICTURES TO OTHER WRESTLERS BEFORE...
CLENCH
LET'S DO THIS!
SNAP

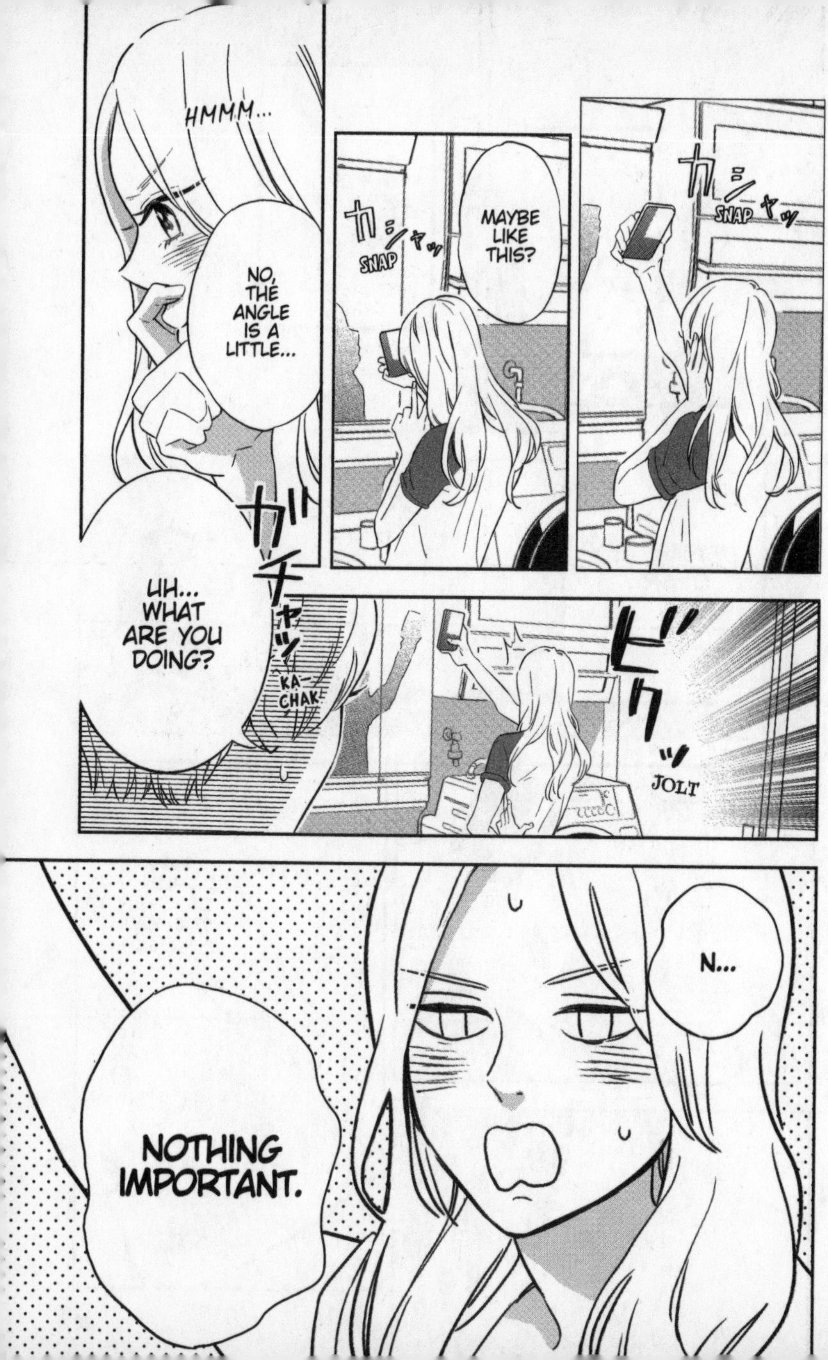
カシャッ
SNAP
MAYBE LIKE THIS?
カシャッ
SNAP
HMMM...
NO, THE ANGLE IS A LITTLE...
ビクッ
JOLT
ガチャッ
KA-CHAK
UH... WHAT ARE YOU DOING?
N...
NOTHING IMPORTANT.

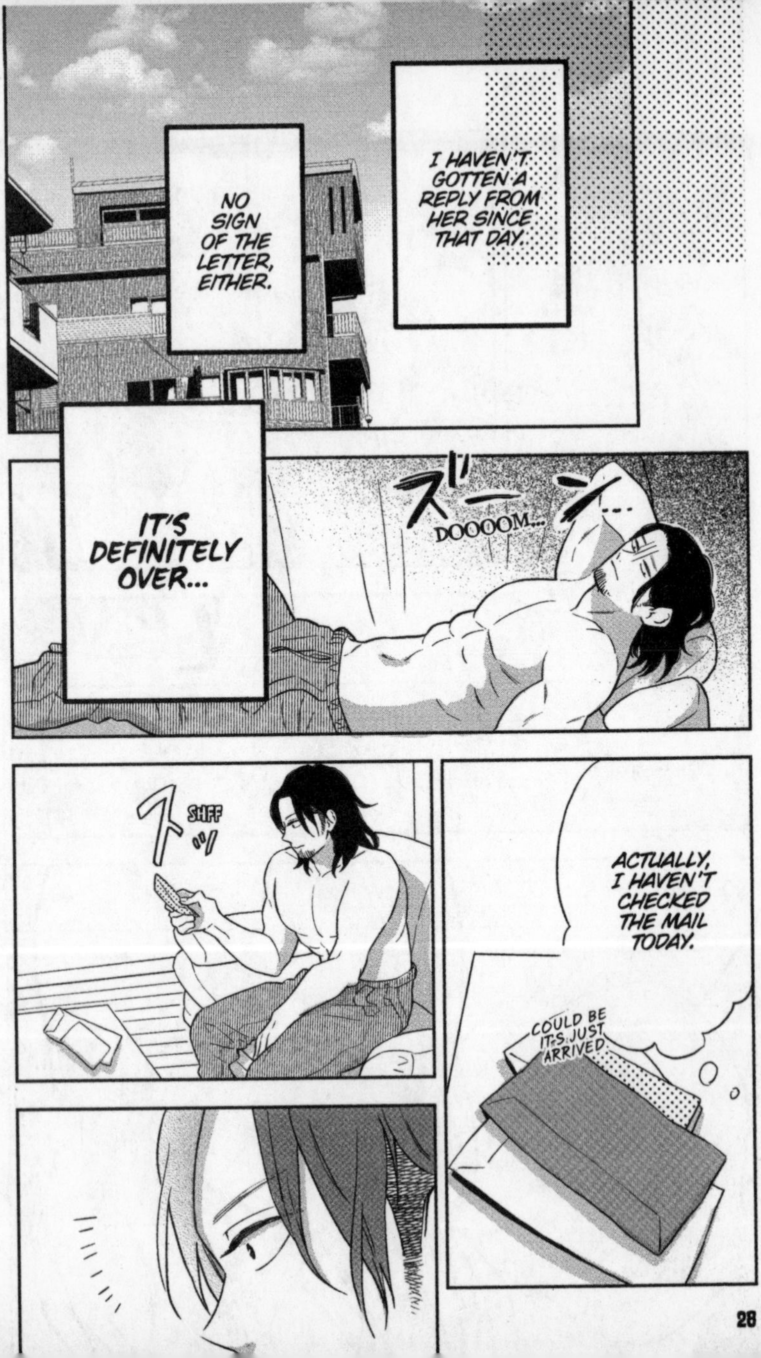

I HAVEN'T GOTTEN A REPLY FROM HER SINCE THAT DAY.
NO SIGN OF THE LETTER, EITHER.
DOOOOM...
IT'S DEFINITELY OVER...
ACTUALLY, I HAVEN'T CHECKED THE MAIL TODAY.
COULD BE IT'S JUST ARRIVED.
SHFF

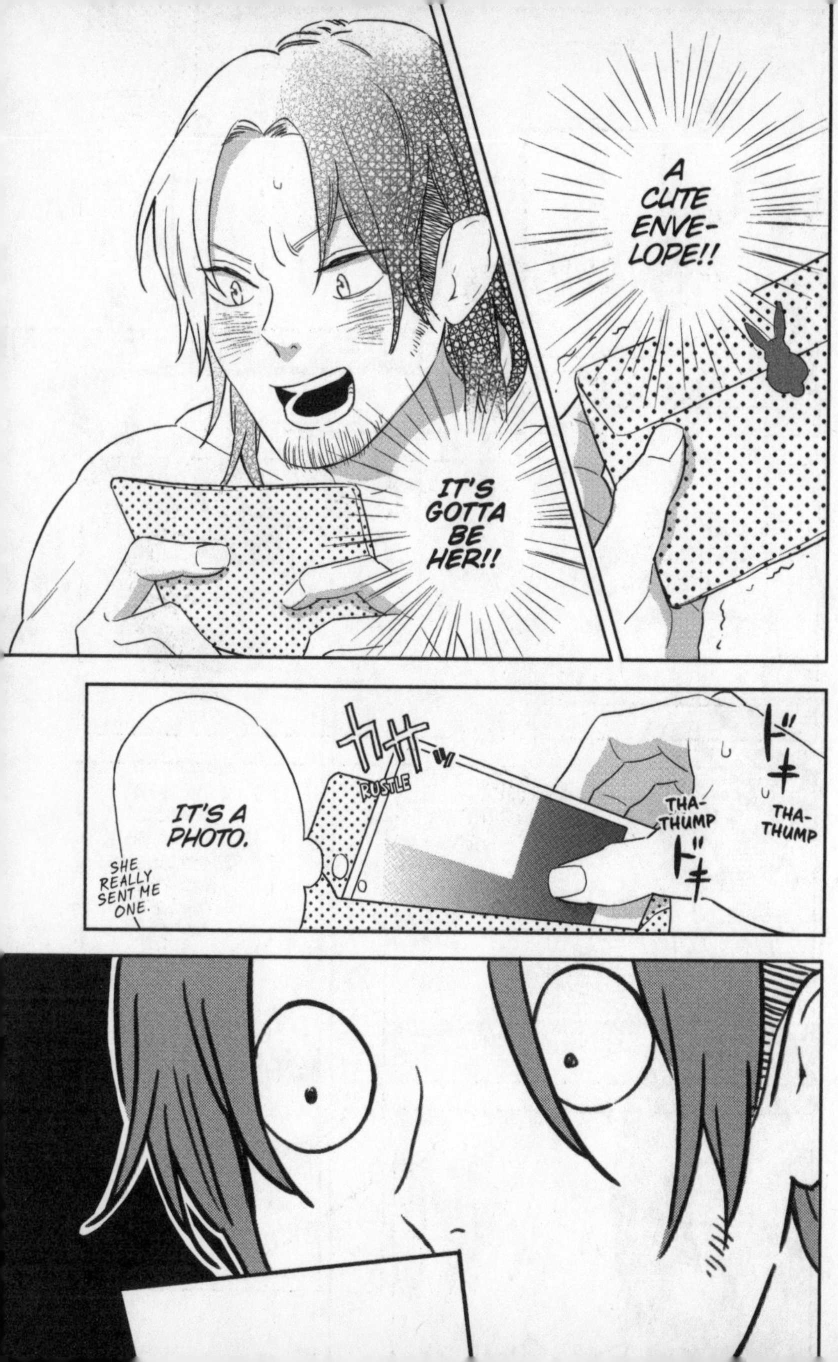
A CUTE ENVELOPE!!
IT'S GOTTA BE HER!!
ドキ
THA-THUMP
ドキ
THA-THUMP
カサ
RUSTLE
IT'S A PHOTO.
SHE REALLY SENT ME ONE.

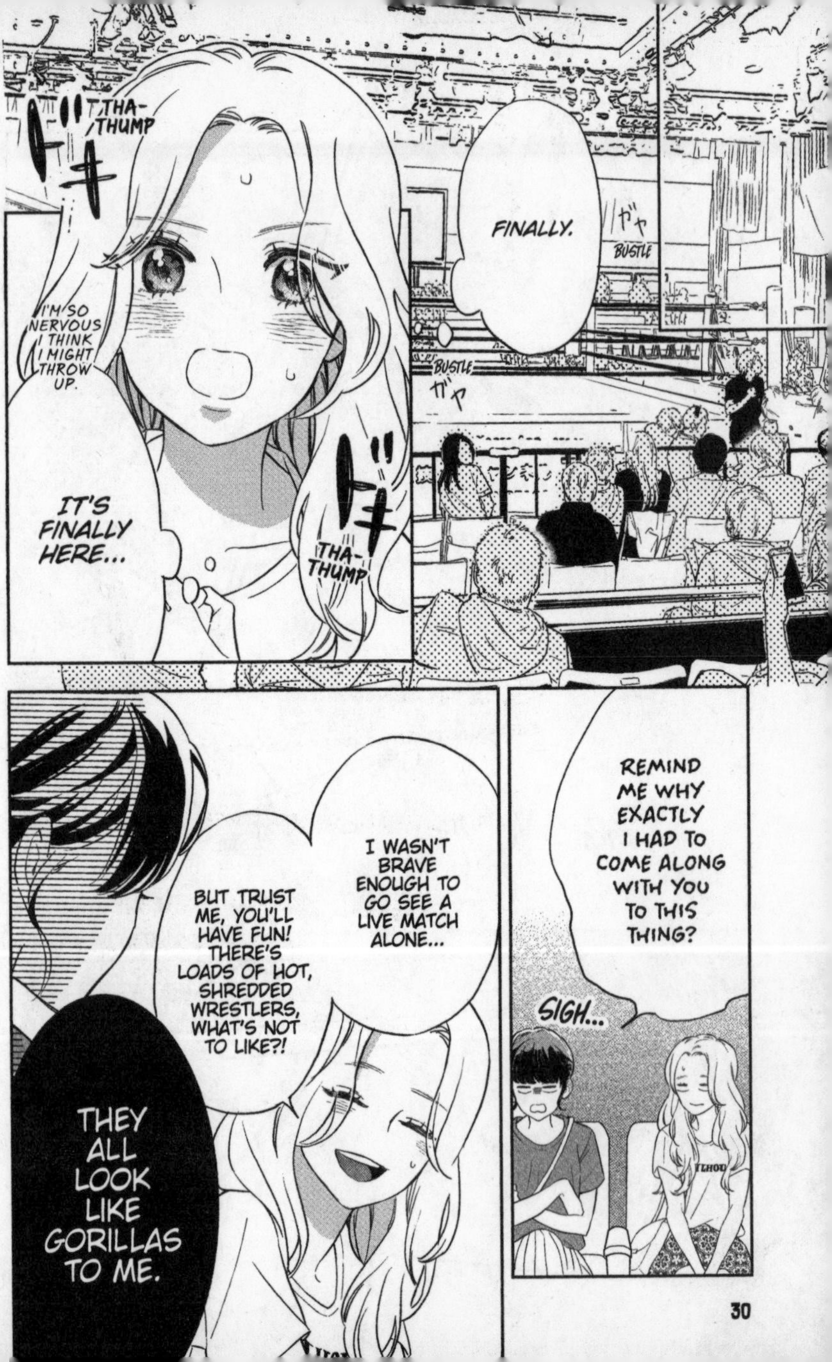
FINALLY.
ガヤ
BUSTLE
BUSTLE
ガヤ
ドキ
THA-THUMP
I'M SO NERVOUS I THINK I MIGHT THROW UP.
IT'S FINALLY HERE...
ドキ
THA-THUMP
REMIND ME WHY EXACTLY I HAD TO COME ALONG WITH YOU TO THIS THING?
SIGH...
I WASN'T BRAVE ENOUGH TO GO SEE A LIVE MATCH ALONE...
BUT TRUST ME, YOU'LL HAVE FUN! THERE'S LOADS OF HOT, SHREDDED WRESTLERS, WHAT'S NOT TO LIKE?!
THEY ALL LOOK LIKE GORILLAS TO ME.

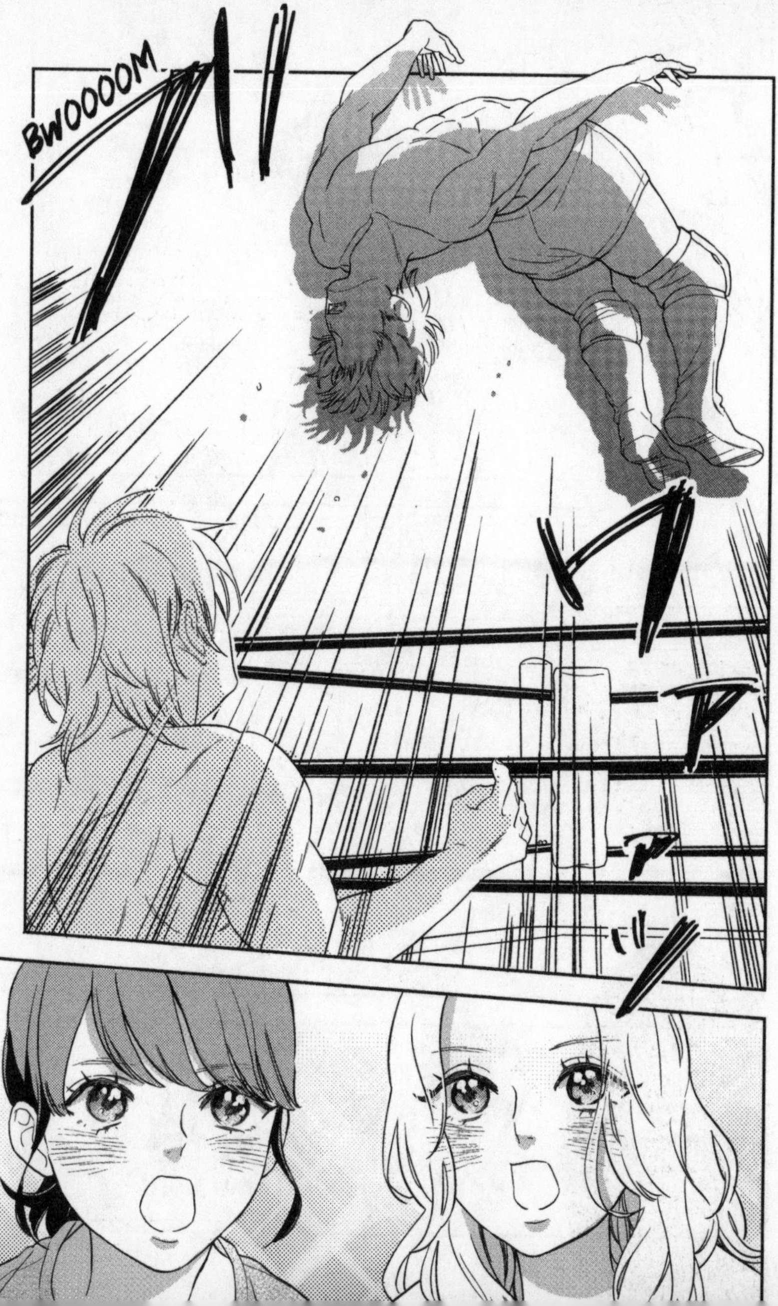
BWOOOOM

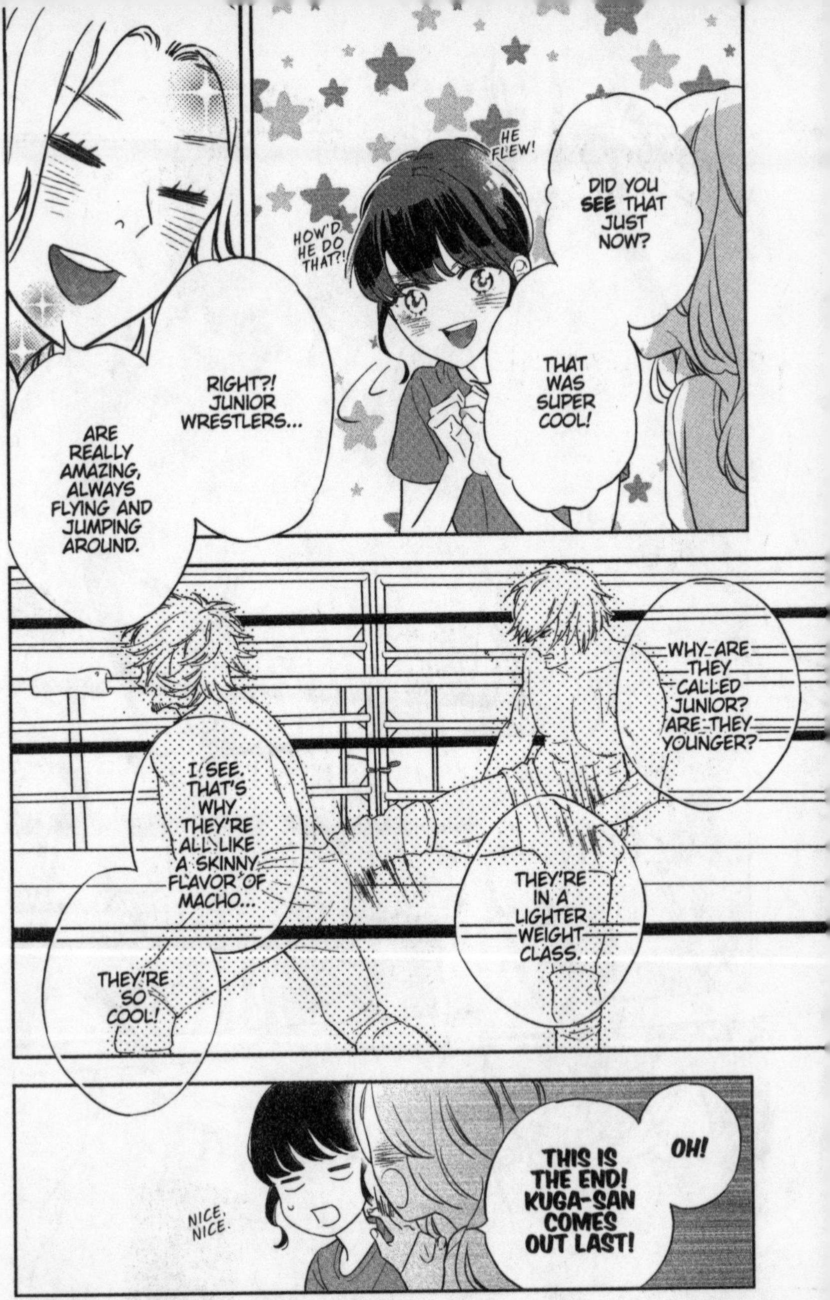
DID YOU SEE THAT JUST NOW?
HE FLEW!
HOW'D HE DO THAT?!
THAT WAS SUPER COOL!
RIGHT?! JUNIOR WRESTLERS...
ARE REALLY AMAZING, ALWAYS FLYING AND JUMPING AROUND.
WHY ARE THEY CALLED JUNIOR? ARE THEY YOUNGER?
THEY'RE IN A LIGHTER WEIGHT CLASS.
I SEE. THAT'S WHY THEY'RE ALL LIKE A SKINNY FLAVOR OF MACHO...
THEY'RE SO COOL!
OH!
THIS IS THE END! KUGA-SAN COMES OUT LAST!
NICE, NICE.

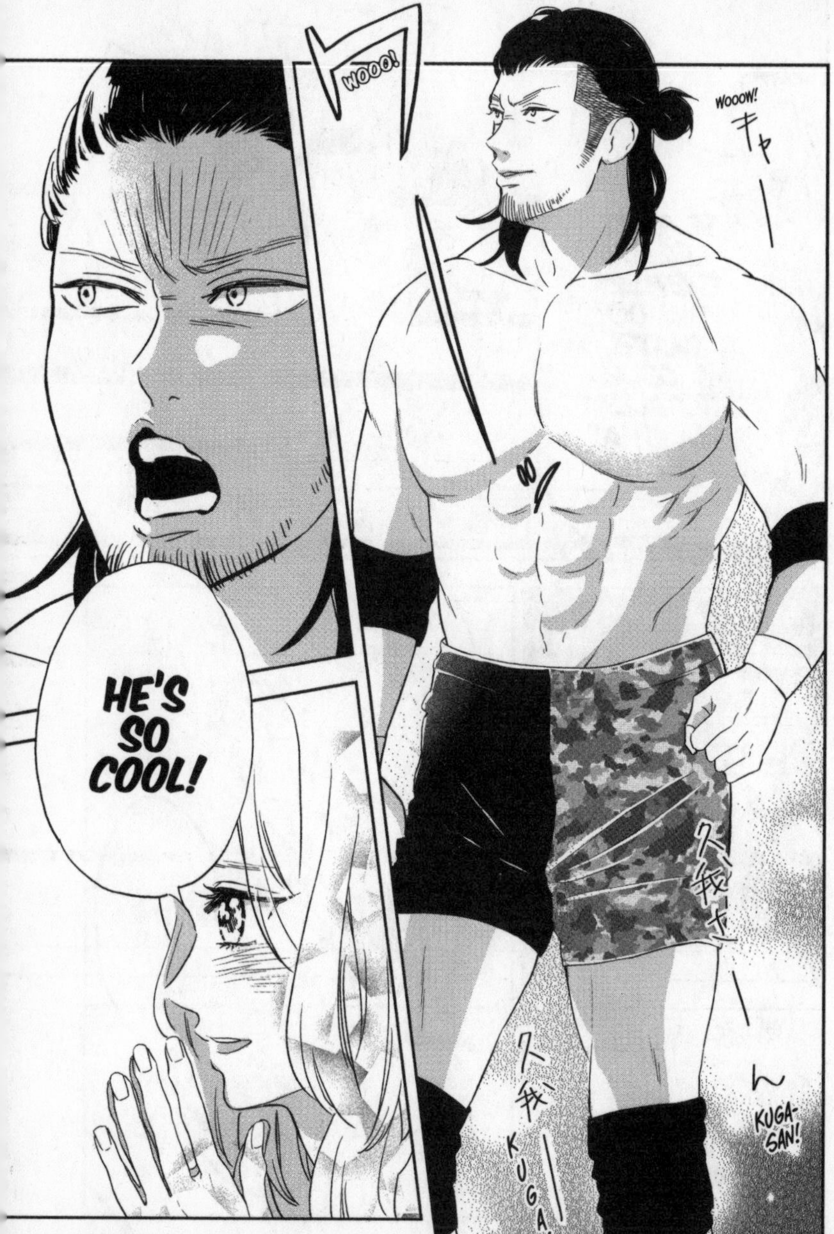
WOOOW!
キャーー
久我さーーん
KUGA-SAN!
久我ーー
KUGA!
WOOO!
HE'S SO COOL!

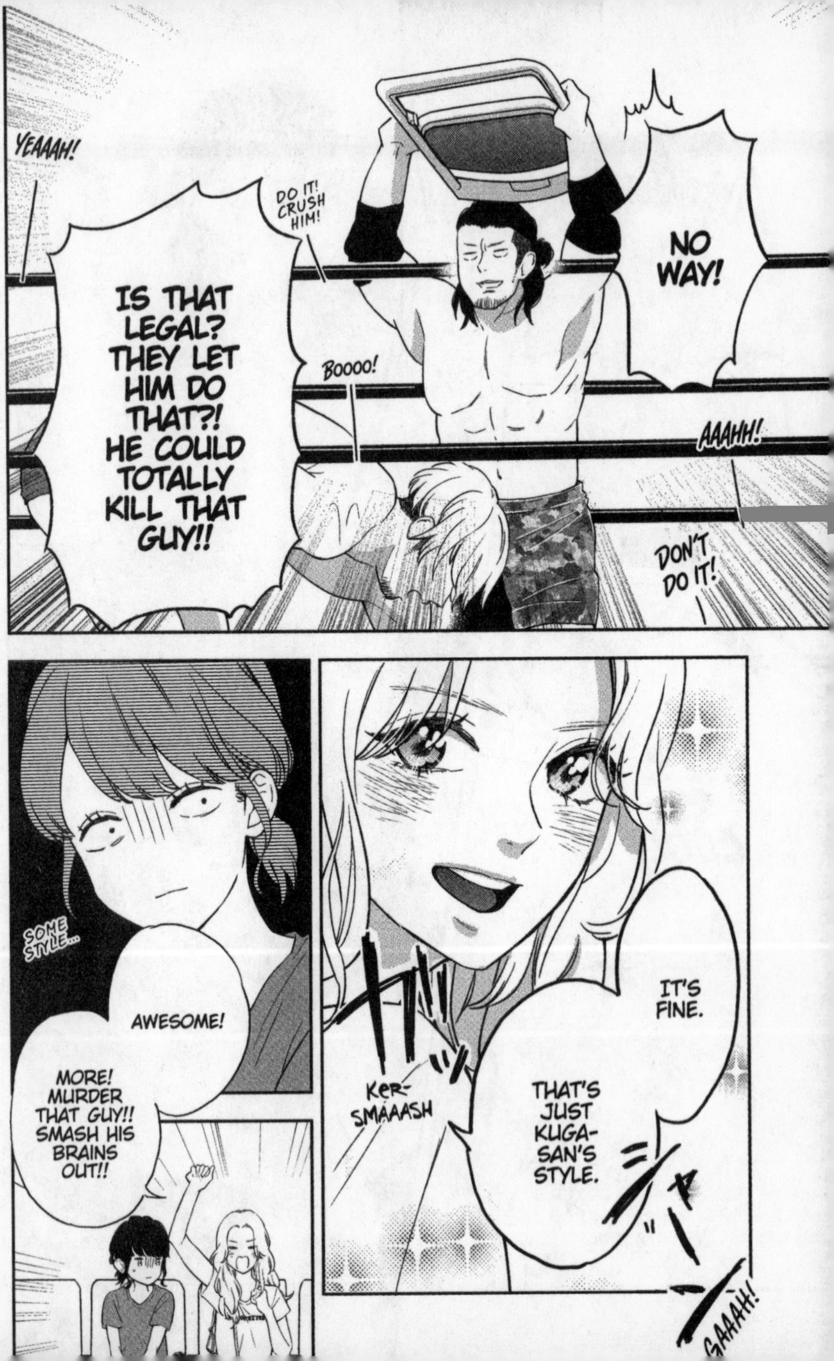
NO WAY!
AAAHH!
DON'T DO IT!
DO IT! CRUSH HIM!
BOOOO!
YEAAAH!
IS THAT LEGAL? THEY LET HIM DO THAT?! HE COULD TOTALLY KILL THAT GUY!!
IT'S FINE.
THAT'S JUST KUGA-SAN'S STYLE.
KER-SMAAASH
GAAAH!
SOME STYLE...
AWESOME!
MORE! MURDER THAT GUY!! SMASH HIS BRAINS OUT!!

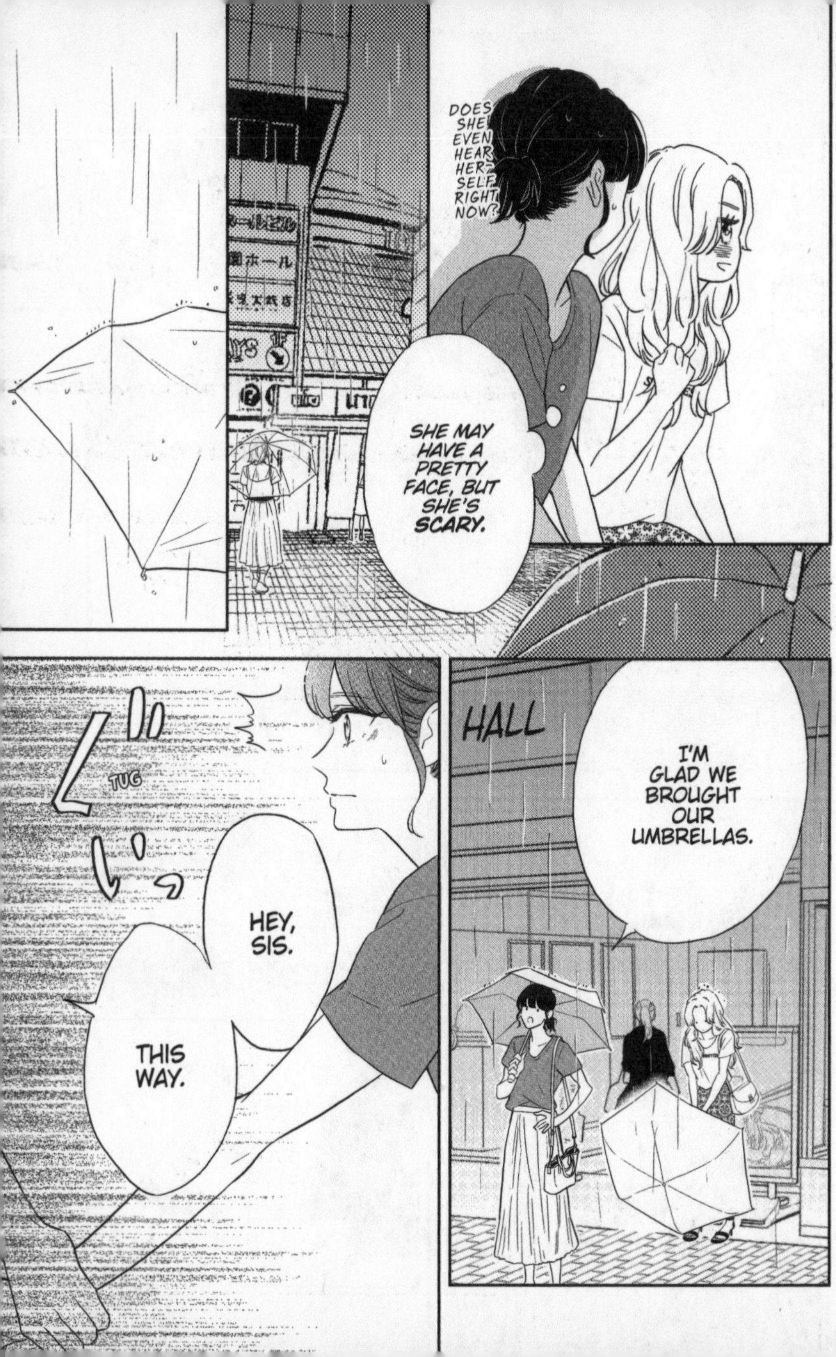
DOES SHE EVEN HEAR HER-SELF RIGHT NOW?
SHE MAY HAVE A PRETTY FACE, BUT SHE'S SCARY.
HALL
I'M GLAD WE BROUGHT OUR UMBRELLAS.
TUG
HEY, SIS.
THIS WAY.

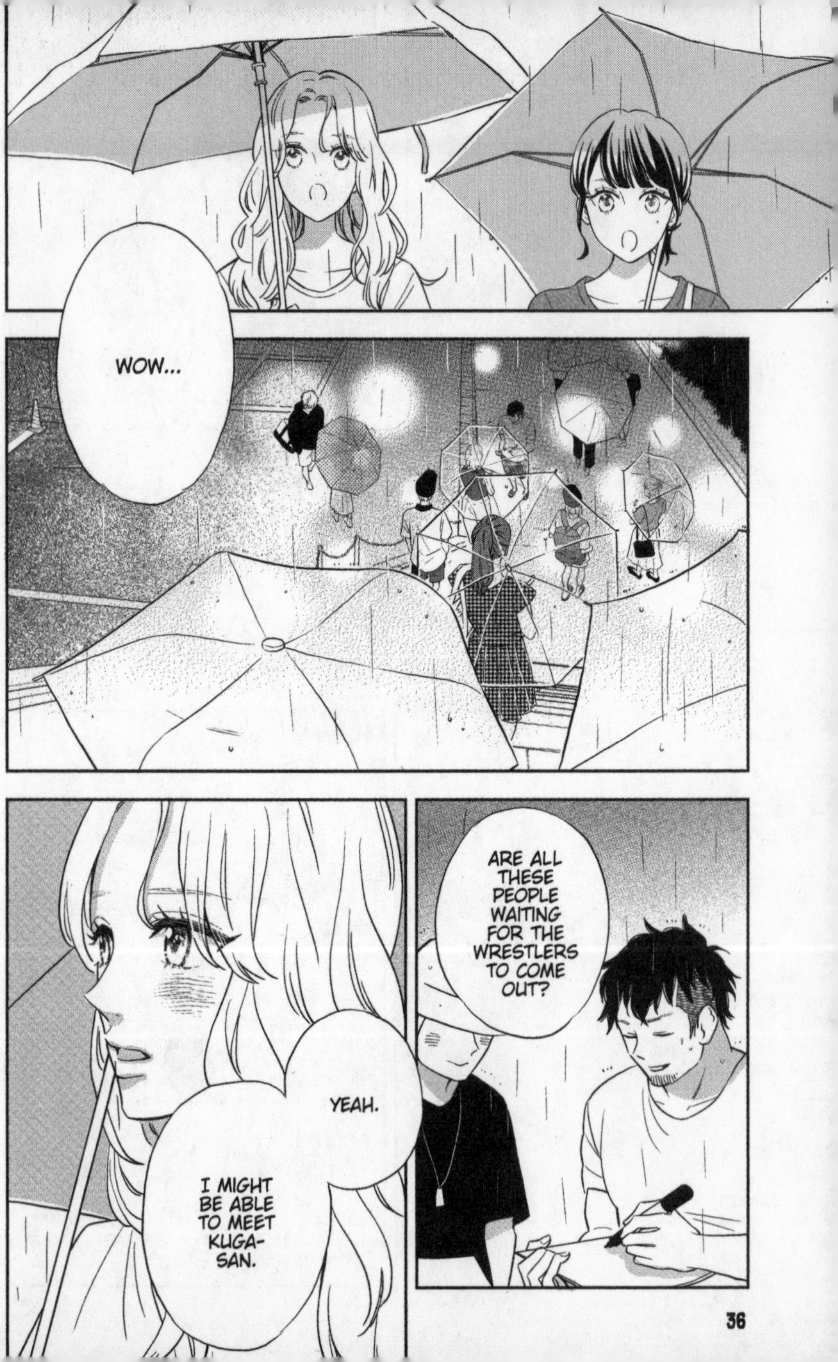
WOW...
ARE ALL THESE PEOPLE WAITING FOR THE WRESTLERS TO COME OUT?
YEAH.
I MIGHT BE ABLE TO MEET KUGA-SAN.

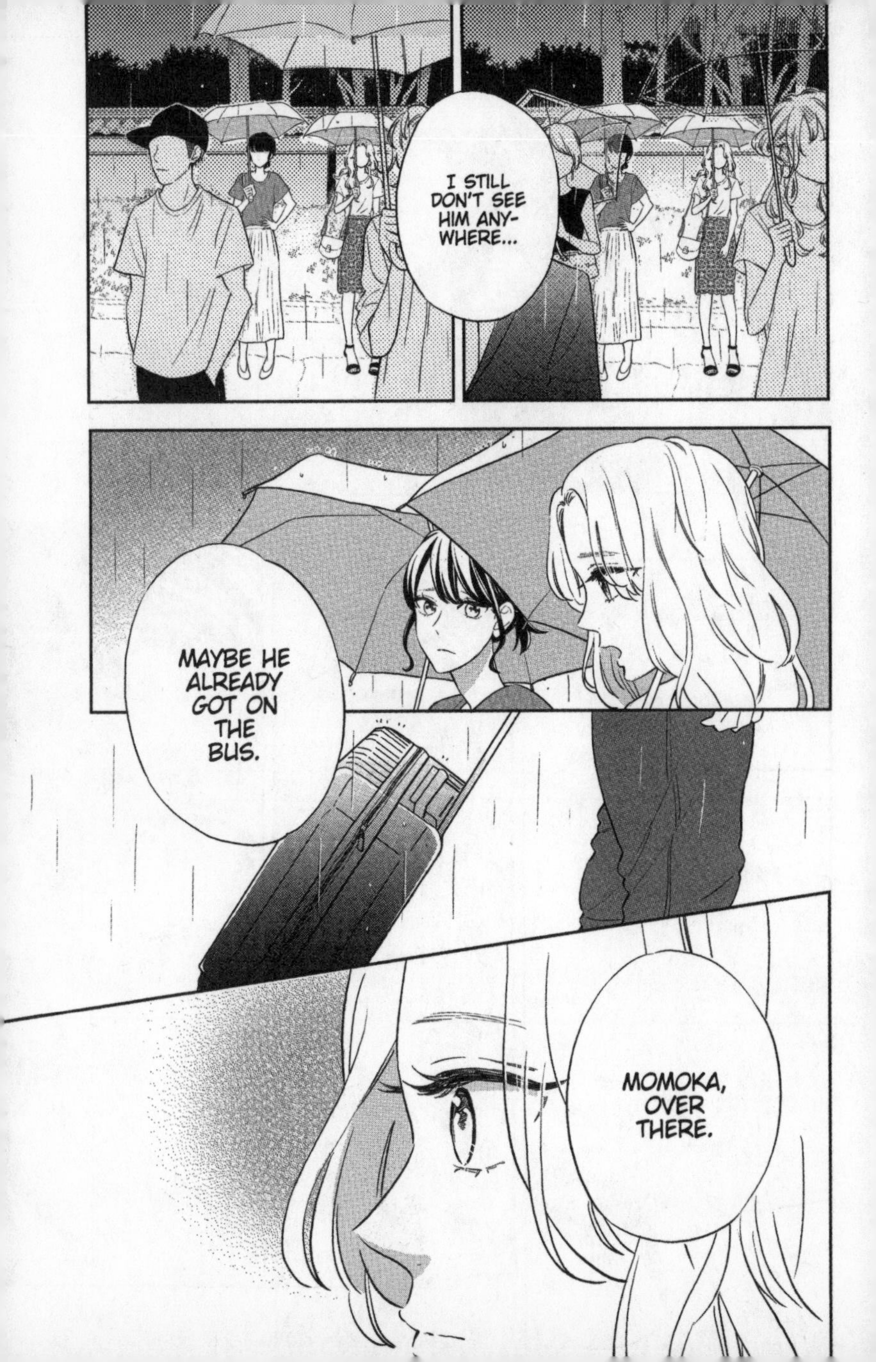
I STILL DON'T SEE HIM ANY-WHERE...
MAYBE HE ALREADY GOT ON THE BUS.
MOMOKA, OVER THERE.

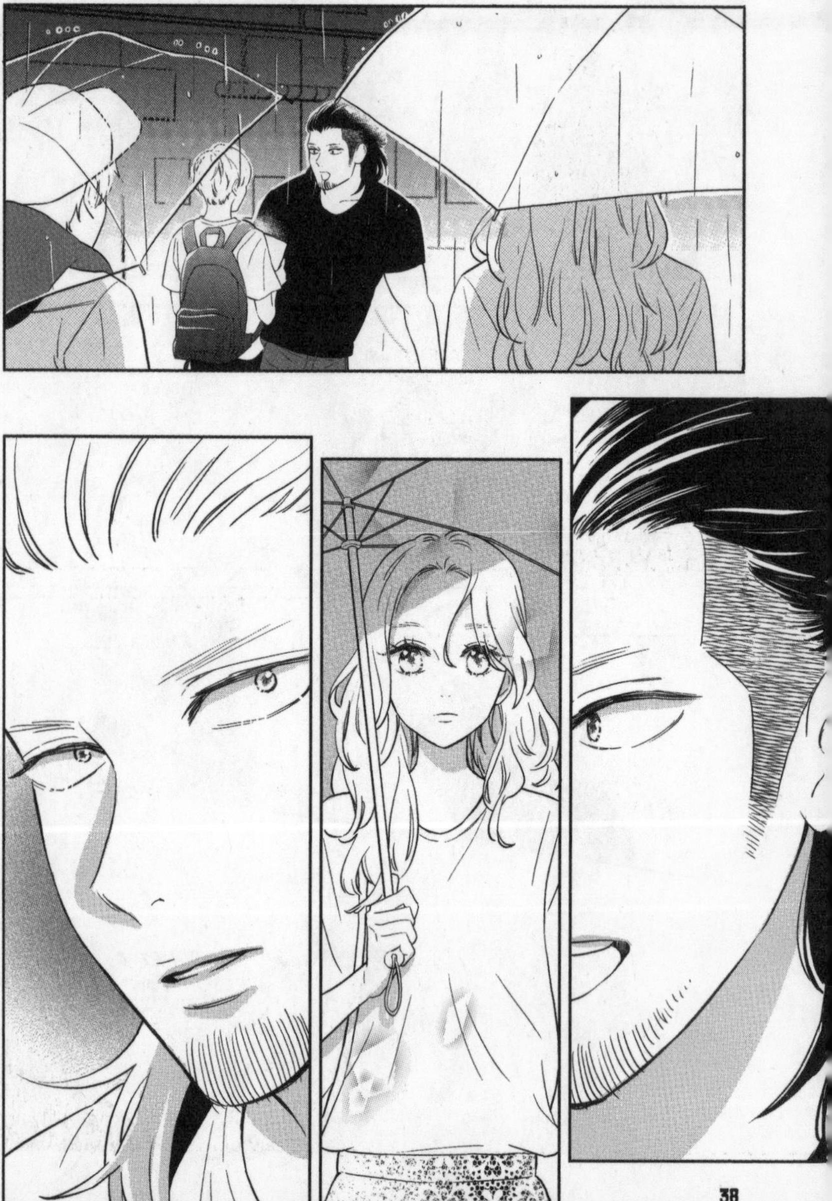

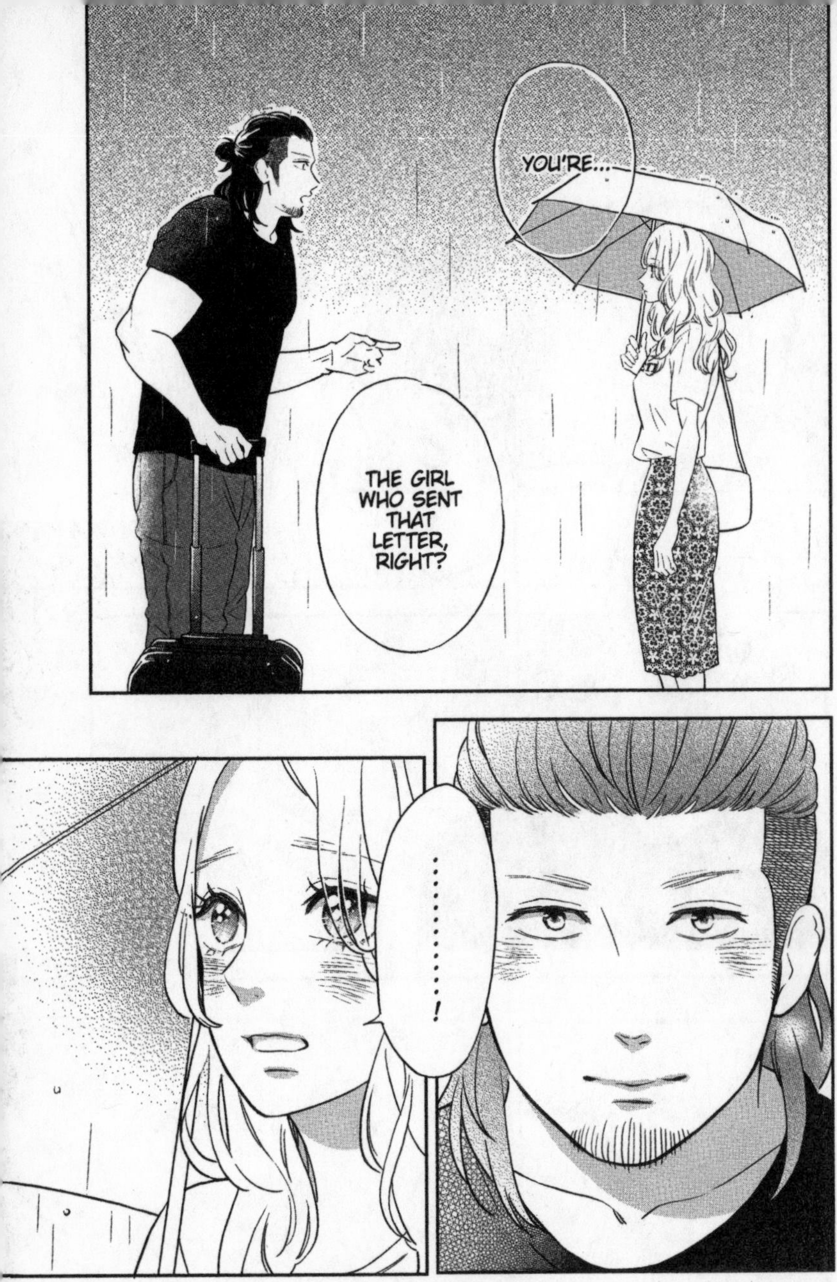
YOU'RE...
THE GIRL WHO SENT THAT LETTER, RIGHT?
......!

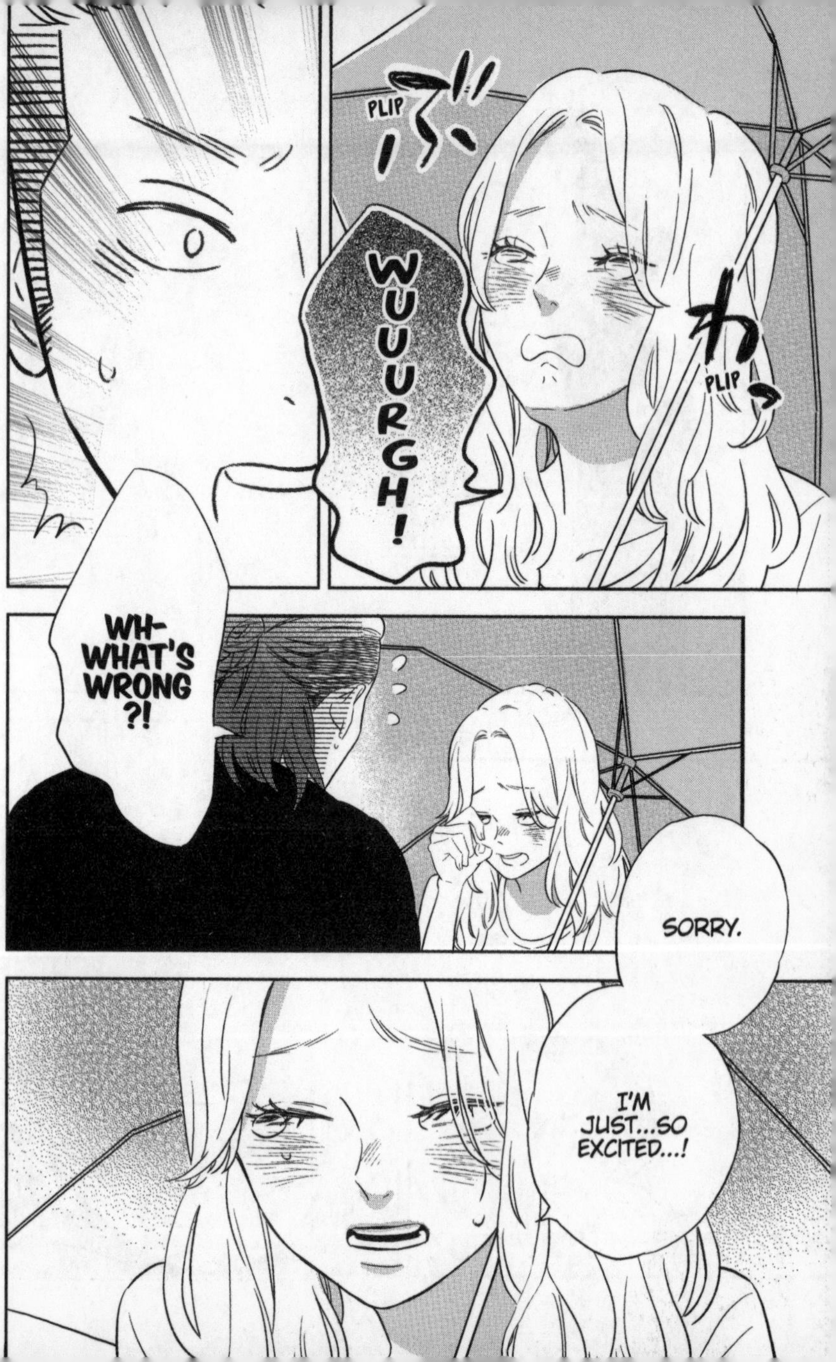

PLIP
PLIP
WUUURGH!
WH-WHAT'S WRONG?!
SORRY.
I'M JUST...SO EXCITED...!

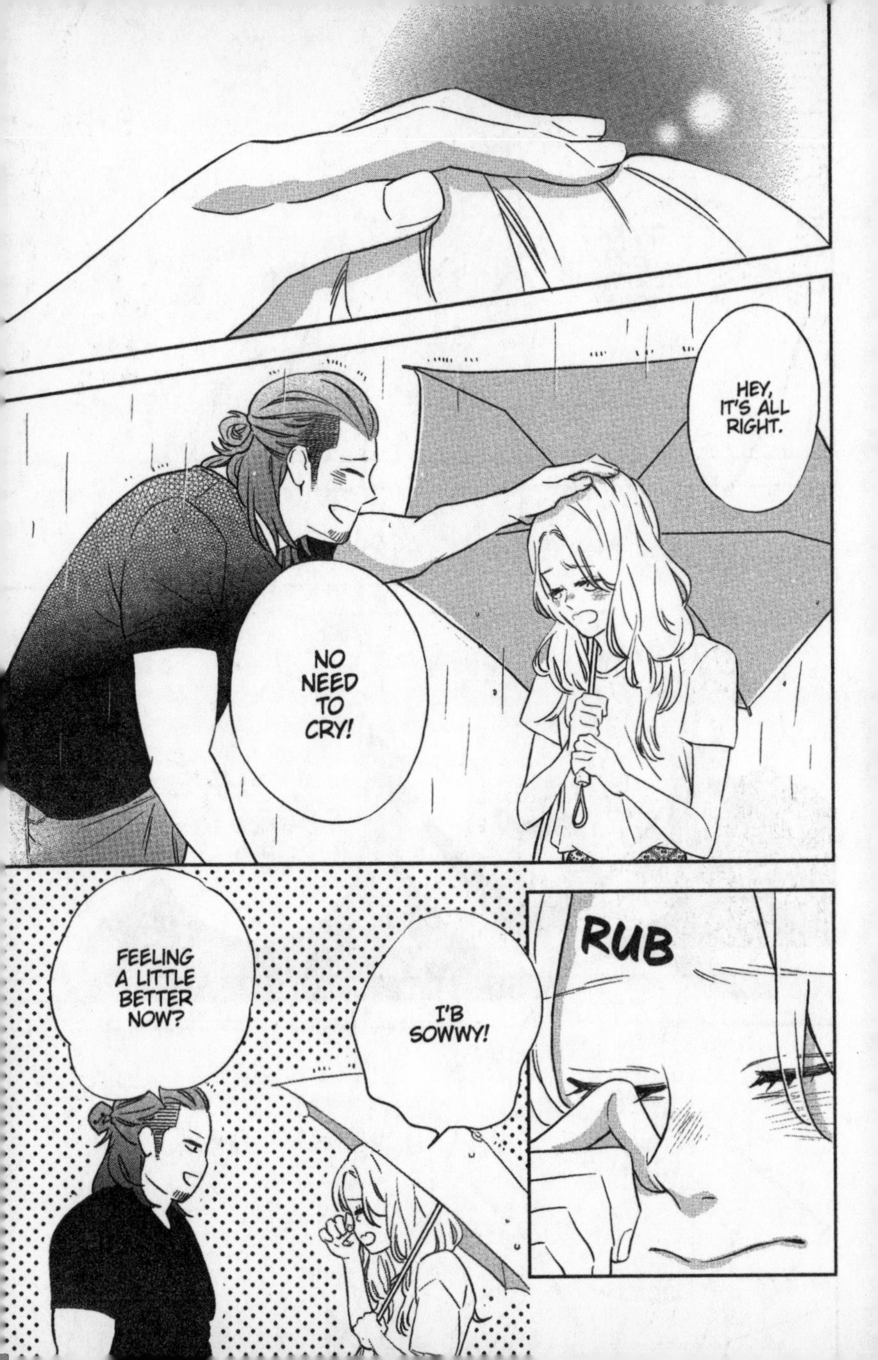
HEY, IT'S ALL RIGHT.
NO NEED TO CRY!
RUB
I'B SOWWY!
FEELING A LITTLE BETTER NOW?

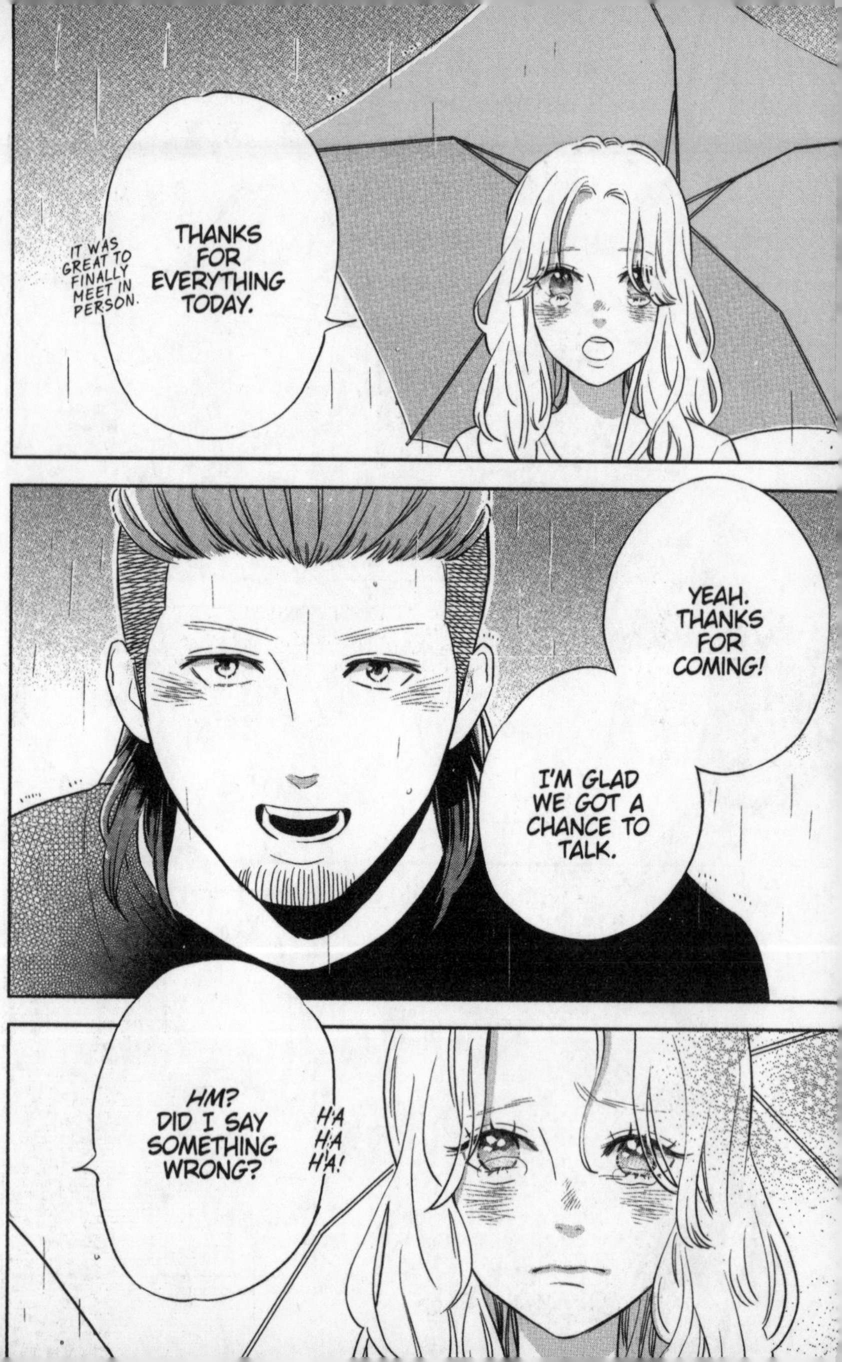
THANKS FOR EVERYTHING TODAY.
IT WAS GREAT TO FINALLY MEET IN PERSON.
YEAH. THANKS FOR COMING!
I'M GLAD WE GOT A CHANCE TO TALK.
HA HA HA!
HM? DID I SAY SOMETHING WRONG?

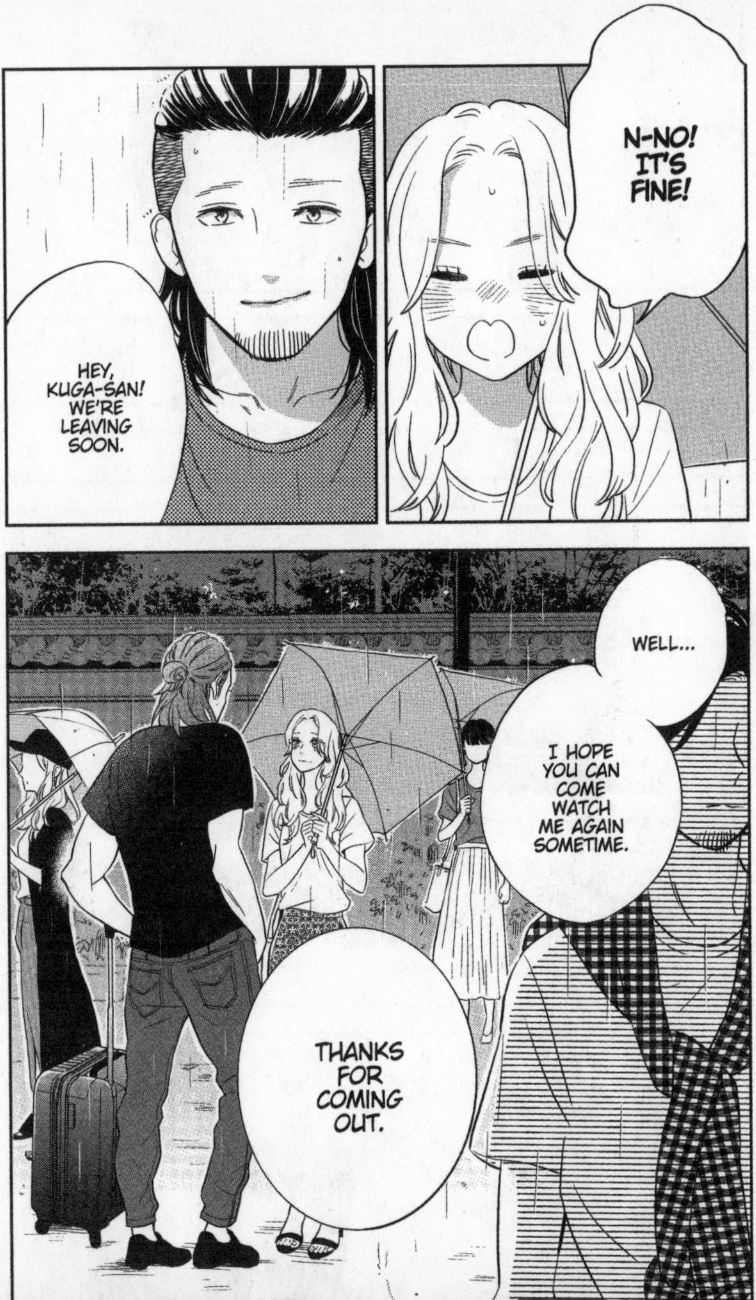
N-NO! IT'S FINE!
HEY, KUGA-SAN! WE'RE LEAVING SOON.
WELL...
I HOPE YOU CAN COME WATCH ME AGAIN SOMETIME.
THANKS FOR COMING OUT.

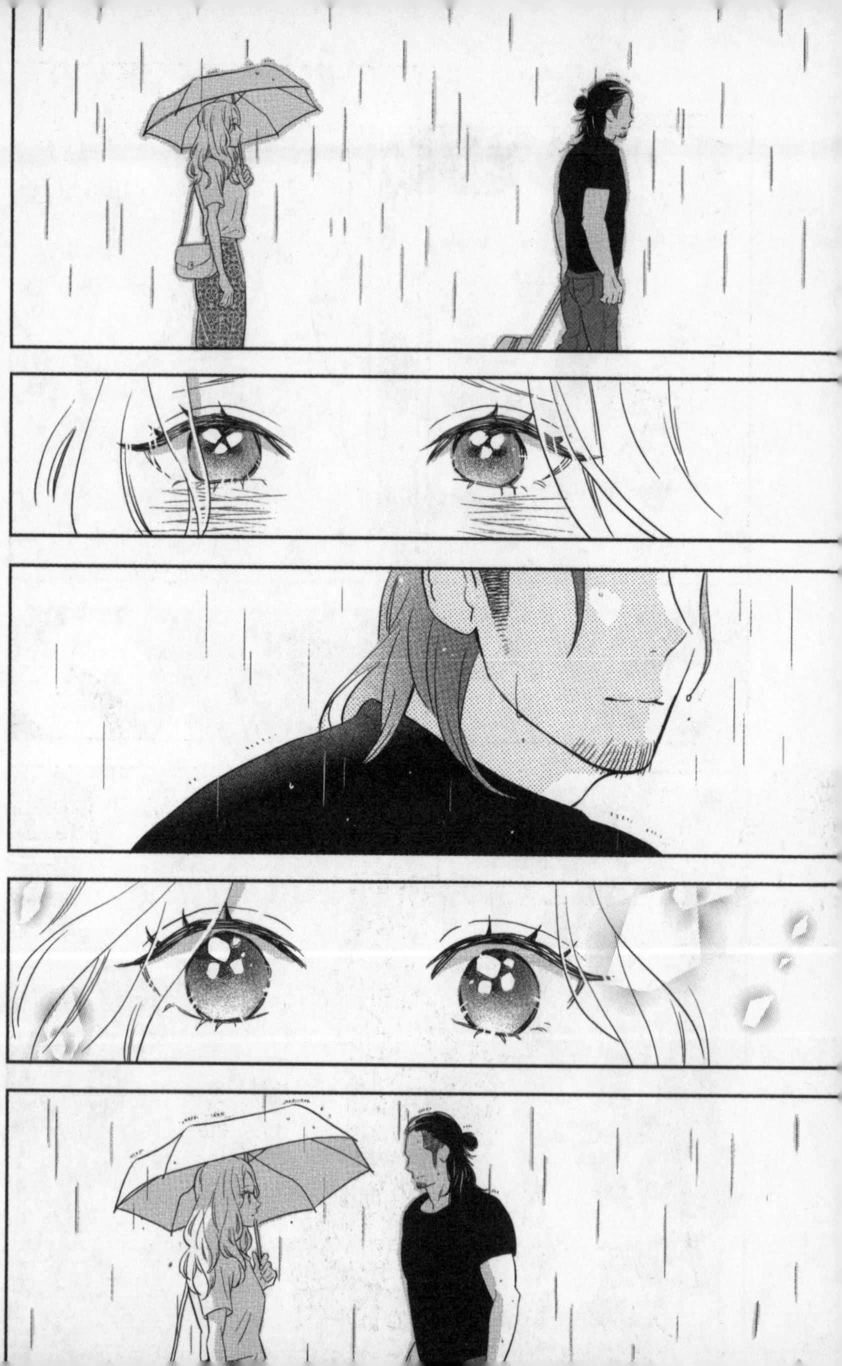

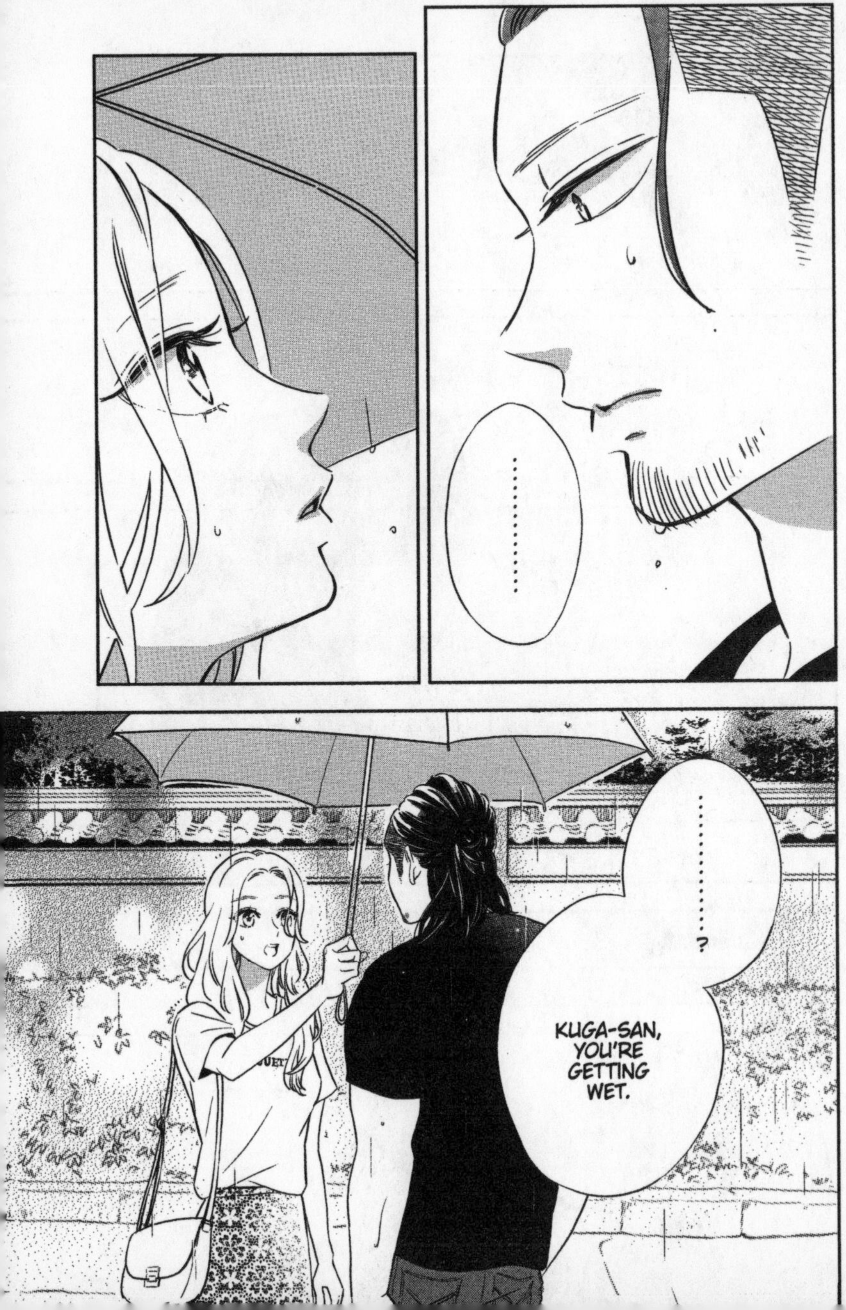
......
......?
KUGA-SAN, YOU'RE GETTING WET.

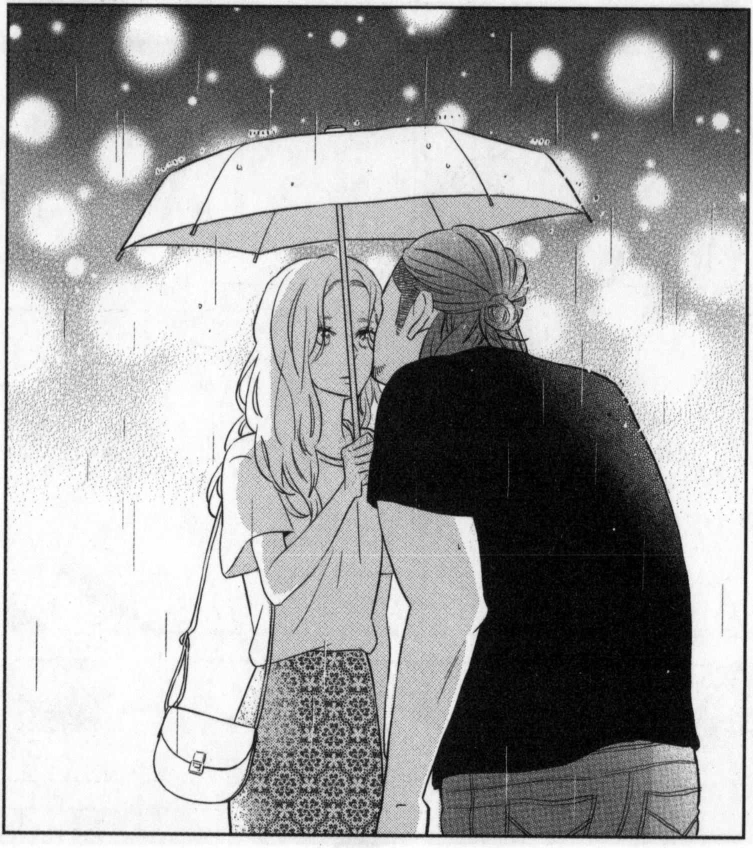
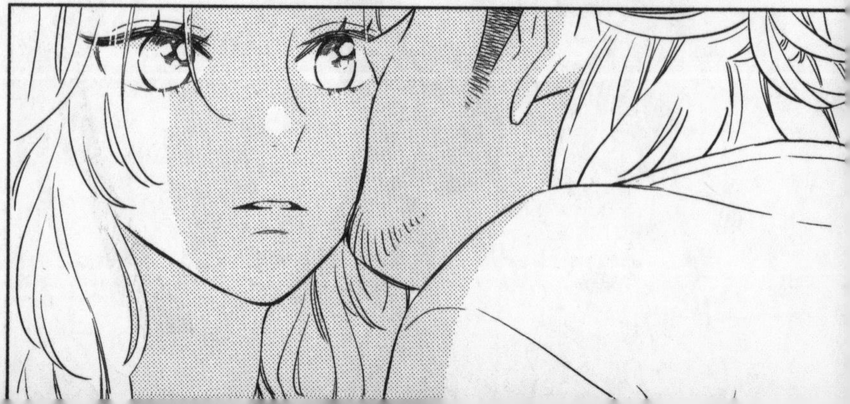

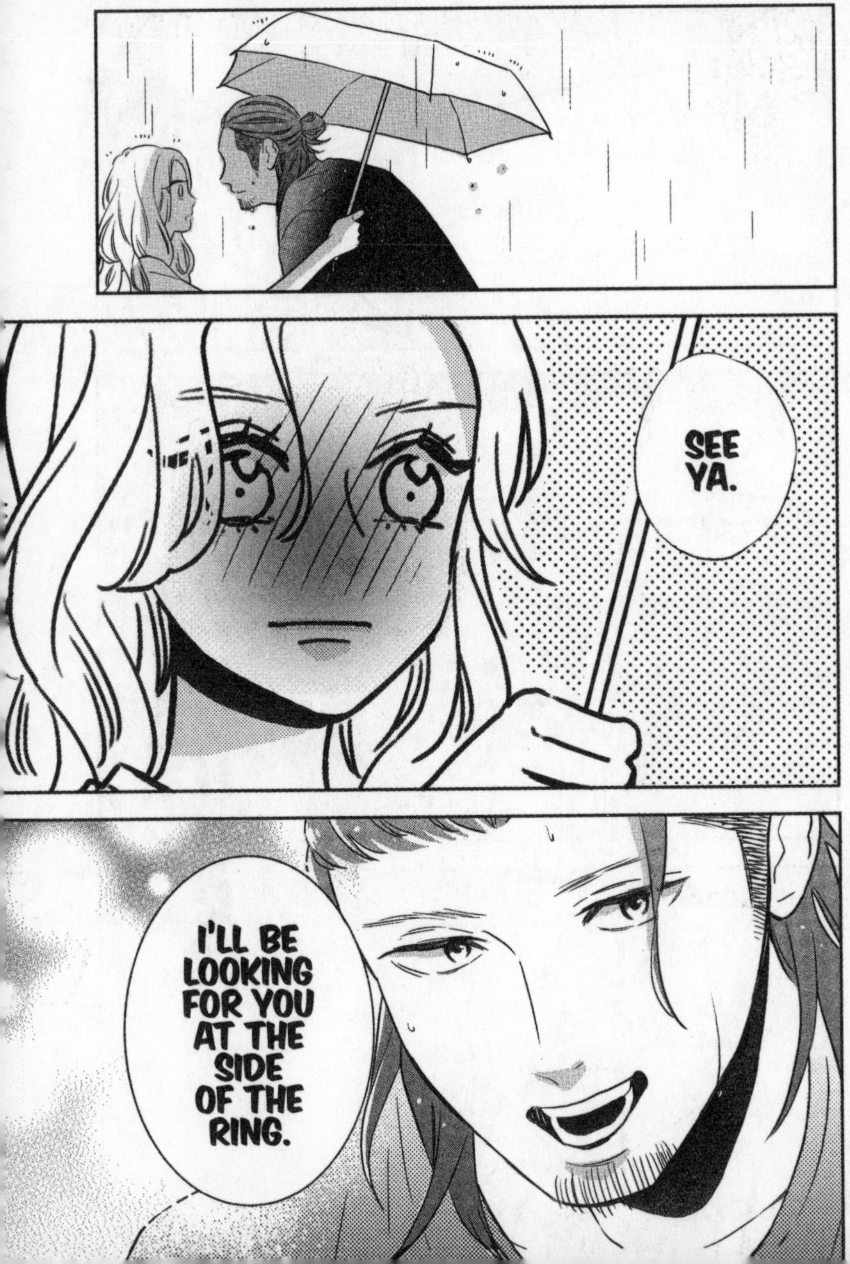
SEE YA.
I'LL BE LOOKING FOR YOU AT THE SIDE OF THE RING.

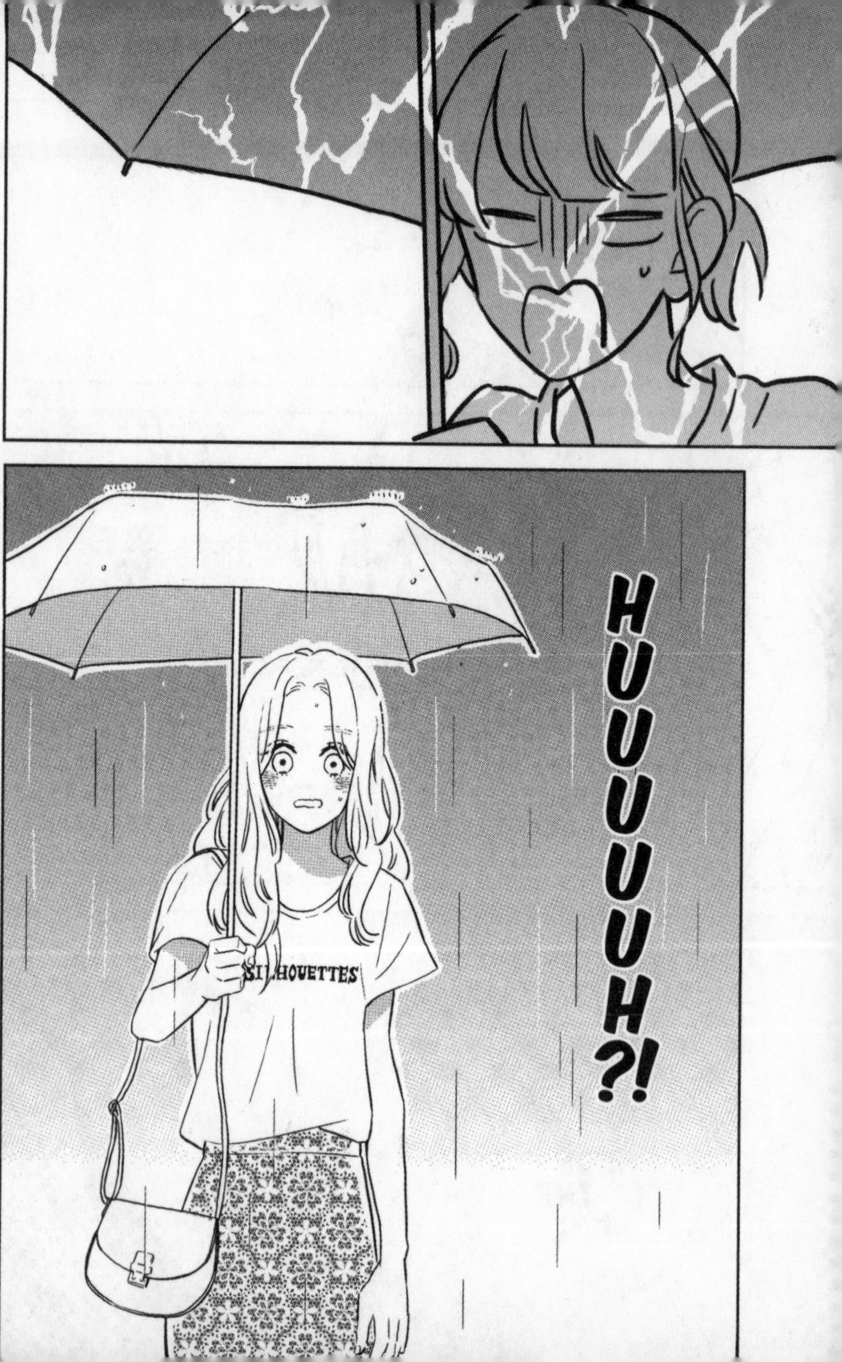
HUUUUUUH?!
SILHOUETTES

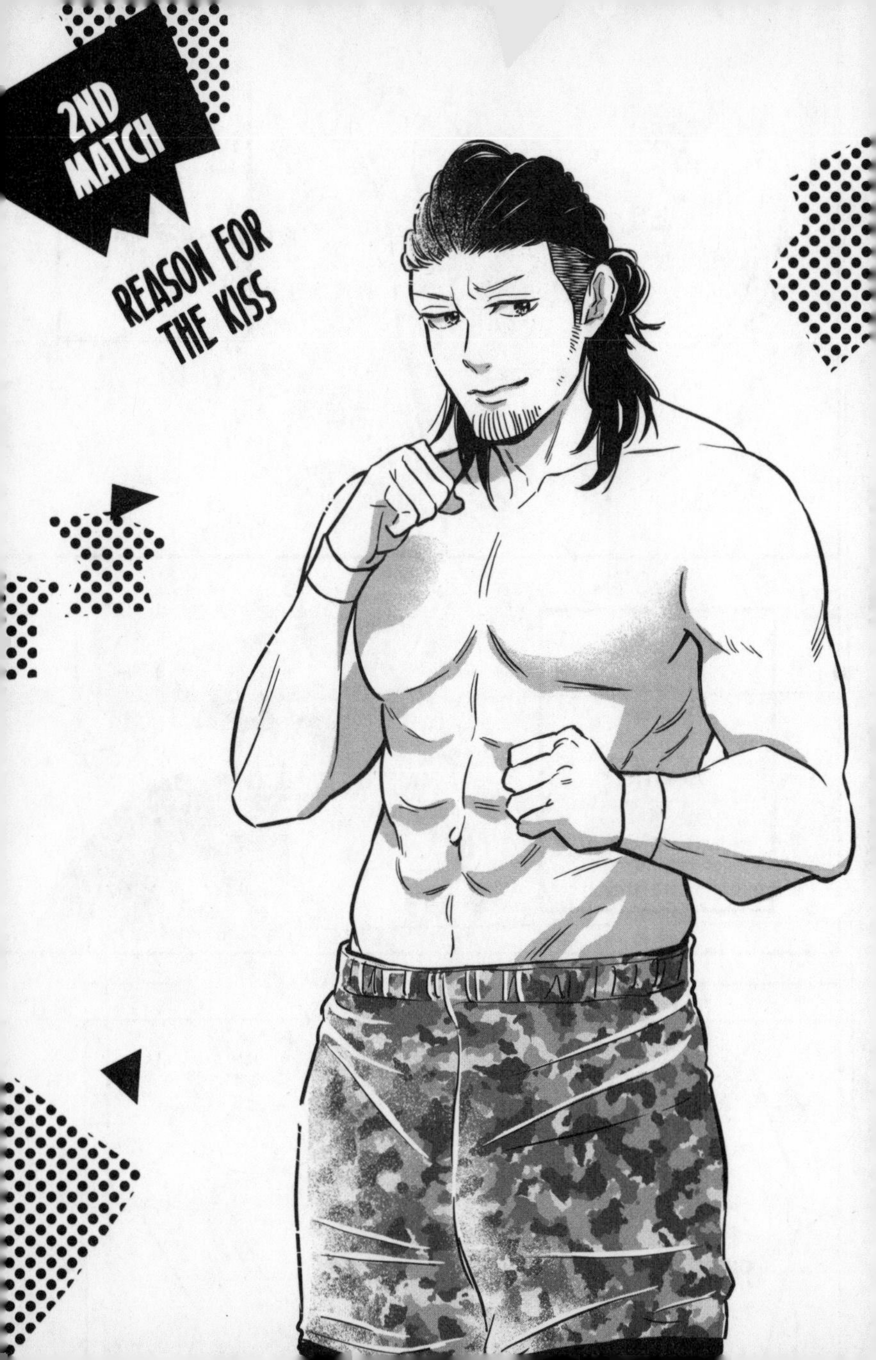
2ND MATCH
REASON FOR THE KISS

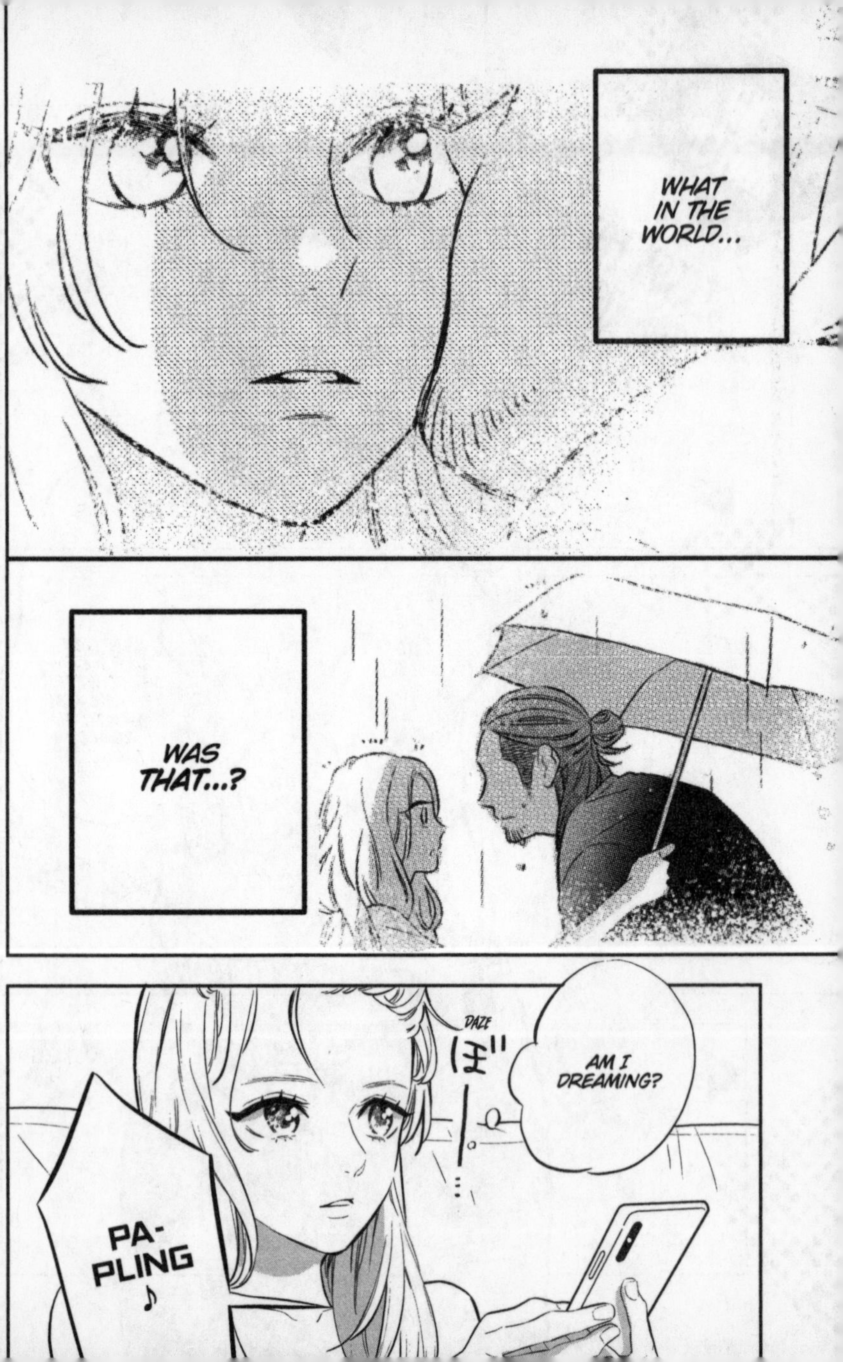
WHAT IN THE WORLD...
WAS THAT...?
AM I DREAMING?
DAZE
ぼ゛ー
PA-PLING ♪

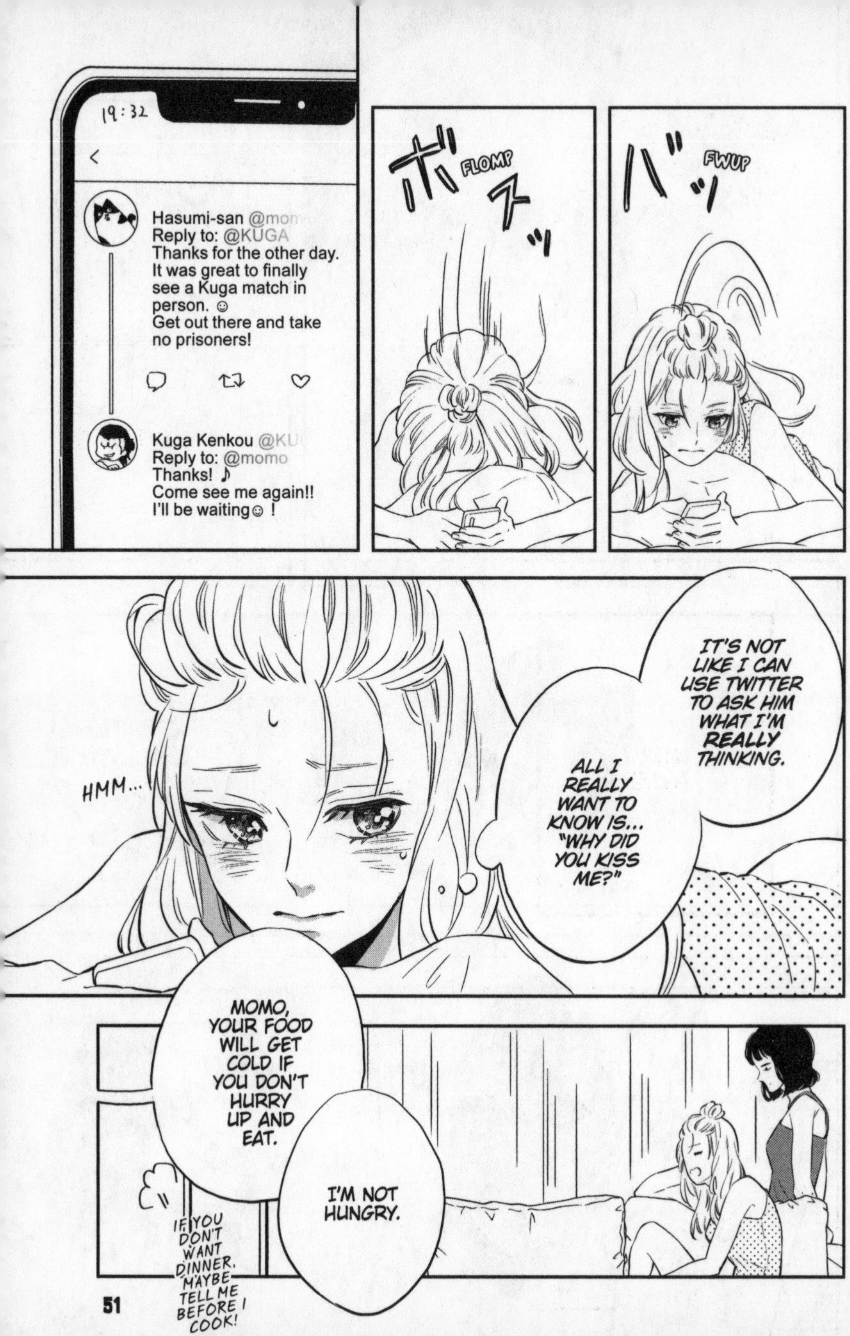

バッ
FWUP
ボスッ
FLOMP
19:32
Hasumi-san @mom
Reply to: @KUGA
Thanks for the other day. It was great to finally see a Kuga match in person. ☺ Get out there and take no prisoners!
Kuga Kenkou @KU
Reply to: @momo
Thanks! ♪ Come see me again!! I'll be waiting☺ !
IT'S NOT LIKE I CAN USE TWITTER TO ASK HIM WHAT I'M REALLY THINKING.
ALL I REALLY WANT TO KNOW IS... "WHY DID YOU KISS ME?"
HMM...
MOMO, YOUR FOOD WILL GET COLD IF YOU DON'T HURRY UP AND EAT.
I'M NOT HUNGRY.
IF YOU DON'T WANT DINNER, MAYBE TELL ME BEFORE I COOK!

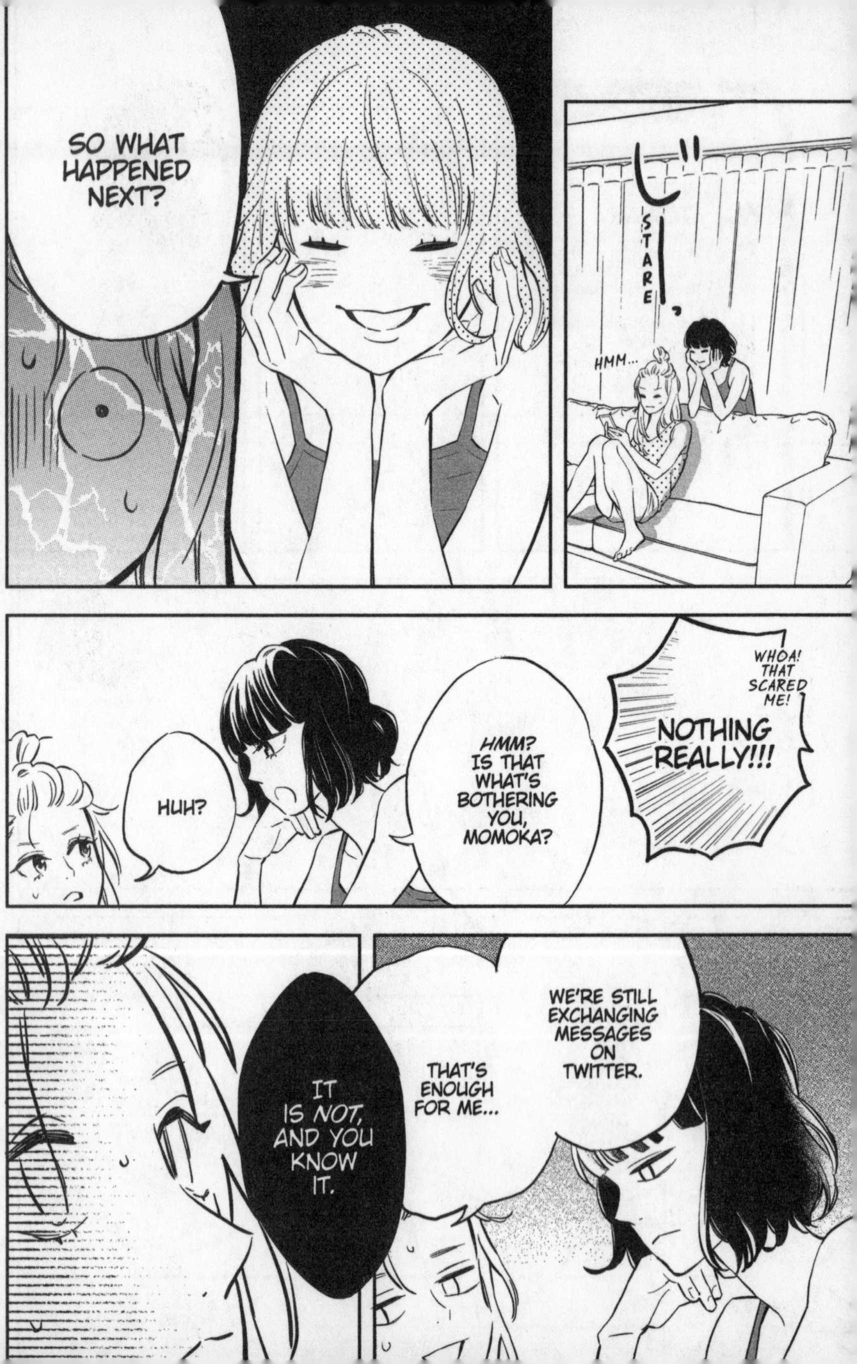
STARE
HMM...
SO WHAT HAPPENED NEXT?
WHOA! THAT SCARED ME!
NOTHING REALLY!!!
HMM? IS THAT WHAT'S BOTHERING YOU, MOMOKA?
HUH?
WE'RE STILL EXCHANGING MESSAGES ON TWITTER.
THAT'S ENOUGH FOR ME...
IT IS *NOT*, AND YOU KNOW IT.

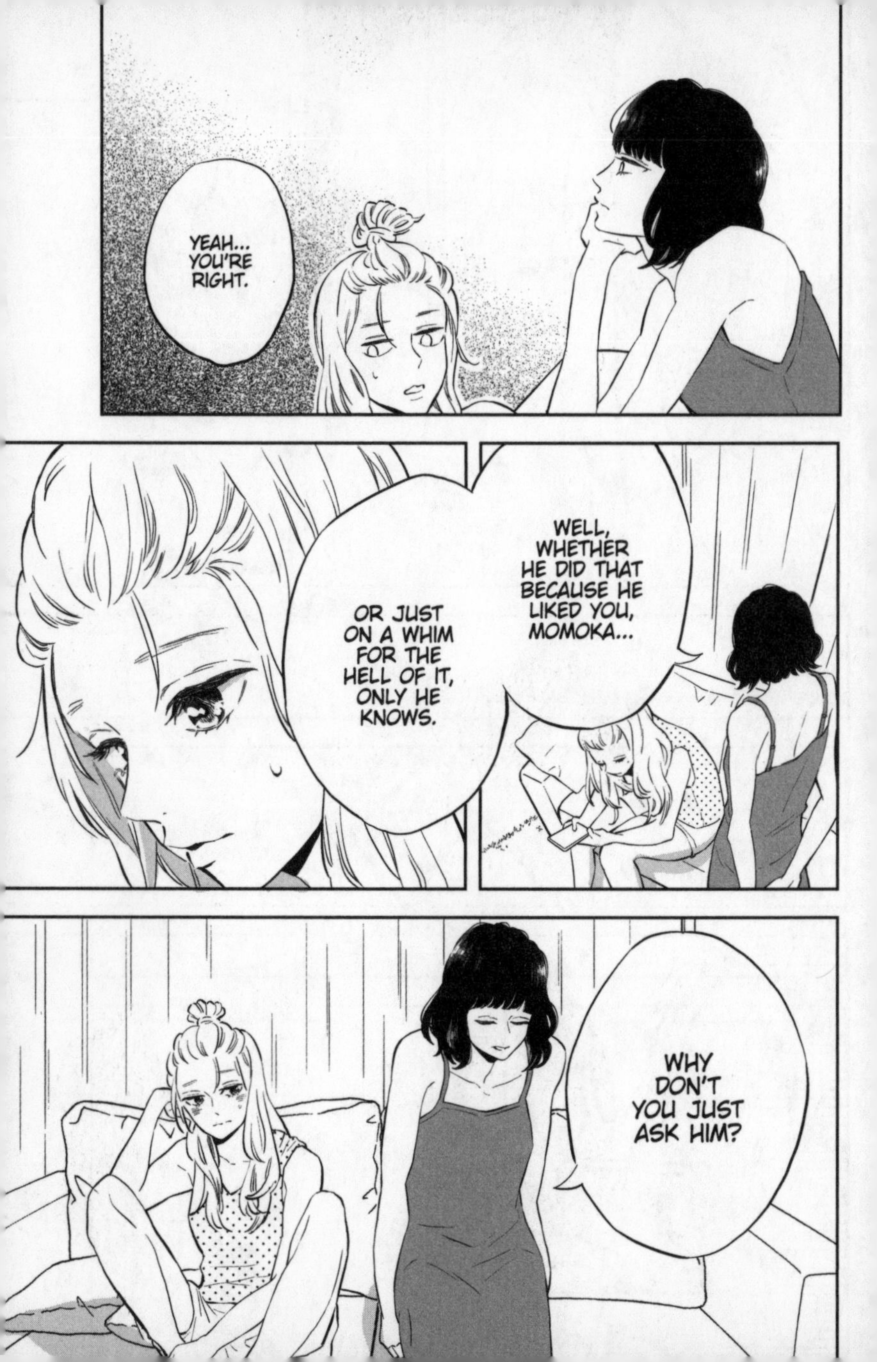
YEAH... YOU'RE RIGHT.
WELL, WHETHER HE DID THAT BECAUSE HE LIKED YOU, MOMOKA...
OR JUST ON A WHIM FOR THE HELL OF IT, ONLY HE KNOWS.
WHY DON'T YOU JUST ASK HIM?

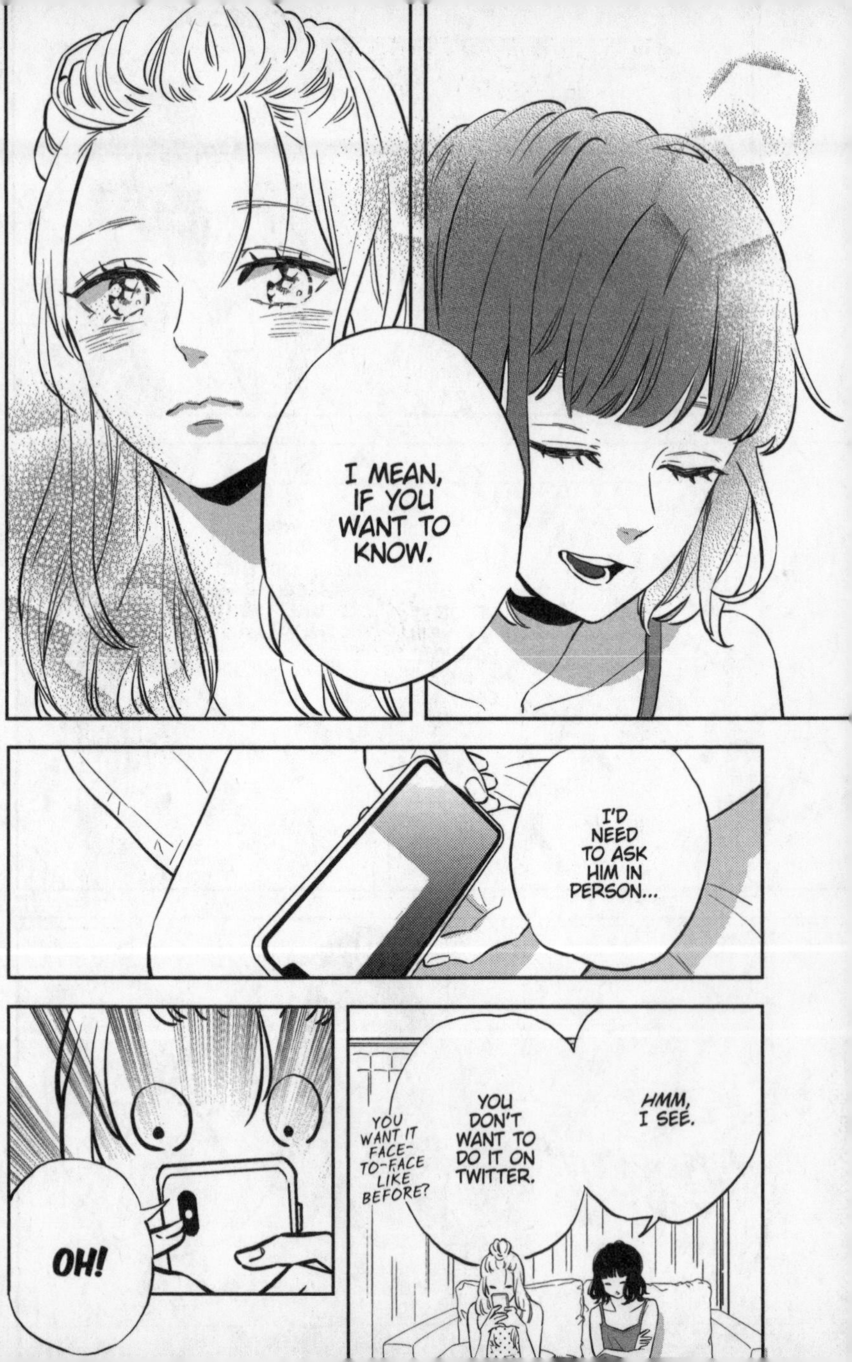
I MEAN, IF YOU WANT TO KNOW.
I'D NEED TO ASK HIM IN PERSON...
HMM, I SEE.
YOU DON'T WANT TO DO IT ON TWITTER.
YOU WANT IT FACE-TO-FACE LIKE BEFORE?
OH!

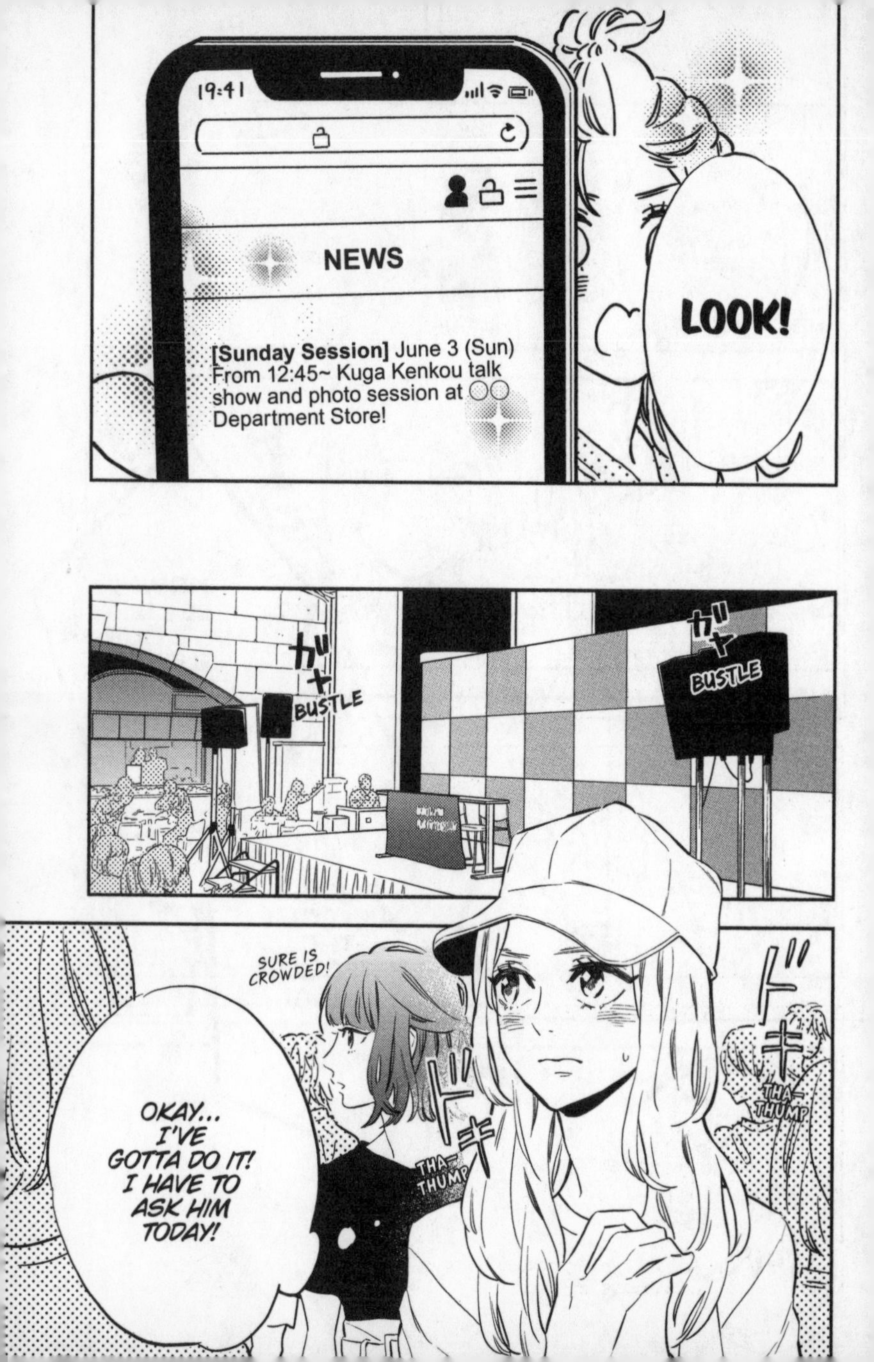
LOOK!
19:41
NEWS
[Sunday Session] June 3 (Sun) From 12:45~ Kuga Kenkou talk show and photo session at ◯◯ Department Store!
ガヤ
BUSTLE
ガヤ
BUSTLE
SURE IS CROWDED!
ドキ
THA-THUMP
ドキ
THA-THUMP
OKAY... I'VE GOTTA DO IT! I HAVE TO ASK HIM TODAY!

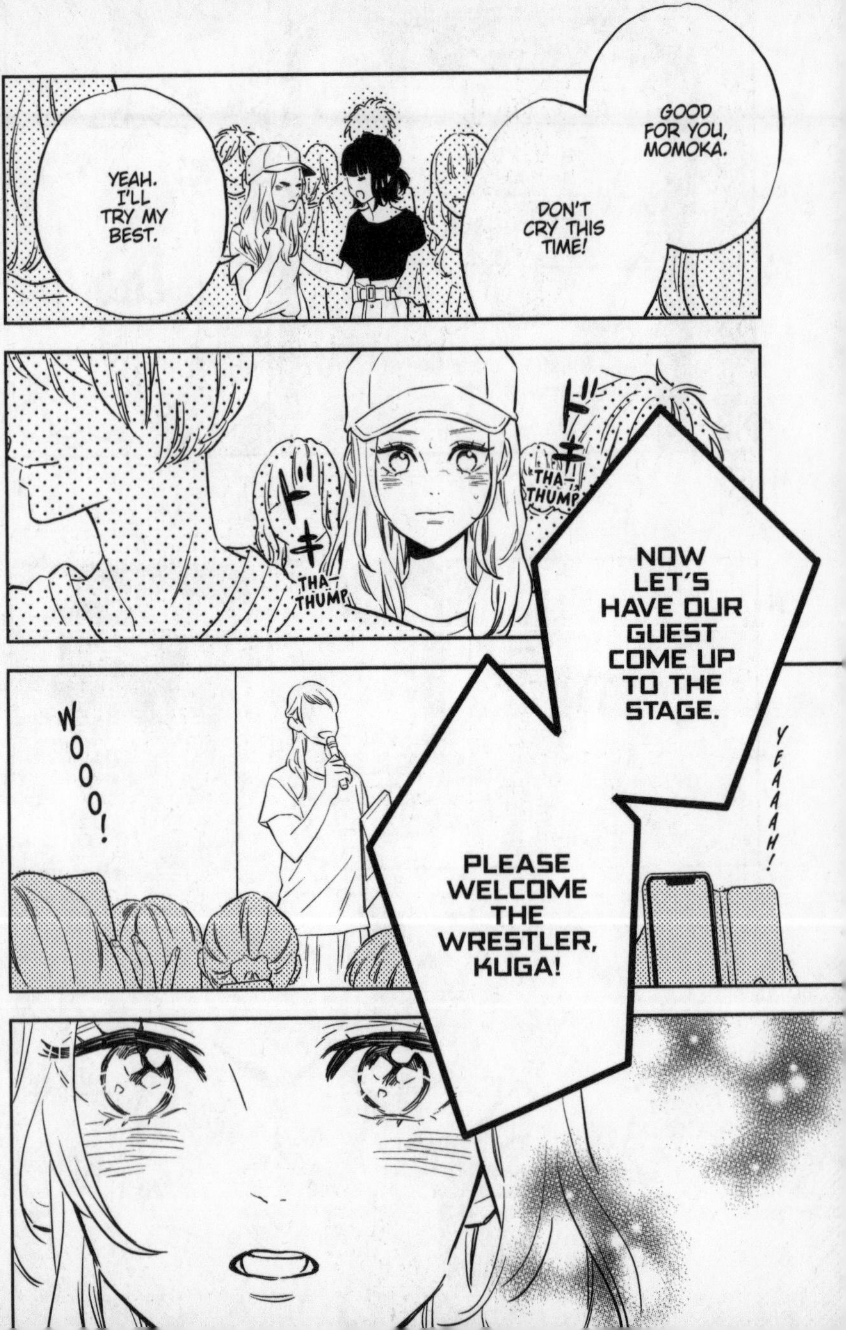
GOOD FOR YOU, MOMOKA.
DON'T CRY THIS TIME!
YEAH. I'LL TRY MY BEST.
THA-THUMP
THA-THUMP
NOW LET'S HAVE OUR GUEST COME UP TO THE STAGE.
YEAAAAH!
PLEASE WELCOME THE WRESTLER, KUGA!
WOOO!

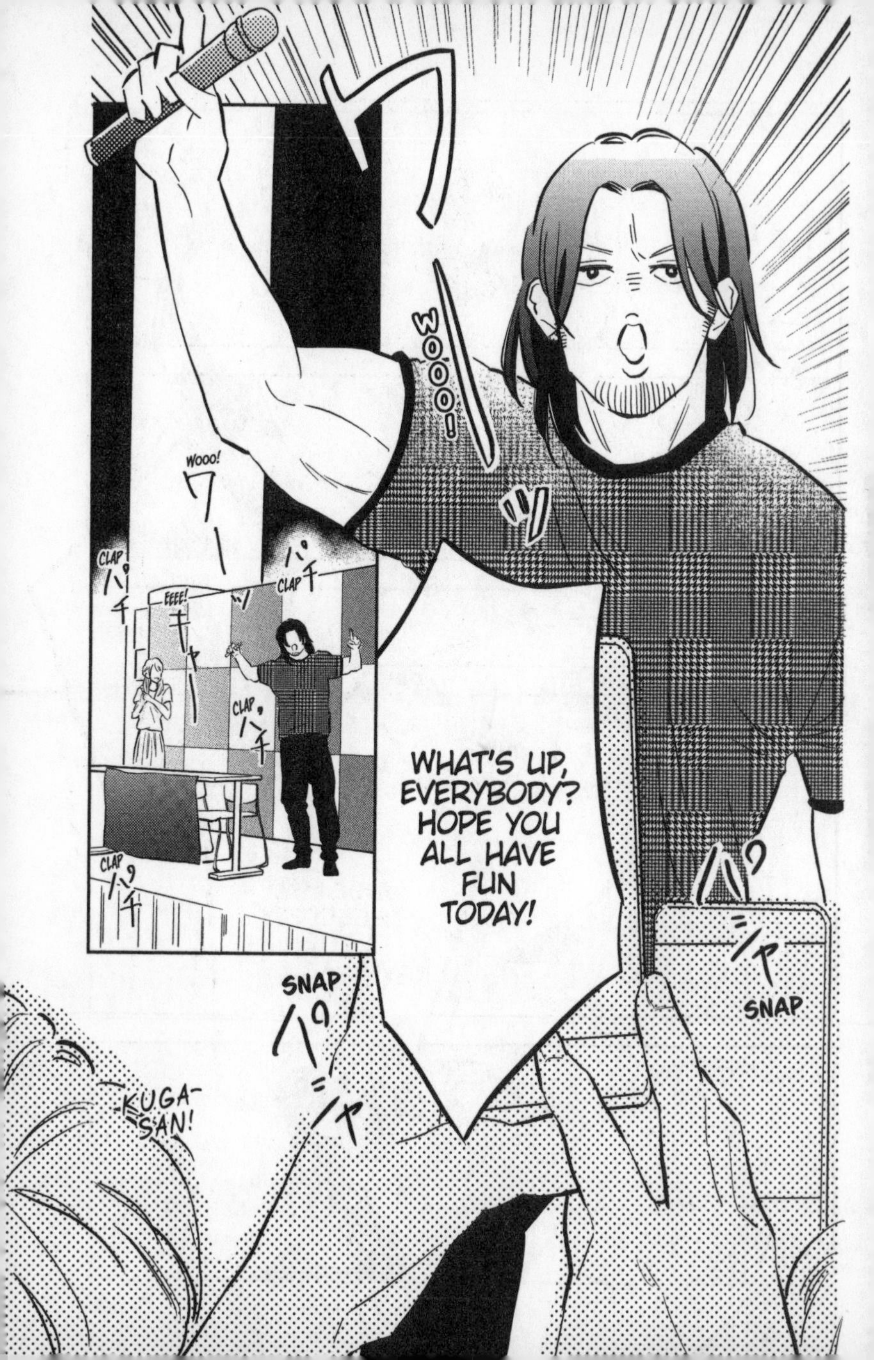

WOOOO!
WHAT'S UP, EVERYBODY? HOPE YOU ALL HAVE FUN TODAY!
SNAP
SNAP
KUGA-SAN!
WOOO!
CLAP
CLAP
EEEE!
CLAP
CLAP

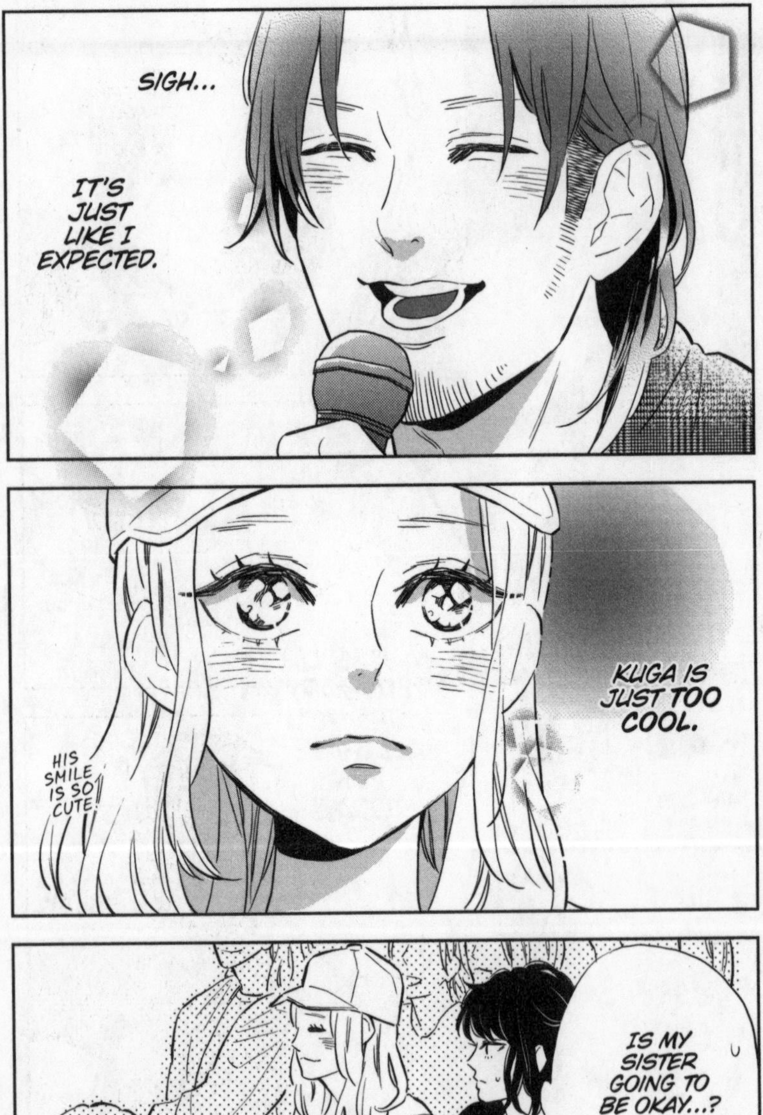
SIGH...
IT'S JUST LIKE I EXPECTED.
KUGA IS JUST TOO COOL.
HIS SMILE IS SO CUTE!
IS MY SISTER GOING TO BE OKAY...?

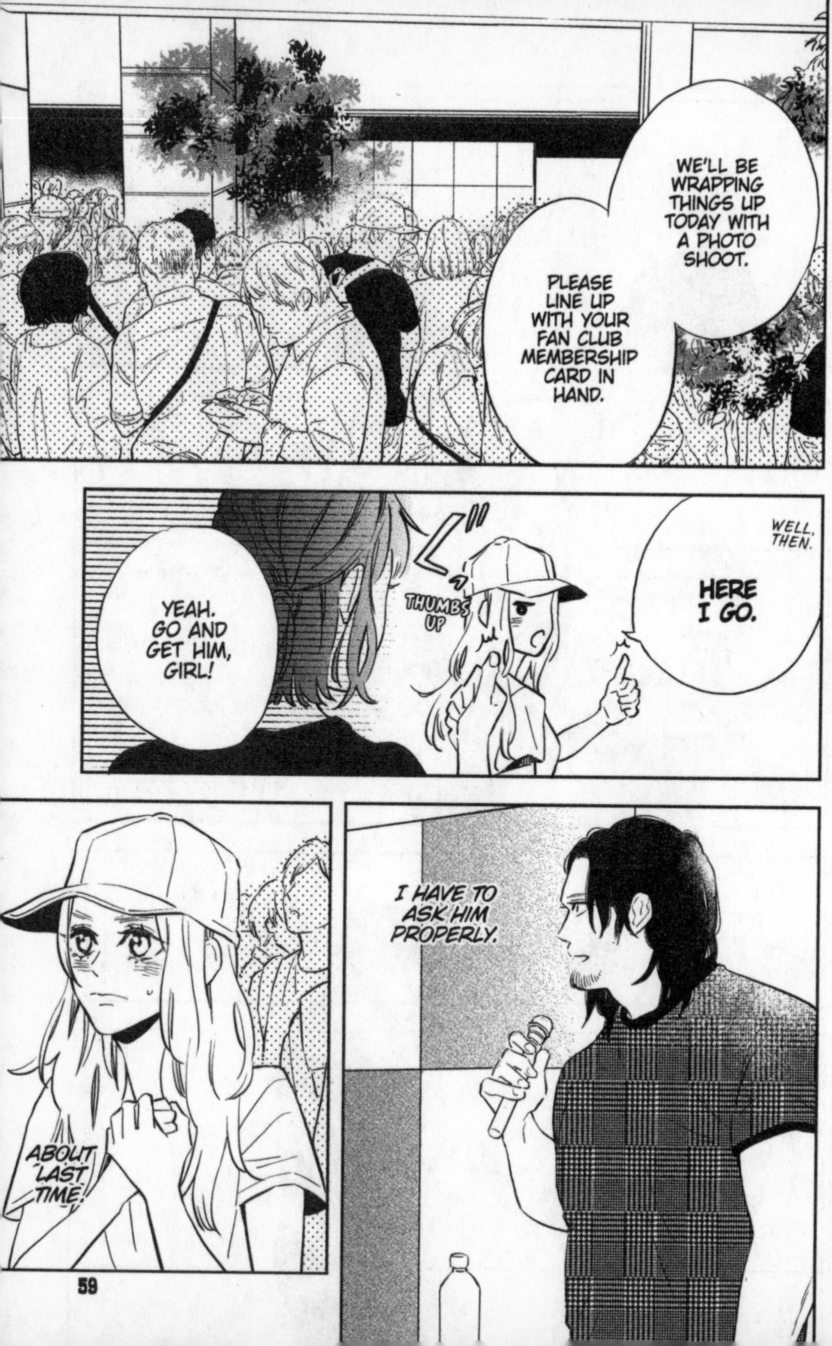
WE'LL BE WRAPPING THINGS UP TODAY WITH A PHOTO SHOOT.
PLEASE LINE UP WITH YOUR FAN CLUB MEMBERSHIP CARD IN HAND.
WELL, THEN.
HERE I GO.
THUMBS UP
YEAH. GO AND GET HIM, GIRL!
I HAVE TO ASK HIM PROPERLY.
ABOUT LAST TIME.

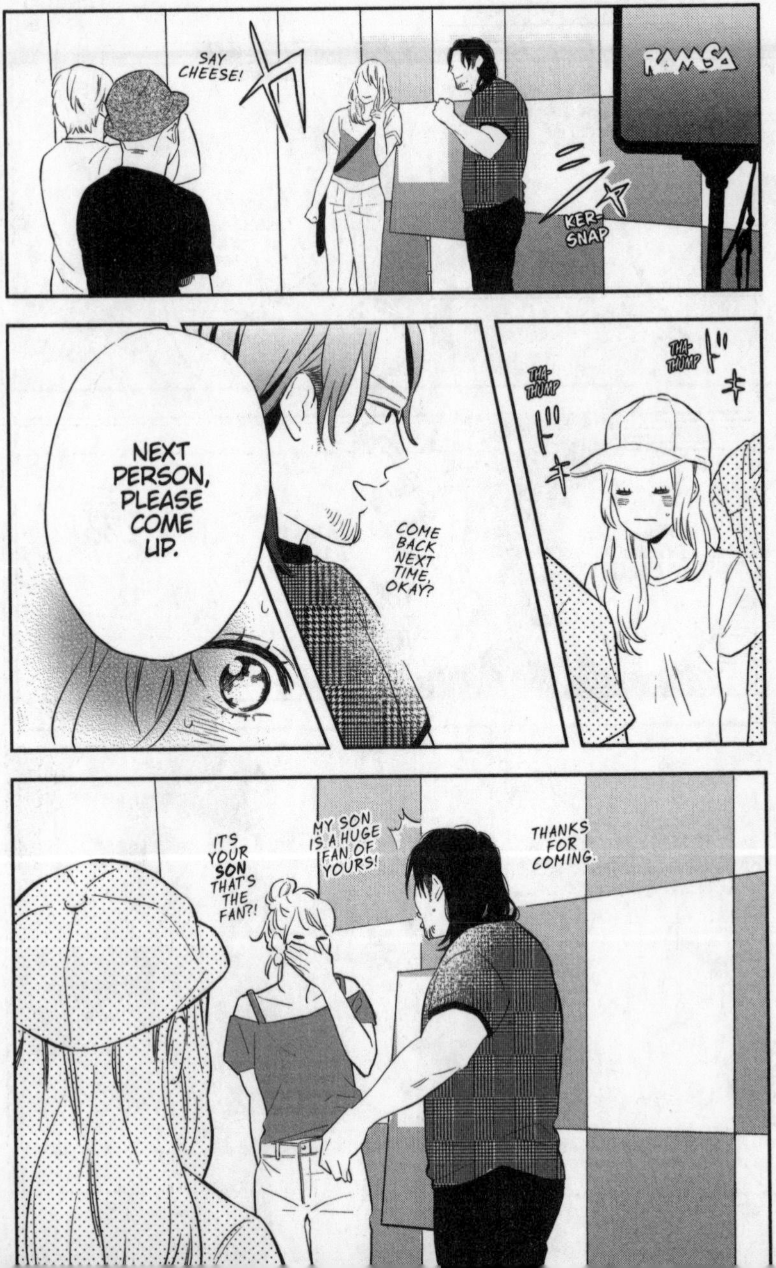
SAY CHEESE!
KER-SNAP
THA-THUMP
THA-THUMP
COME BACK NEXT TIME, OKAY?
NEXT PERSON, PLEASE COME UP.
THANKS FOR COMING.
MY SON IS A HUGE FAN OF YOURS!
IT'S YOUR SON THAT'S THE FAN?!

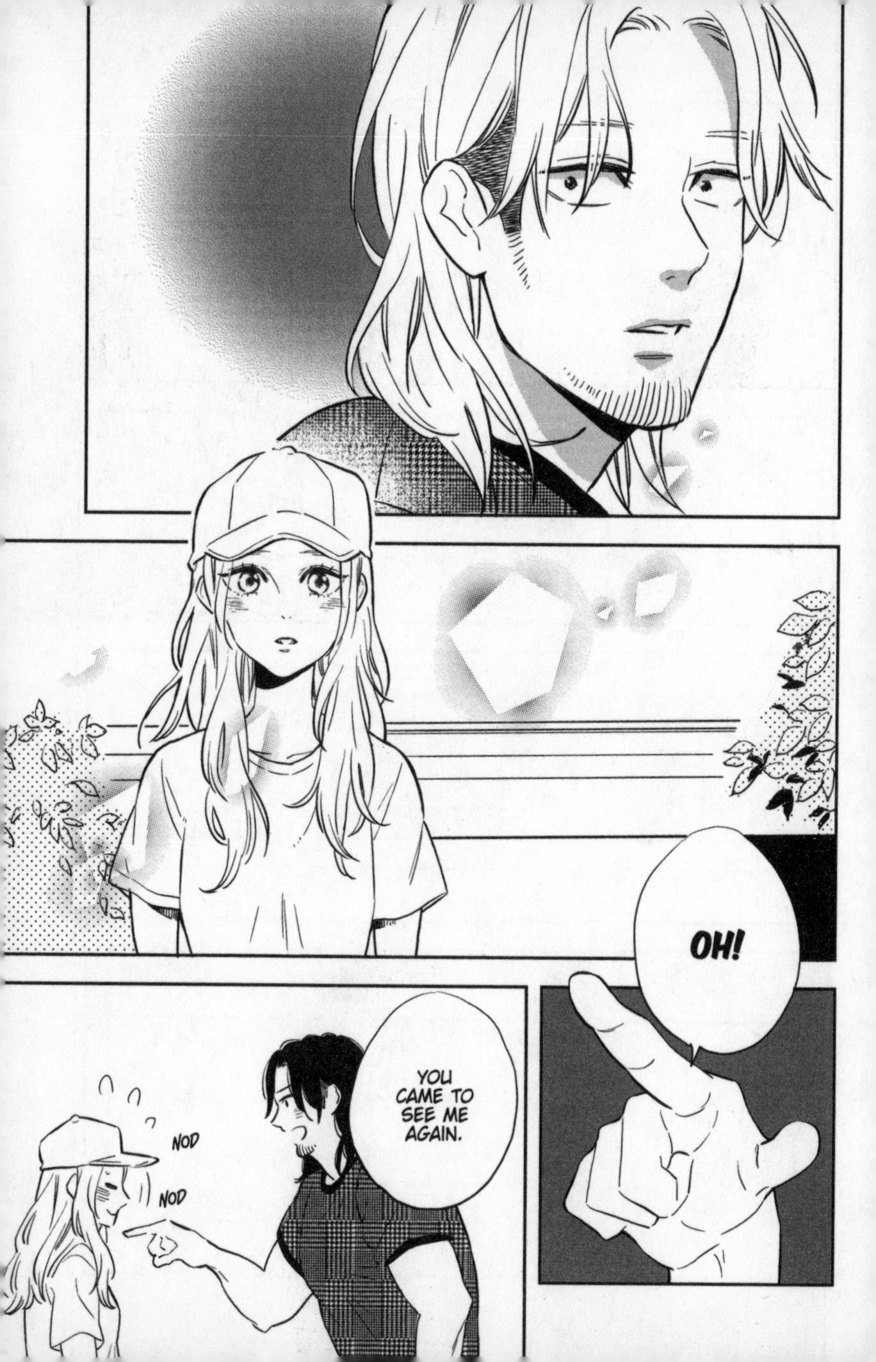
OH!
YOU CAME TO SEE ME AGAIN.
NOD
NOD

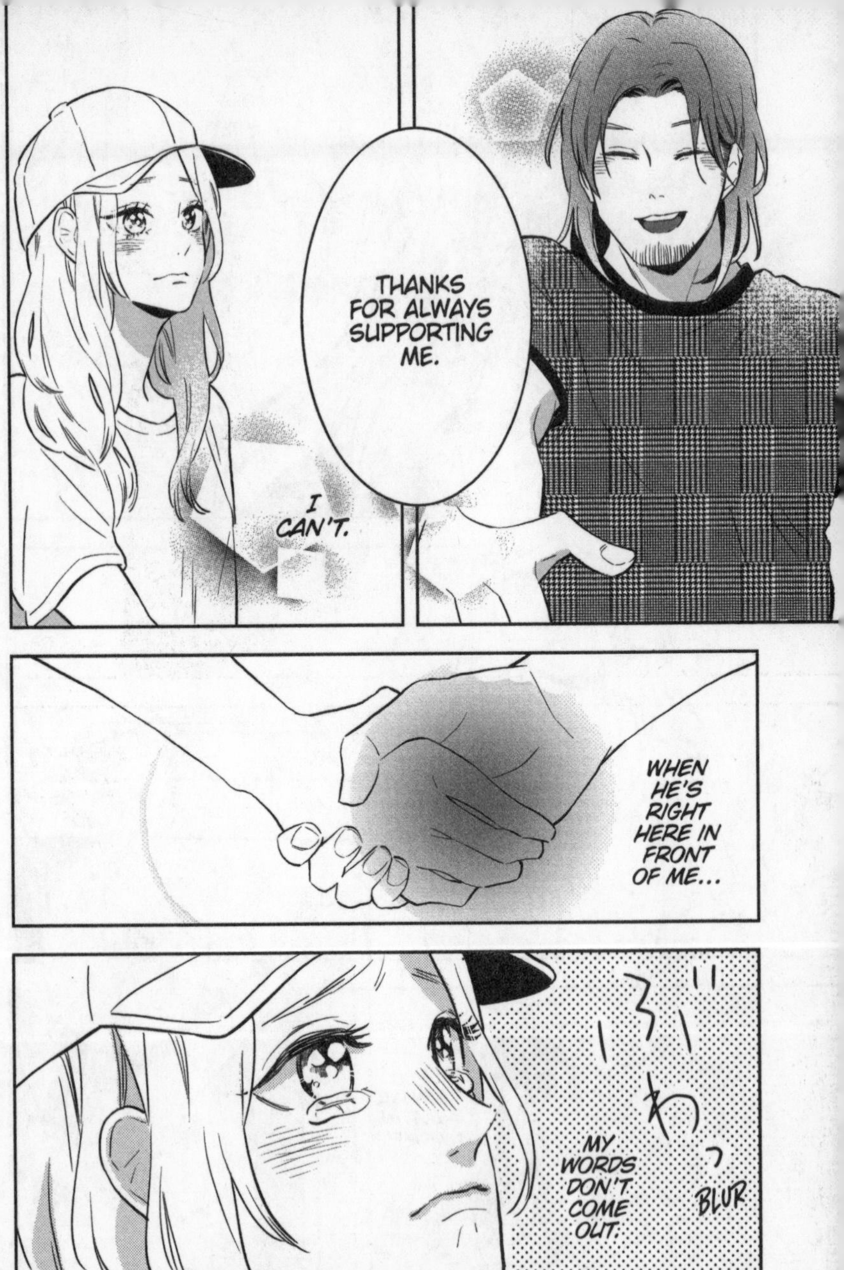
THANKS FOR ALWAYS SUPPORTING ME.
I CAN'T.
WHEN HE'S RIGHT HERE IN FRONT OF ME...
ふわっ
BLUR
MY WORDS DON'T COME OUT.

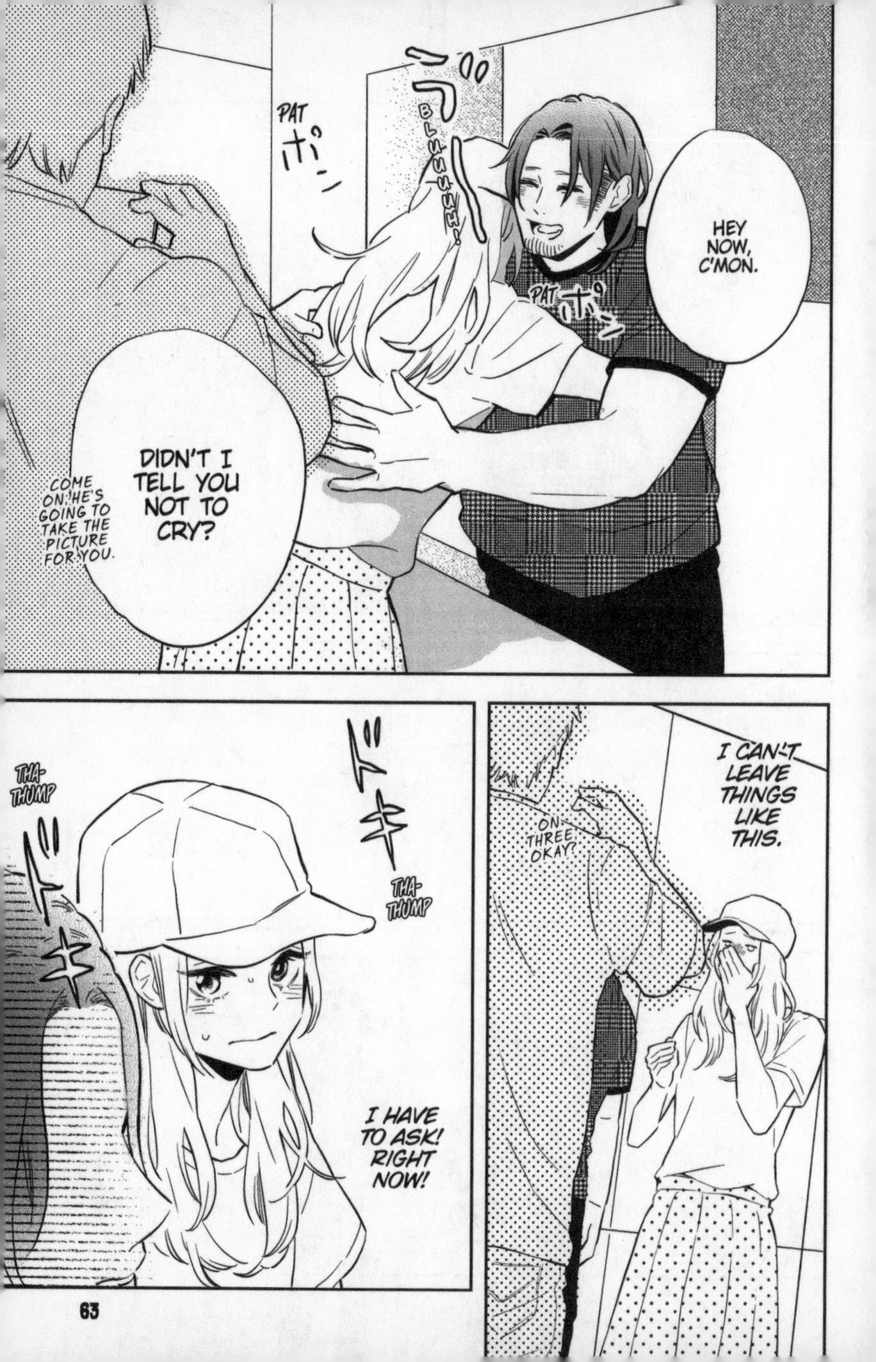
BLUUUUUH!
PAT
HEY NOW, C'MON.
PAT
DIDN'T I TELL YOU NOT TO CRY?
COME ON. HE'S GOING TO TAKE THE PICTURE FOR YOU.
I CAN'T LEAVE THINGS LIKE THIS.
ON THREE OKAY?
THA-THUMP
THA-THUMP
I HAVE TO ASK! RIGHT NOW!

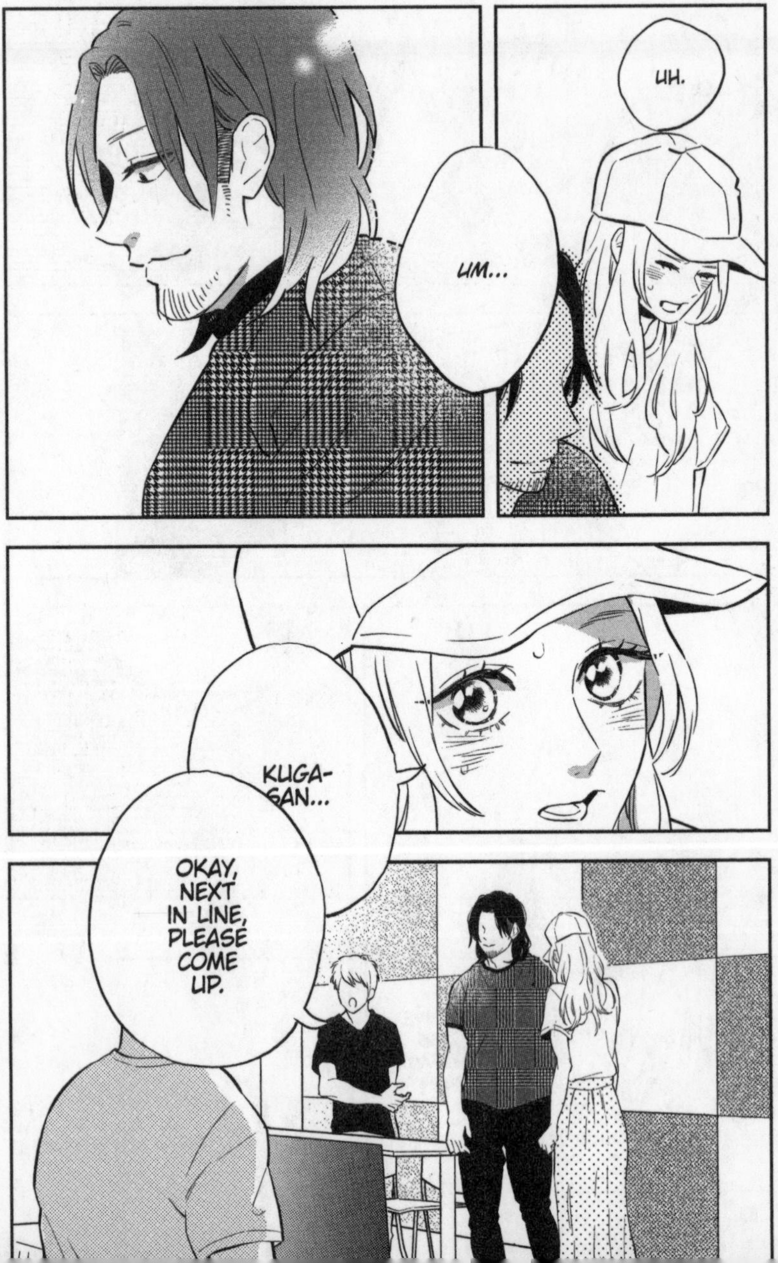
UH.
UM...
KUGA-SAN...
OKAY, NEXT IN LINE, PLEASE COME UP.

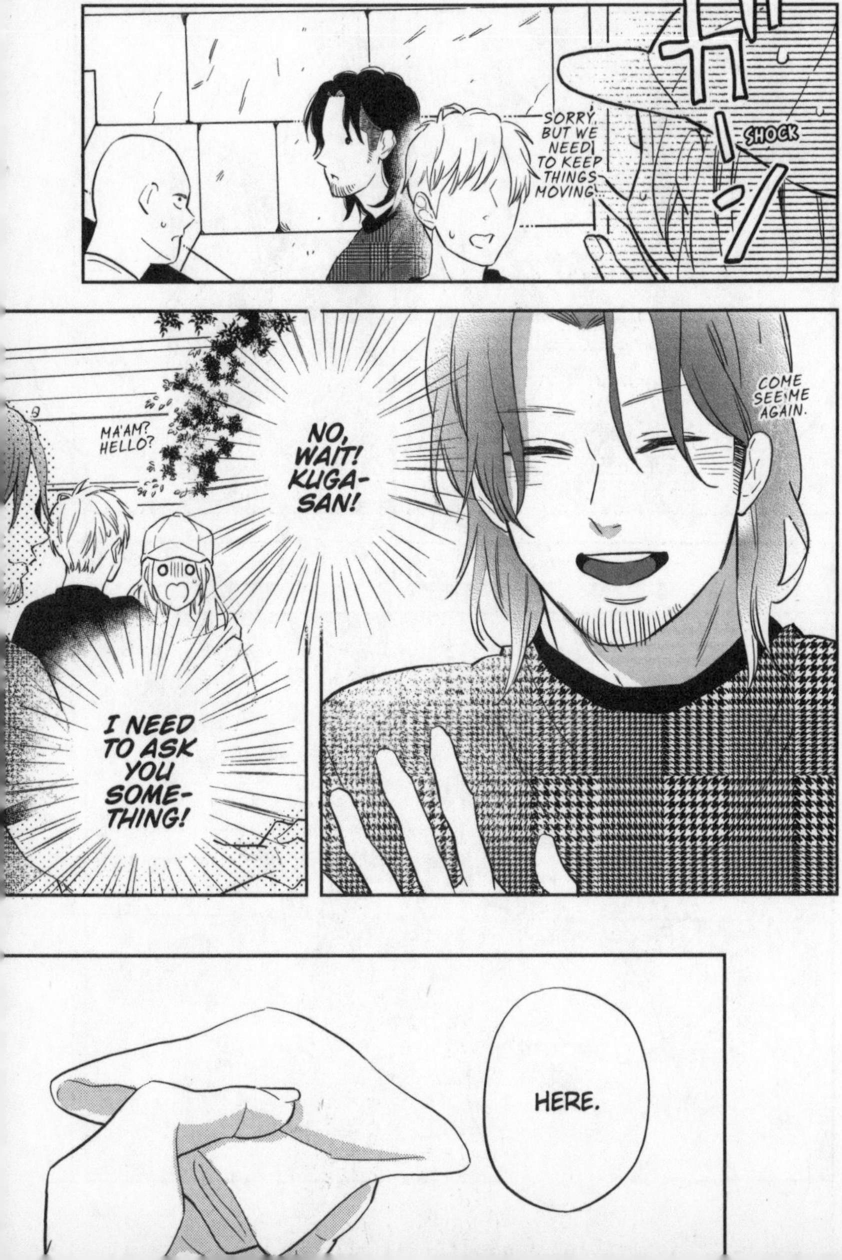
SHOCK
SORRY, BUT WE NEED TO KEEP THINGS MOVING.
COME SEE ME AGAIN.
NO, WAIT! KUGA-SAN!
MA'AM? HELLO?
I NEED TO ASK YOU SOME-THING!
HERE.

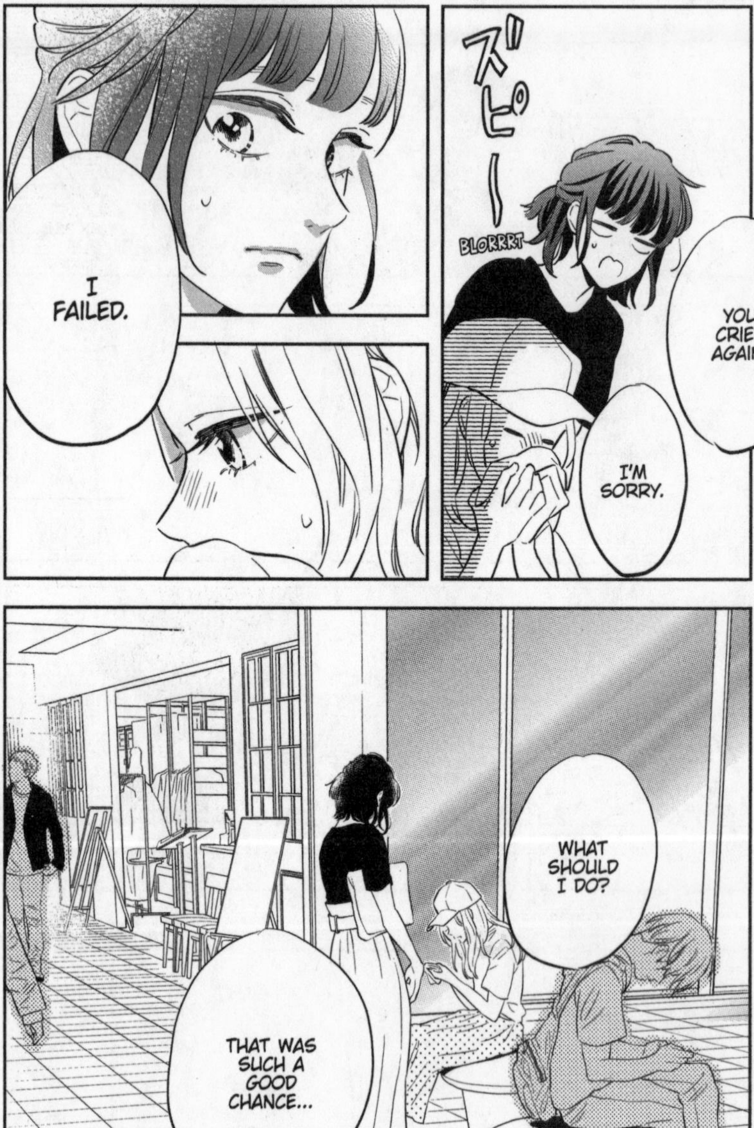
ズピー
BLORRRT
YOU CRIED AGAIN.
I'M SORRY.
I FAILED.
WHAT SHOULD I DO?
THAT WAS SUCH A GOOD CHANCE...

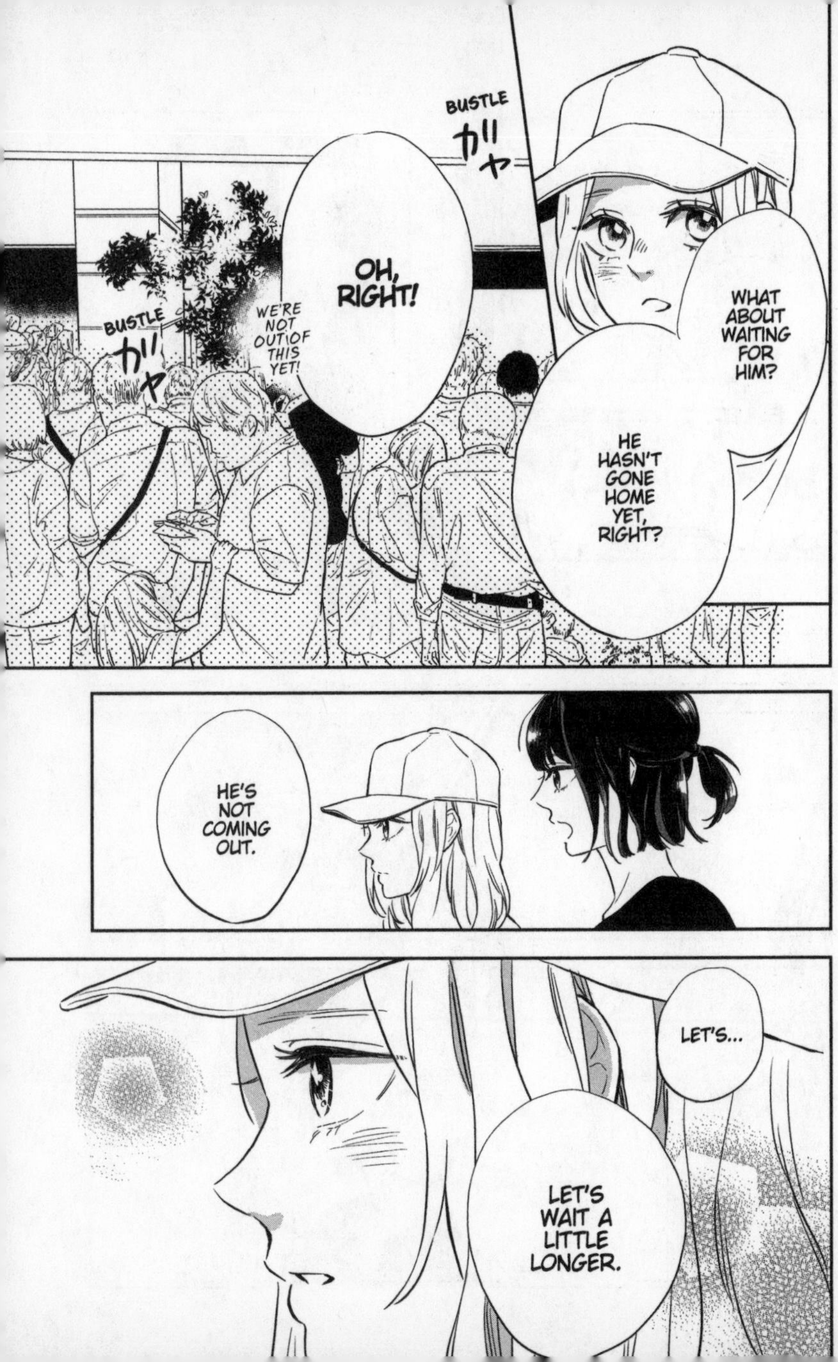
WHAT ABOUT WAITING FOR HIM?
HE HASN'T GONE HOME YET, RIGHT?
BUSTLE
ガヤ
OH, RIGHT!
WE'RE NOT OUT OF THIS YET!
BUSTLE
ガヤ
HE'S NOT COMING OUT.
LET'S...
LET'S WAIT A LITTLE LONGER.

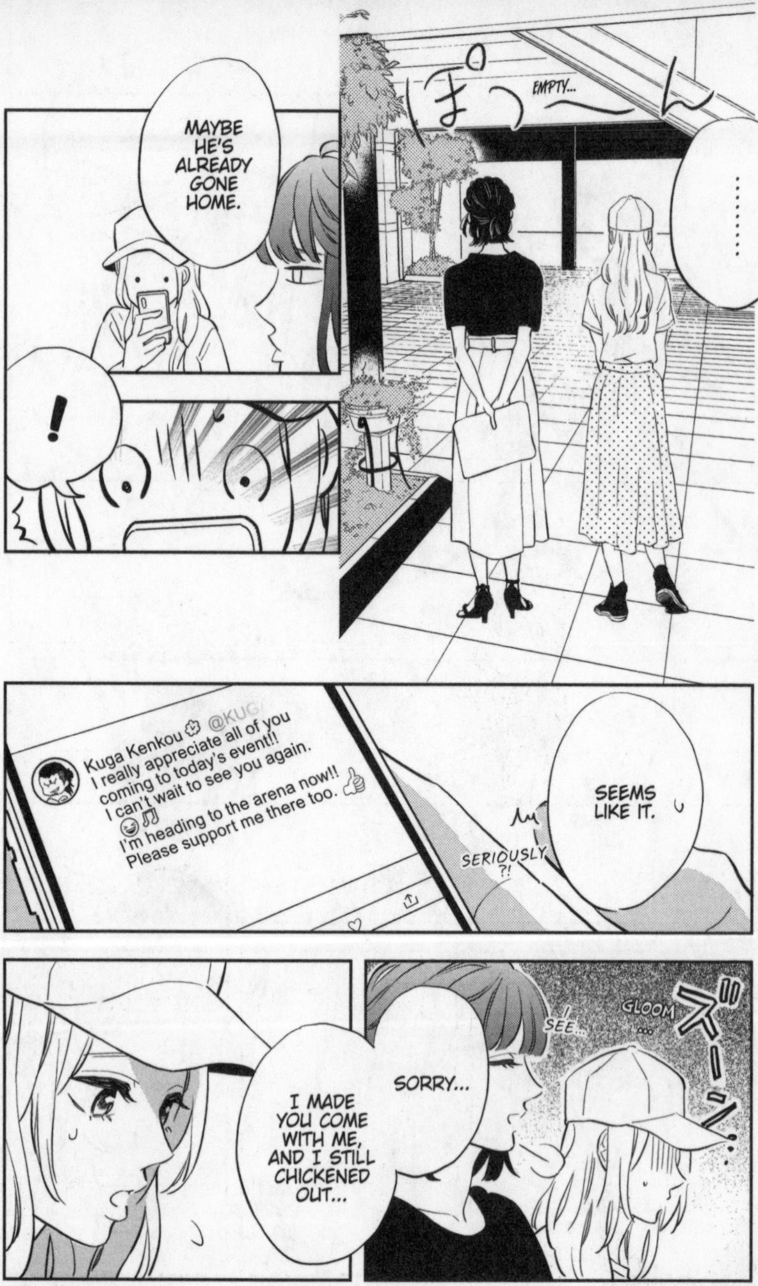
ぽつーん
EMPTY...
......
MAYBE HE'S ALREADY GONE HOME.
!
SEEMS LIKE IT.
SERIOUSLY?!
Kuga Kenkou @KUGI
I really appreciate all of you coming to today's event!! I can't wait to see you again.
I'm heading to the arena now!! Please support me there too.
ズーン
GLOOM...
I SEE...
SORRY...
I MADE YOU COME WITH ME, AND I STILL CHICKENED OUT...

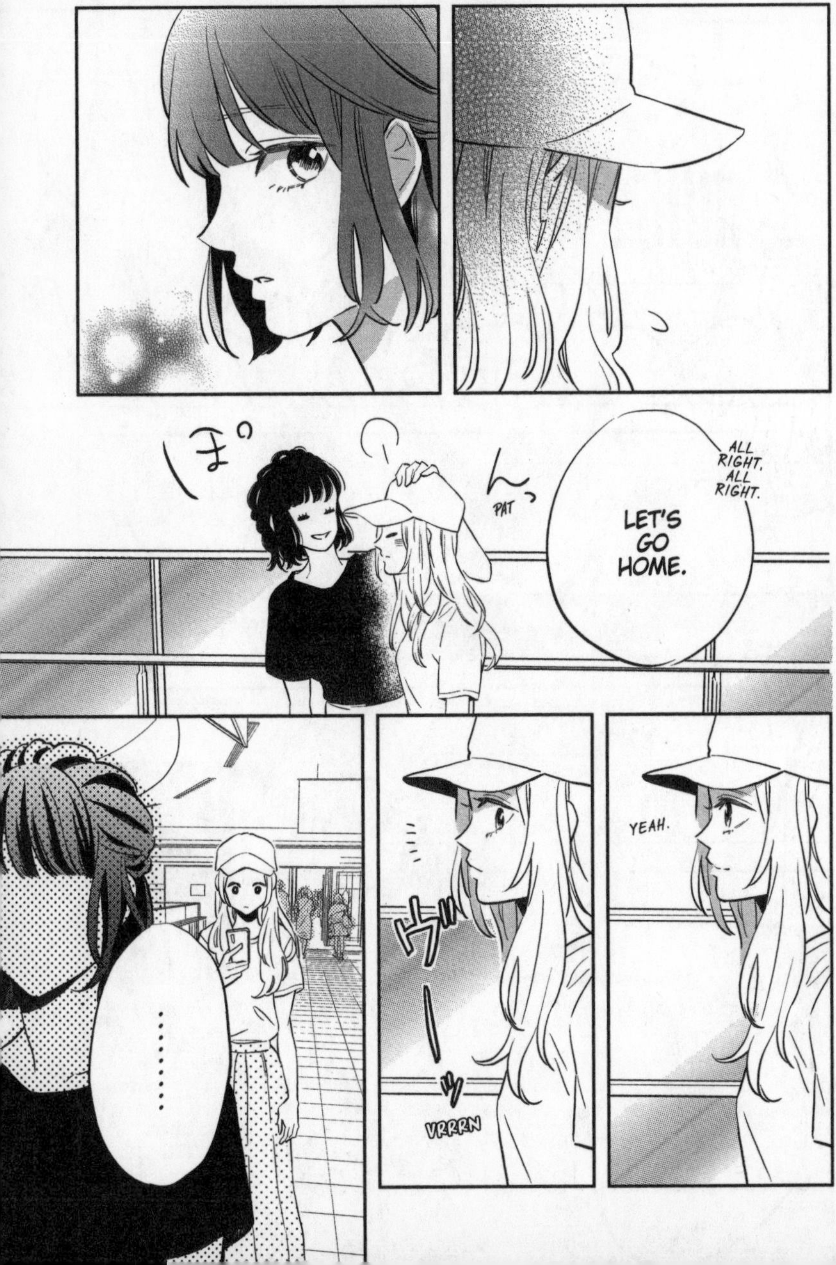
ALL RIGHT, ALL RIGHT.
LET'S GO HOME.
ぽん
PAT
YEAH.
ヴーッ
VRRRN
......

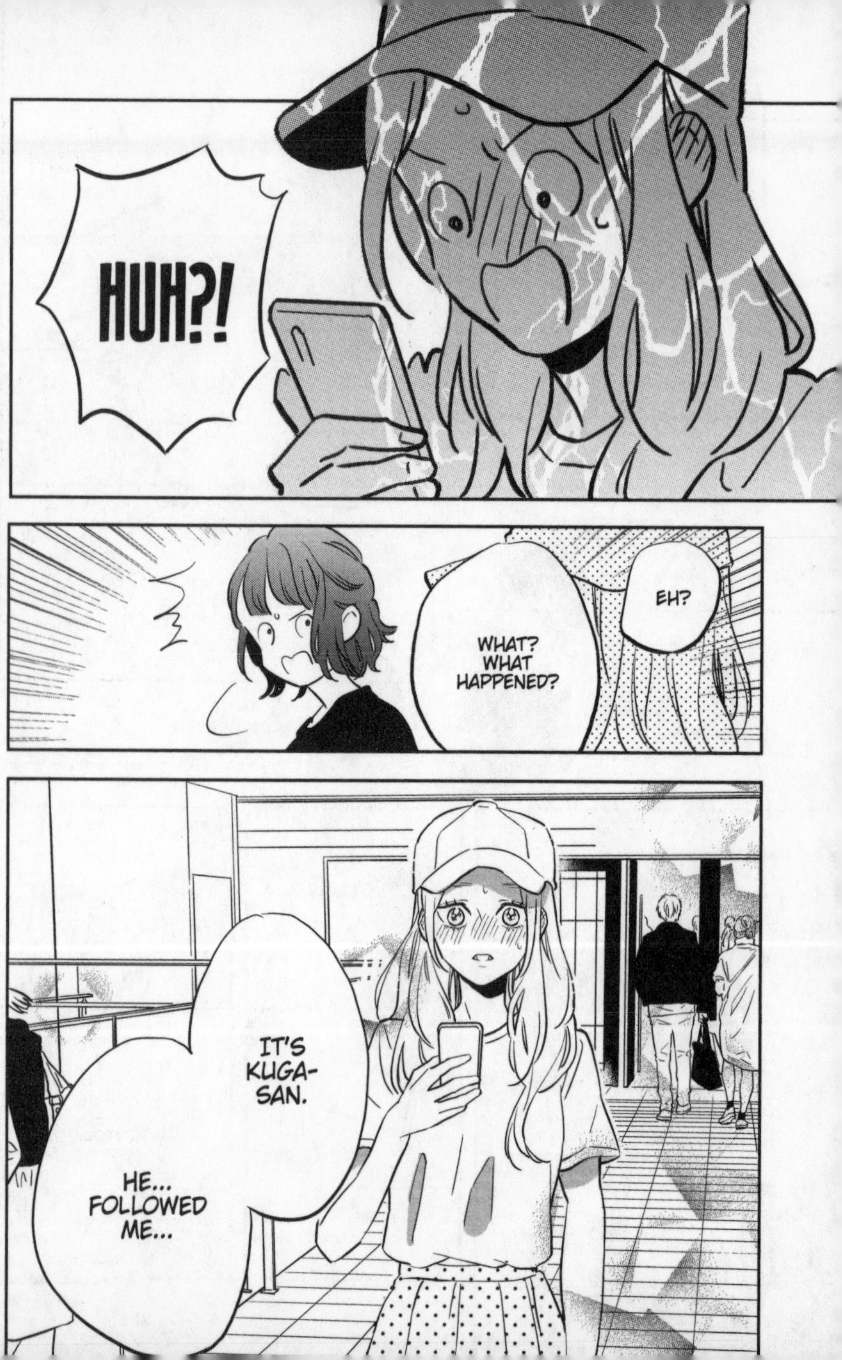
HUH?!
EH?
WHAT? WHAT HAPPENED?
IT'S KUGA-SAN.
HE... FOLLOWED ME...

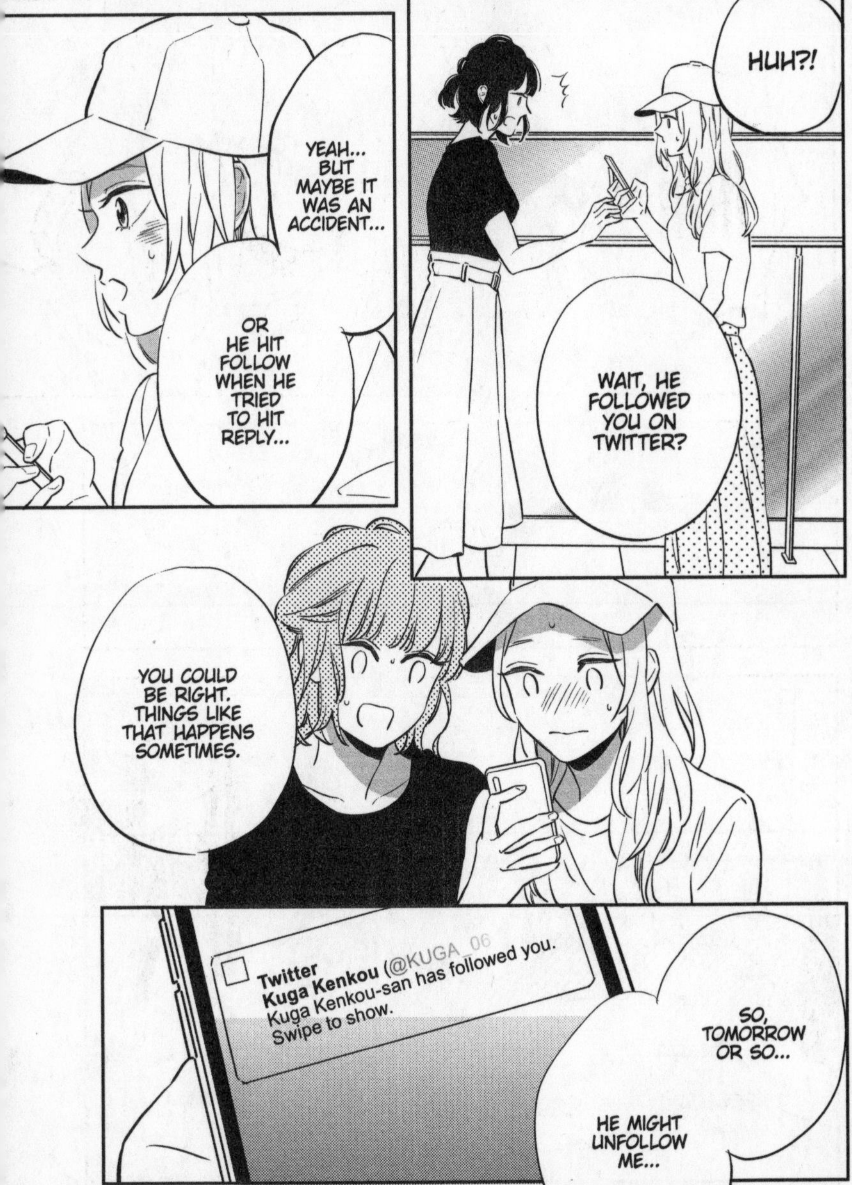
HUH?!
WAIT, HE FOLLOWED YOU ON TWITTER?
YEAH... BUT MAYBE IT WAS AN ACCIDENT...
OR HE HIT FOLLOW WHEN HE TRIED TO HIT REPLY...
YOU COULD BE RIGHT. THINGS LIKE THAT HAPPENS SOMETIMES.
Twitter
Kuga Kenkou (@KUGA_06
Kuga Kenkou-san has followed you.
Swipe to show.
SO, TOMORROW OR SO...
HE MIGHT UNFOLLOW ME...

WELL...

FOR NOW, LET'S GO HOME.

YEAH...

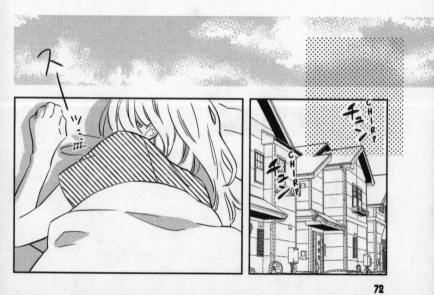

CHIRP

CHIRP

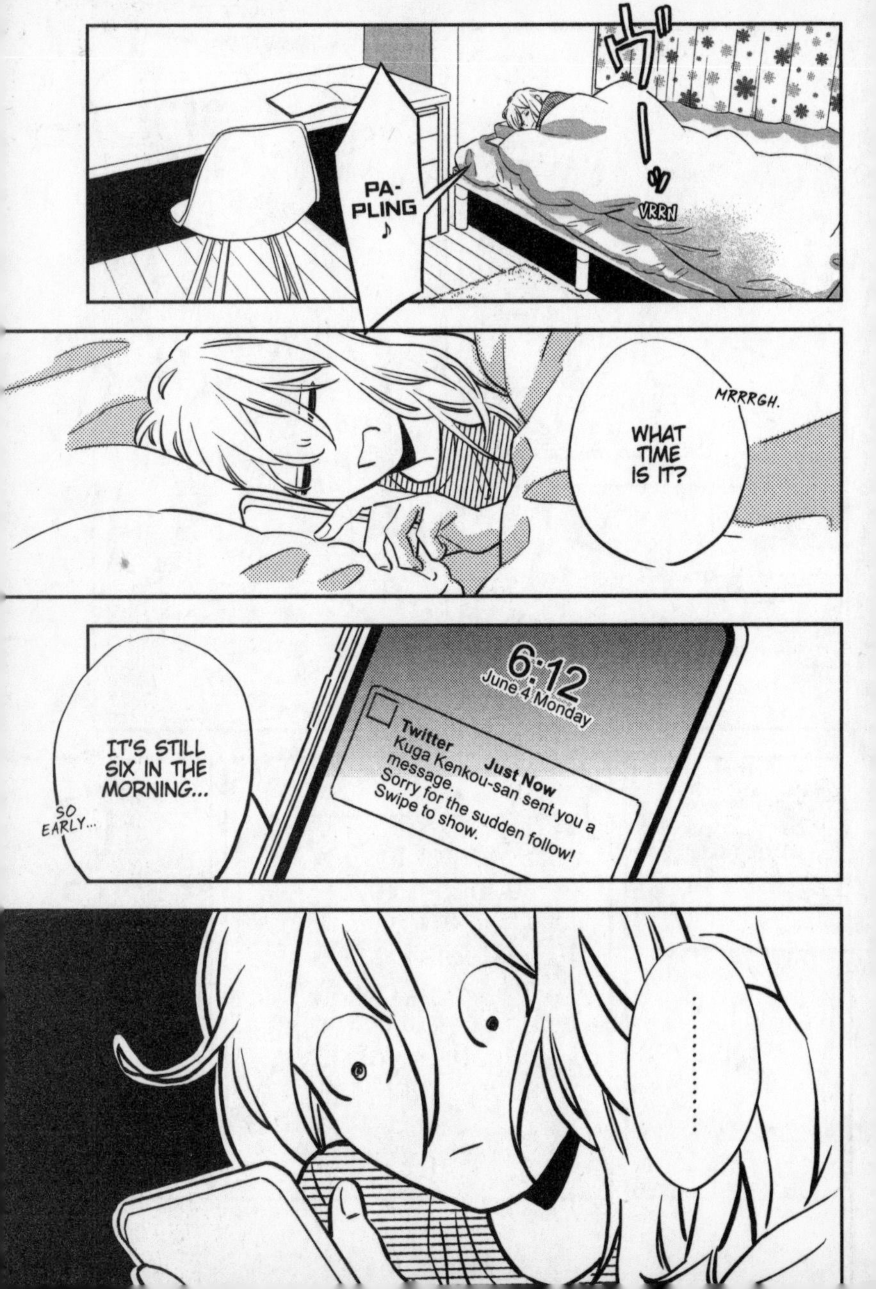
ヴーッ
VRRN
PA-PLING ♪
MRRRGH.
WHAT TIME IS IT?
6:12
June 4 Monday
Twitter
Just Now
Kuga Kenkou-san sent you a message.
Sorry for the sudden follow!
Swipe to show.
IT'S STILL SIX IN THE MORNING...
SO EARLY...
……

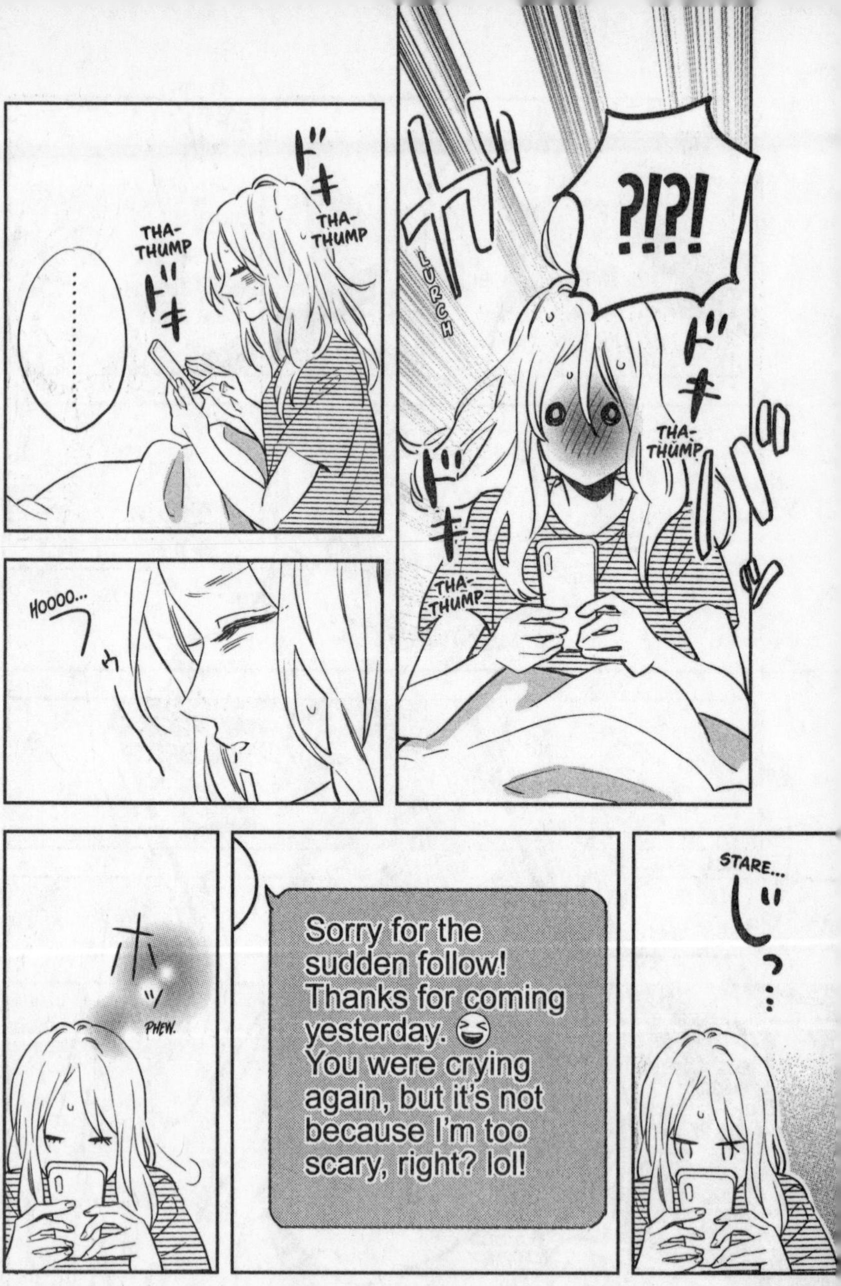
?!?!
LURCH
THA-THUMP
THA-THUMP
……
THA-THUMP
THA-THUMP
HOOOO...
STARE...
Sorry for the sudden follow! Thanks for coming yesterday. 😆 You were crying again, but it's not because I'm too scary, right? lol!
PHEW.

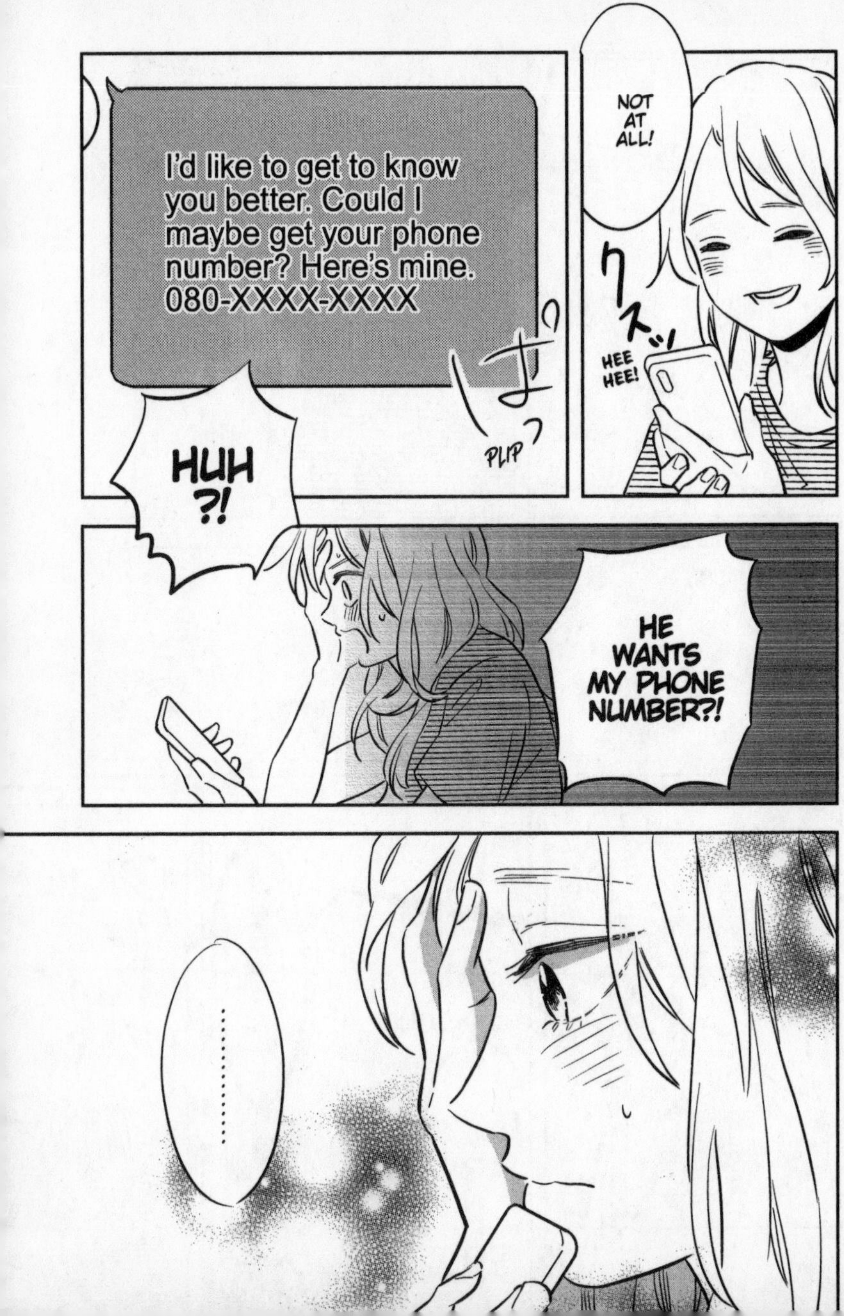
NOT AT ALL!
クスッ
HEE HEE!
I'd like to get to know you better. Could I maybe get your phone number? Here's mine. 080-XXXX-XXXX
PLIP
HUH?!
HE WANTS MY PHONE NUMBER?!
……

e to g[...]
[...]etter. Could I
[...]be get your phone
[...]ber? Here's mine.
[...]-XXXX-XXXX

THAT KISS...

TREMBLE
カタ

BUT...

カタ
TREMBLE

TAP

IF I CALL HIM, I CAN ASK HIM...

SO FAST!

THA-THUMP?

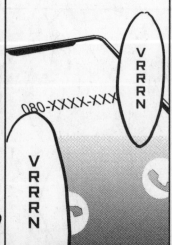

VRRRN

080-XXXX-XXX

VRRRN

HOOOO......

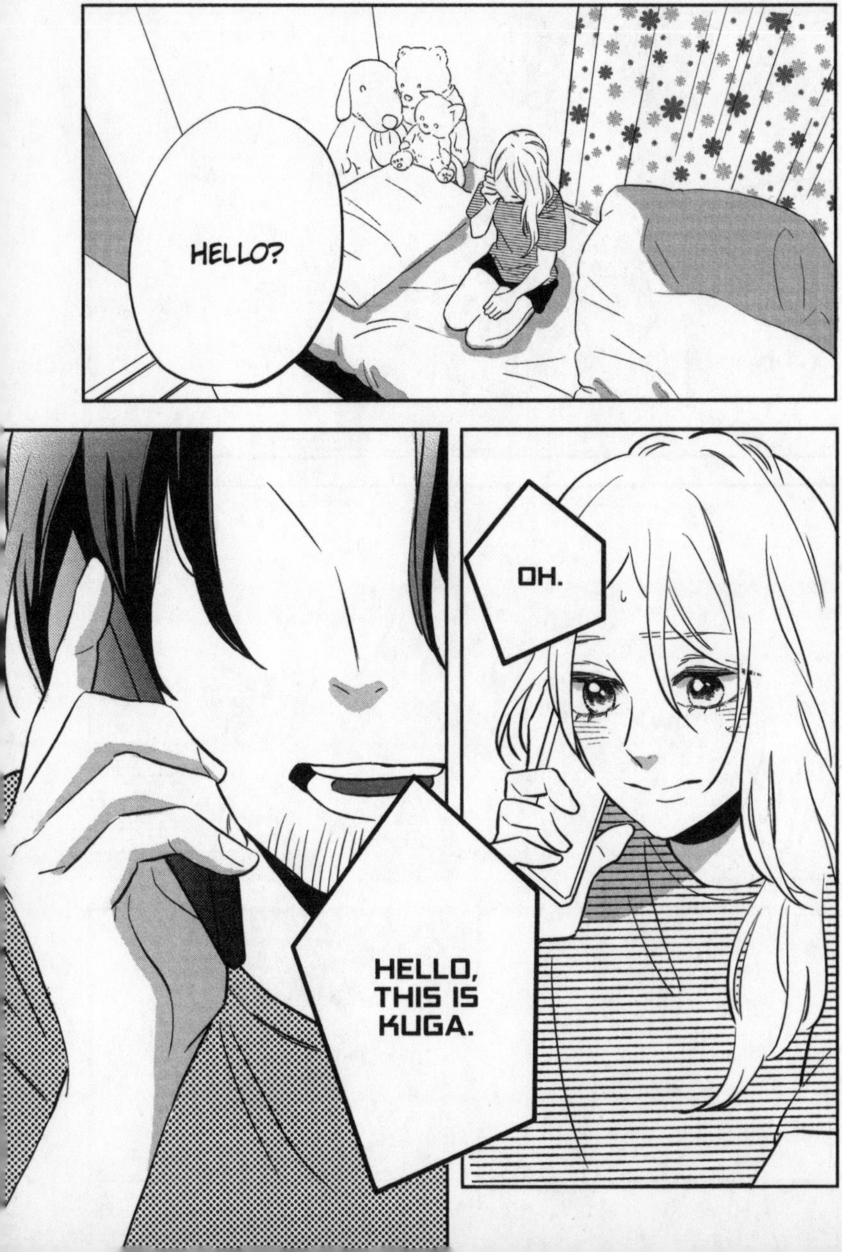
HELLO?
OH.
HELLO, THIS IS KUGA.

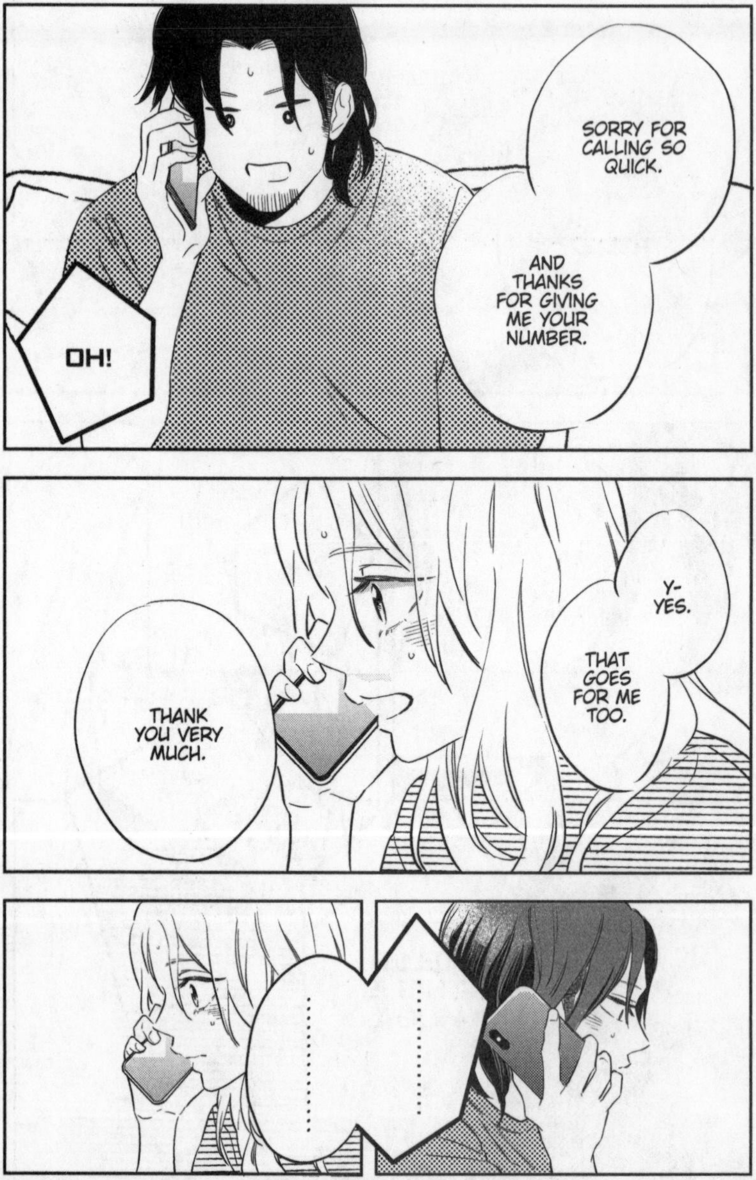
SORRY FOR CALLING SO QUICK.
AND THANKS FOR GIVING ME YOUR NUMBER.
OH!
Y- YES.
THAT GOES FOR ME TOO.
THANK YOU VERY MUCH.
......
......

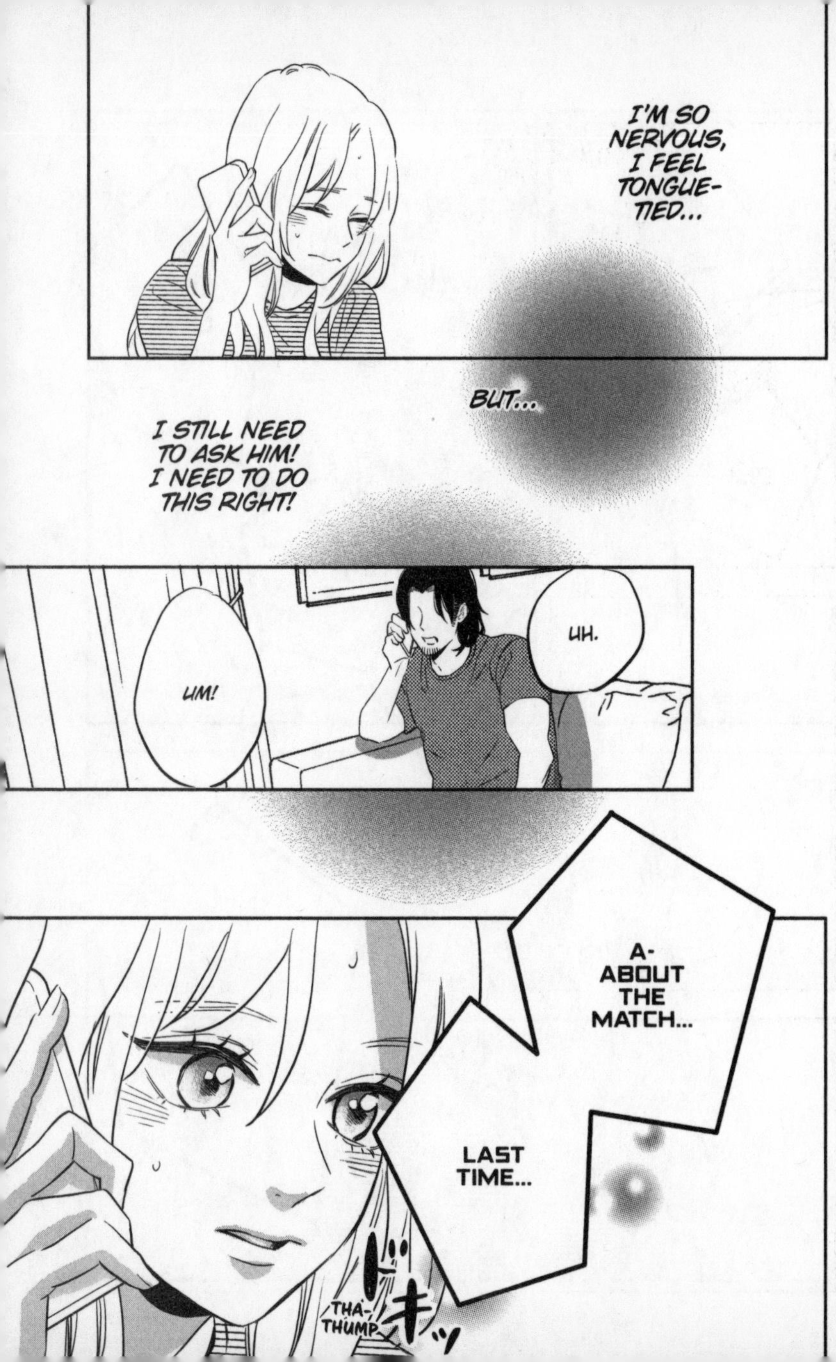
I'M SO NERVOUS, I FEEL TONGUE-TIED...
BUT...
I STILL NEED TO ASK HIM! I NEED TO DO THIS RIGHT!
UH.
UM!
A- ABOUT THE MATCH...
LAST TIME...
THA-THUMP

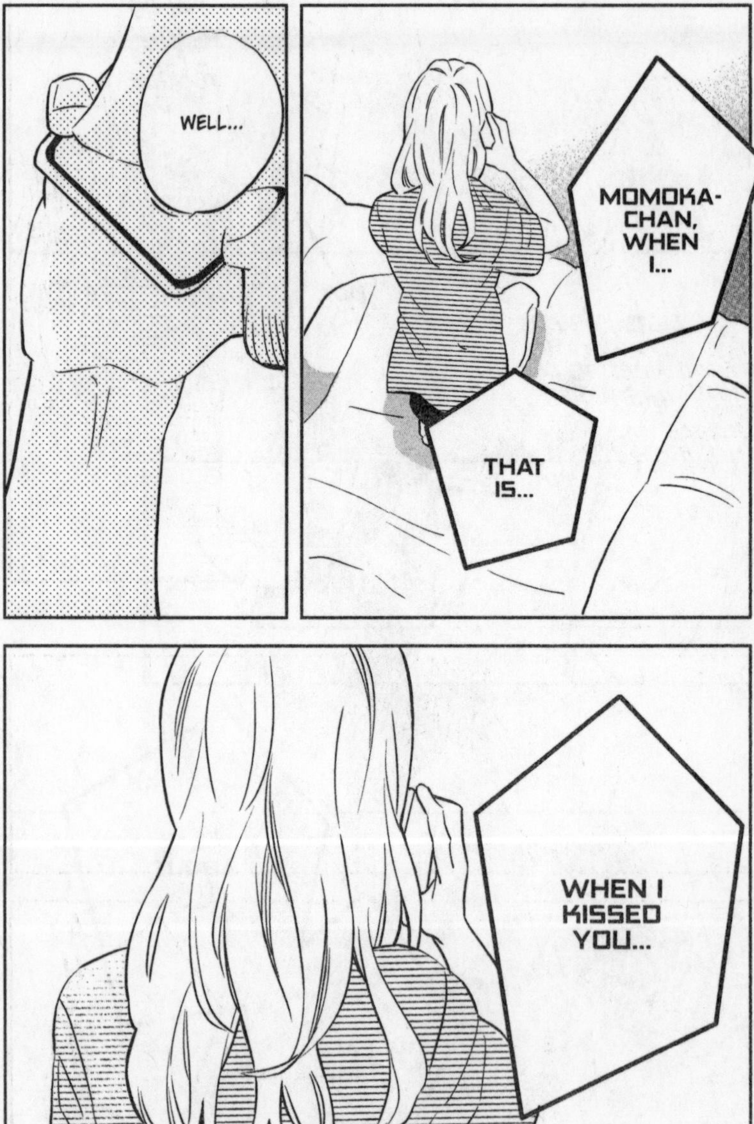
MOMOKA-CHAN, WHEN I...
THAT IS...
WELL...
WHEN I KISSED YOU...

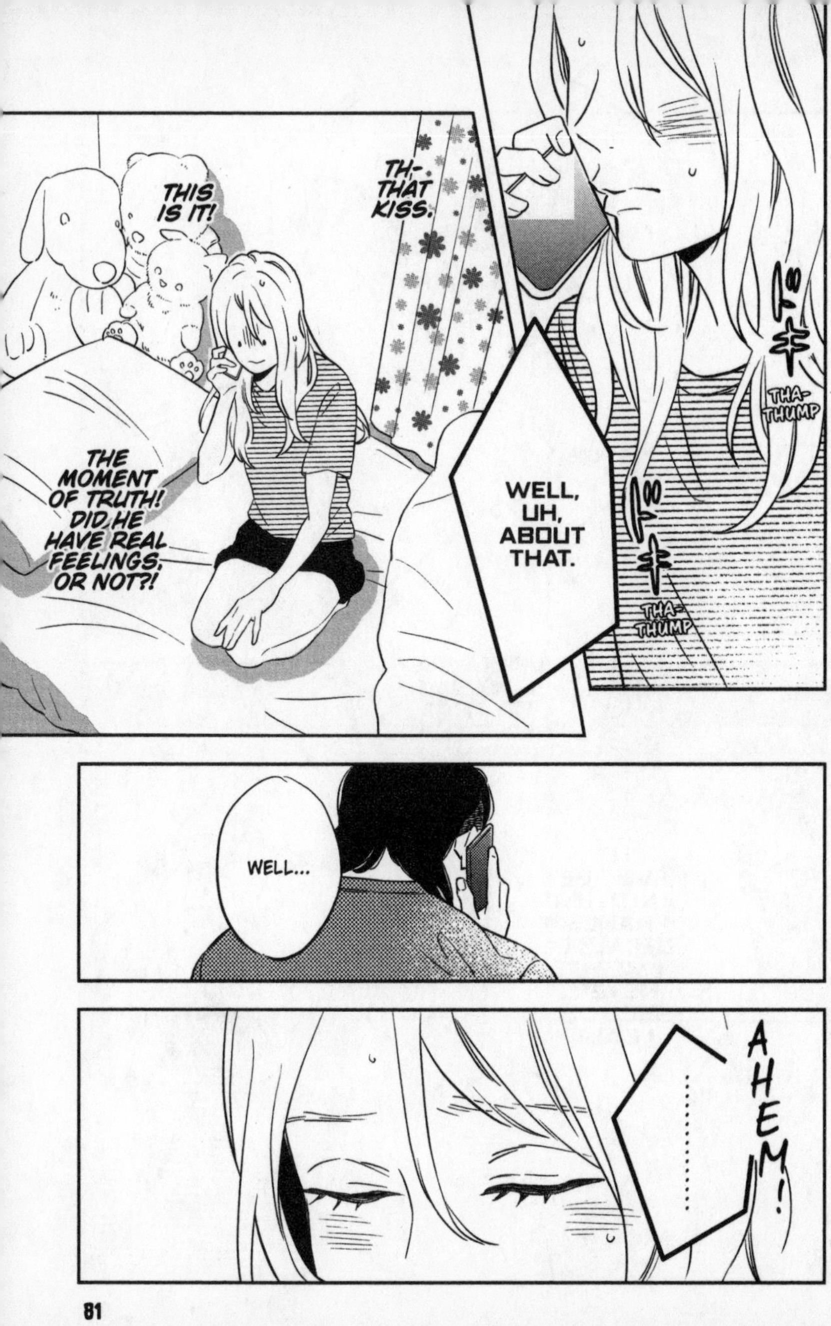
THA-THUMP
WELL, UH, ABOUT THAT.
THA-THUMP
TH-THAT KISS.
THIS IS IT!
THE MOMENT OF TRUTH! DID HE HAVE REAL FEELINGS, OR NOT?!
WELL...
AHEM!
......

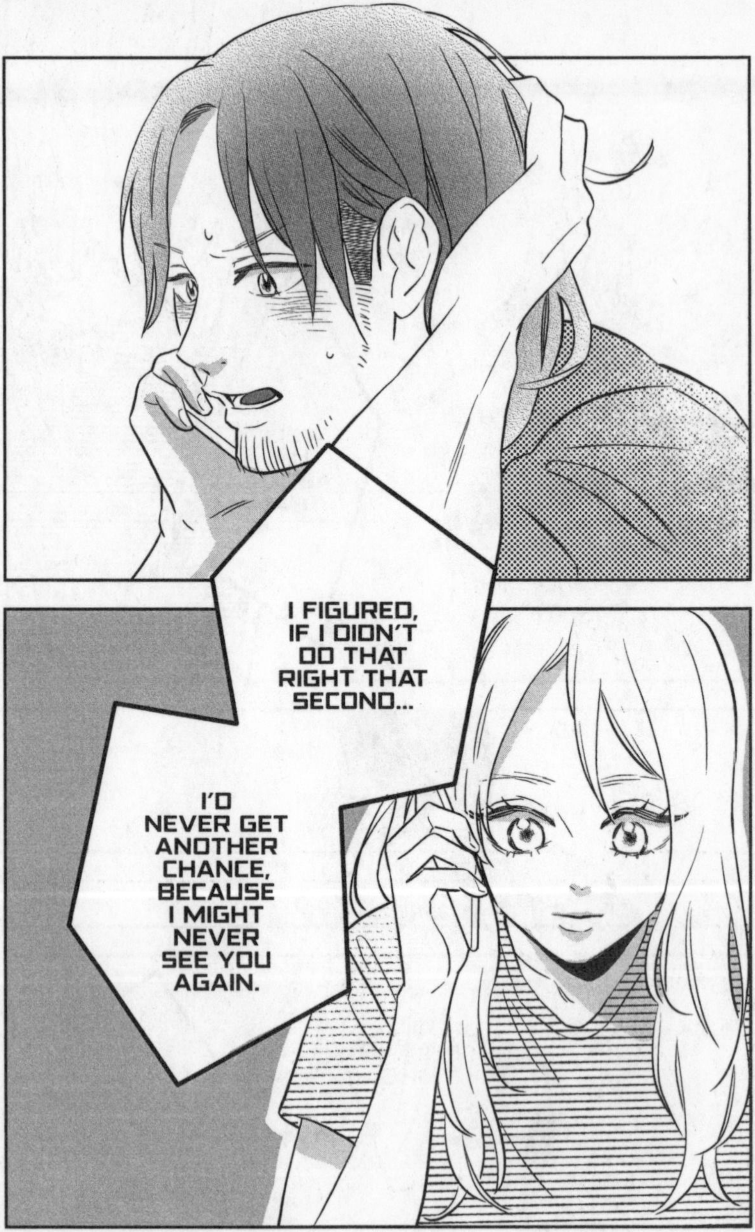
I FIGURED, IF I DIDN'T DO THAT RIGHT THAT SECOND...
I'D NEVER GET ANOTHER CHANCE, BECAUSE I MIGHT NEVER SEE YOU AGAIN.

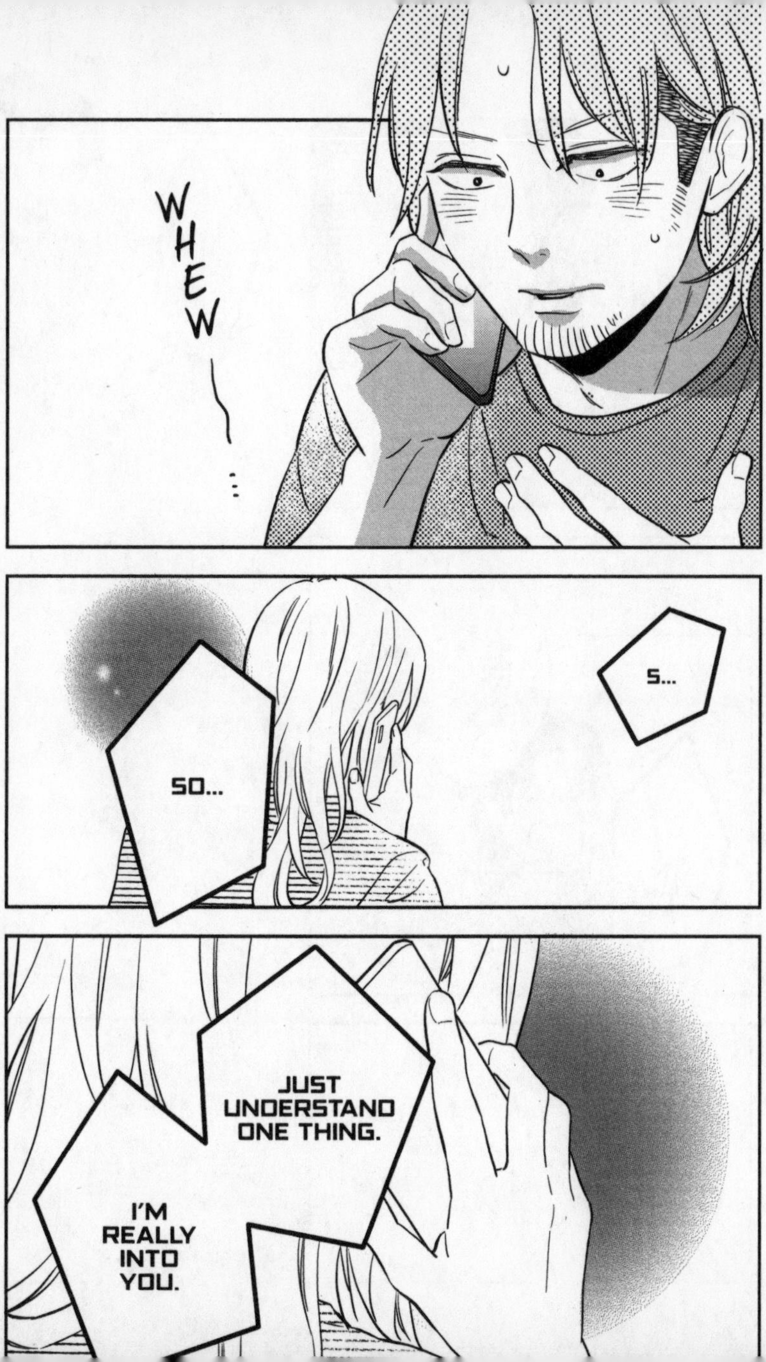
WHEW...
S...
SO...
JUST UNDERSTAND ONE THING.
I'M REALLY INTO YOU.

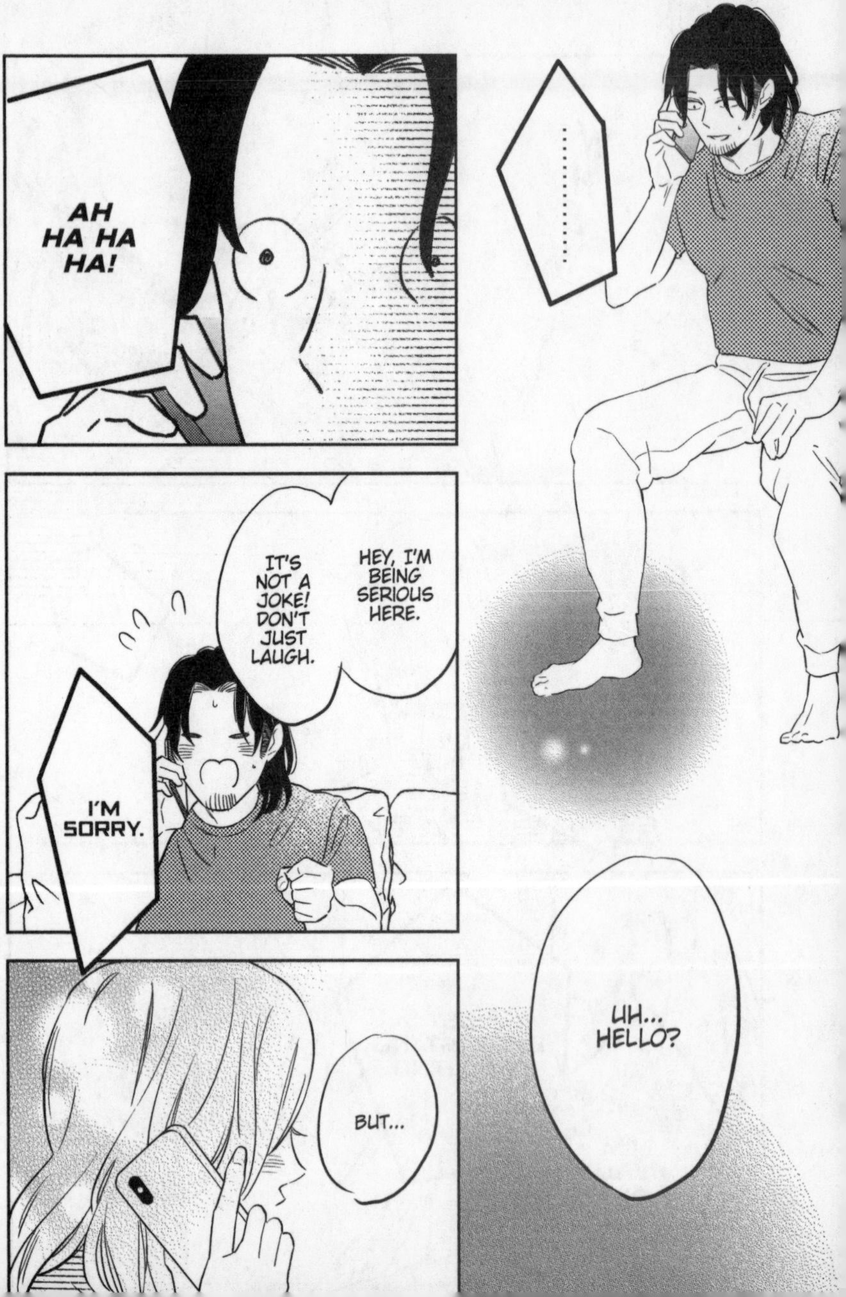
......
UH... HELLO?
AH HA HA HA!
HEY, I'M BEING SERIOUS HERE.
IT'S NOT A JOKE! DON'T JUST LAUGH.
I'M SORRY.
BUT...

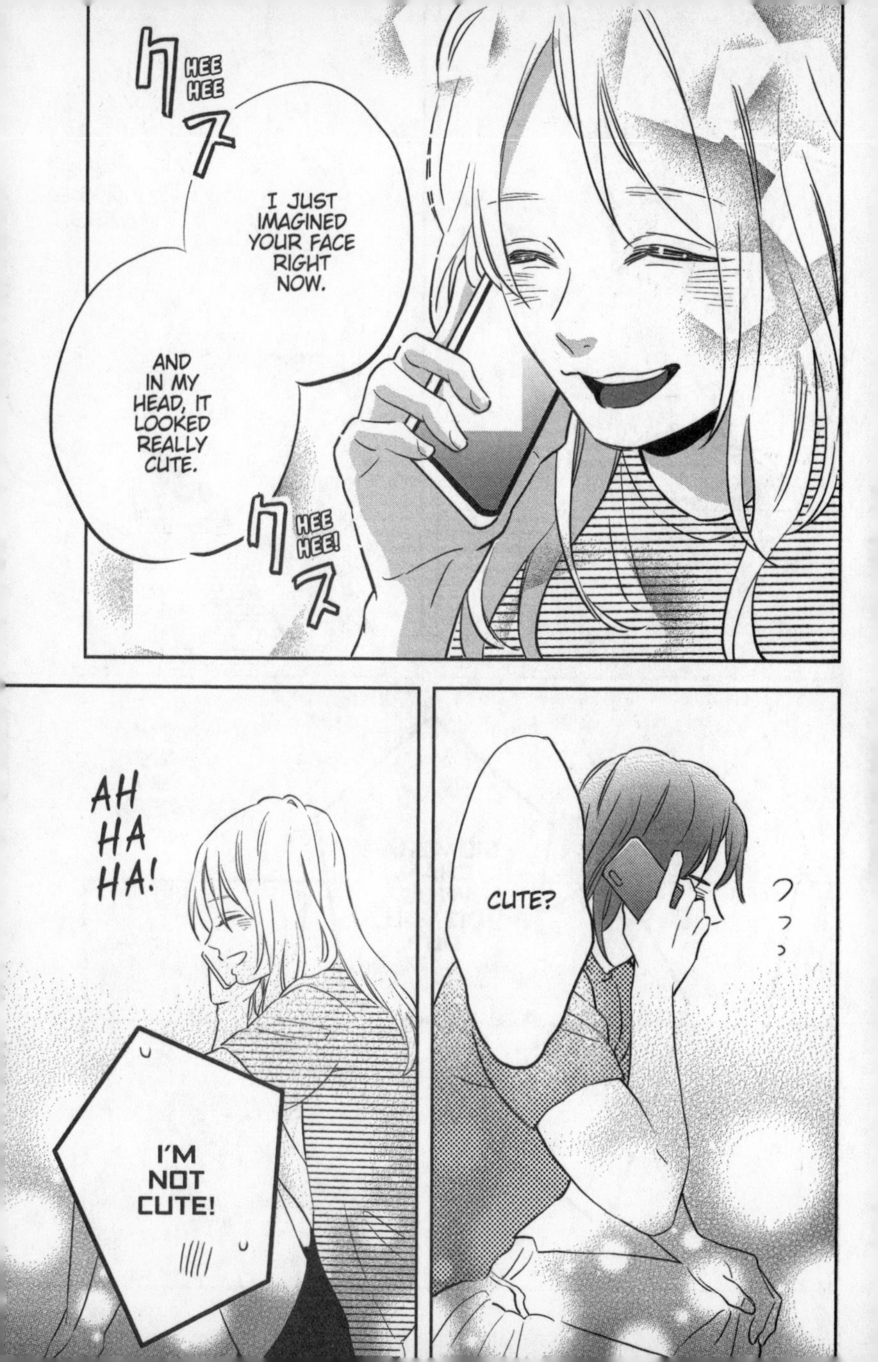
HEE HEE
I JUST IMAGINED YOUR FACE RIGHT NOW.
AND IN MY HEAD, IT LOOKED REALLY CUTE.
HEE HEE!
CUTE?
AH HA HA!
I'M NOT CUTE!

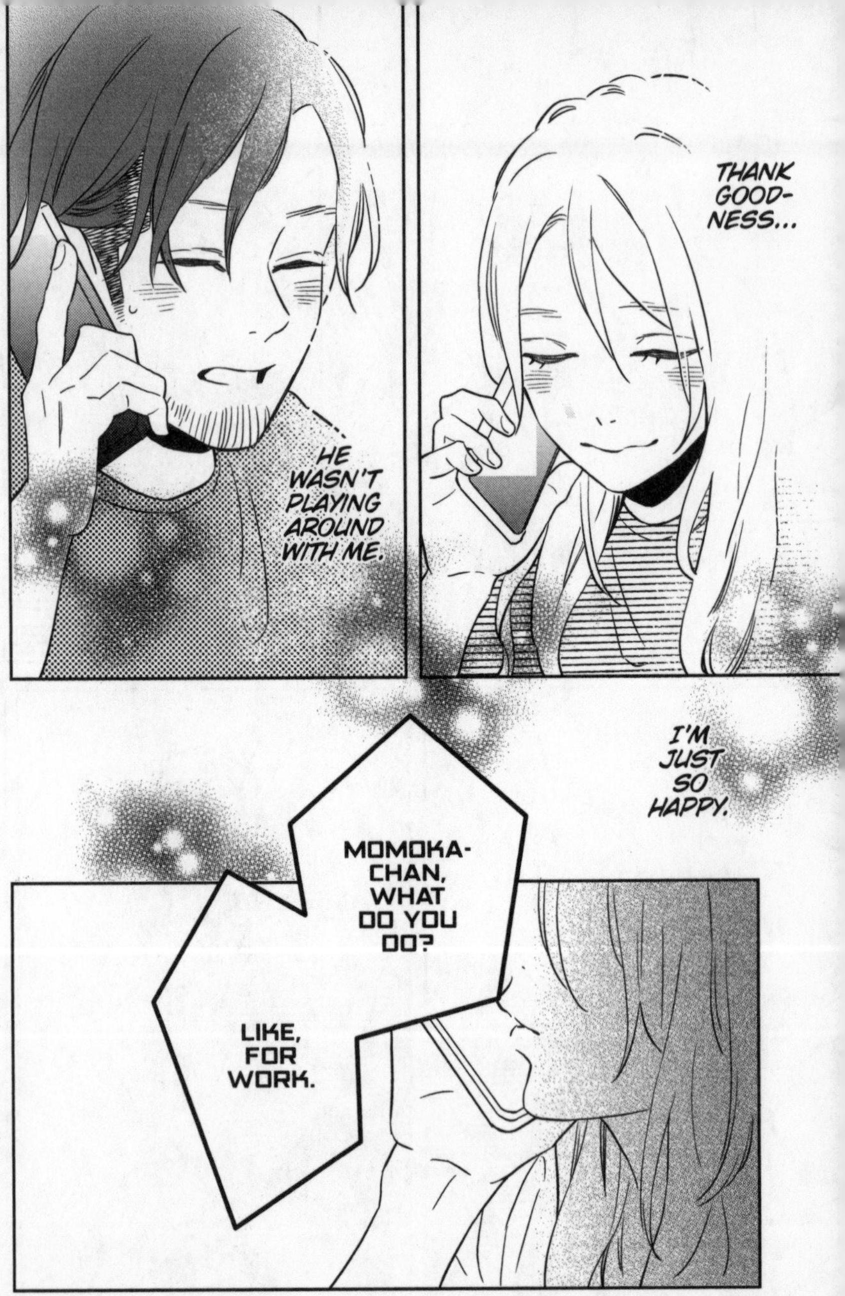
THANK GOOD-NESS...
HE WASN'T PLAYING AROUND WITH ME.
I'M JUST SO HAPPY.
MOMOKA-CHAN, WHAT DO YOU DO?
LIKE, FOR WORK.

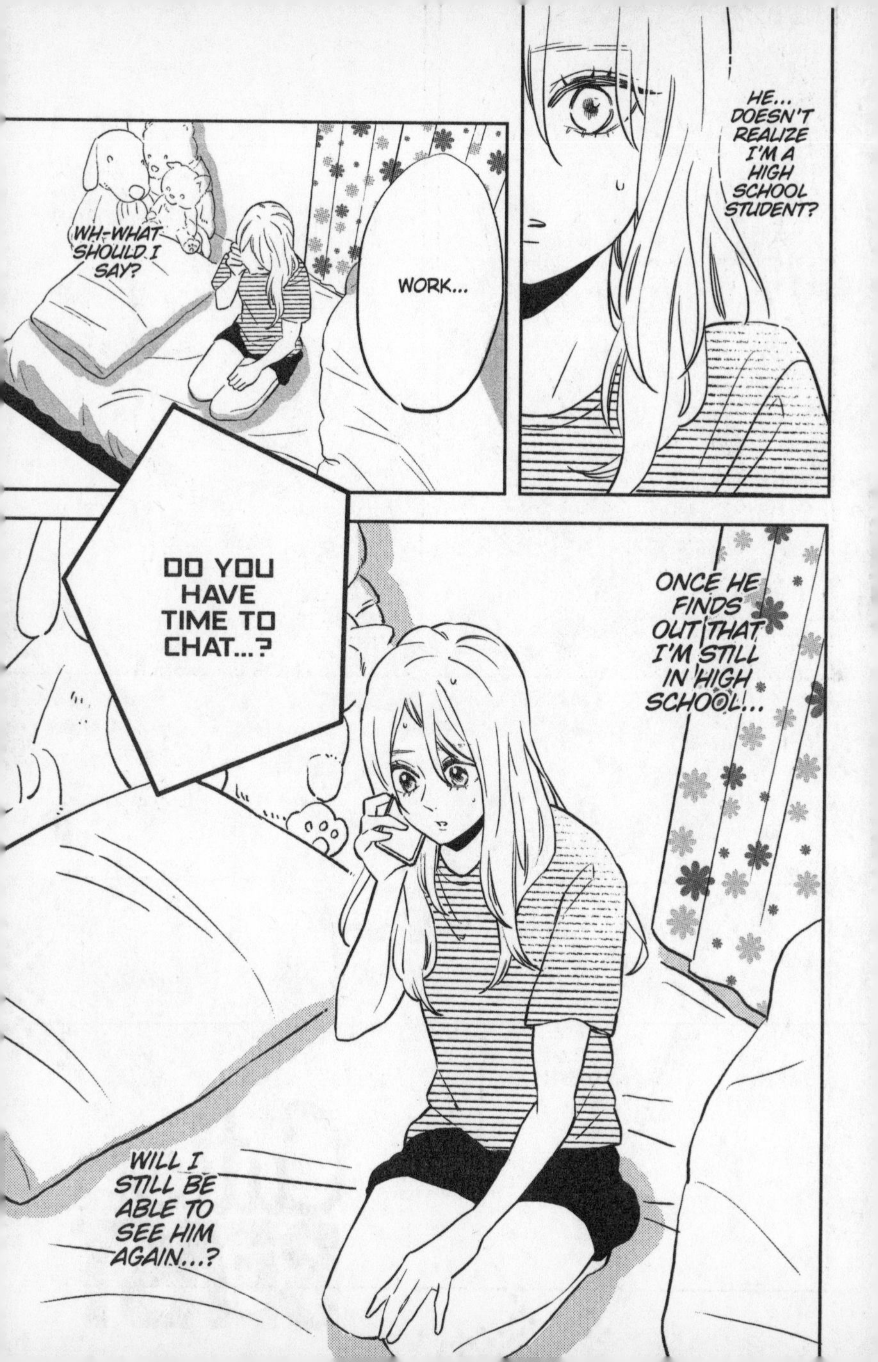
HE... DOESN'T REALIZE I'M A HIGH SCHOOL STUDENT?
WORK...
WH-WHAT SHOULD I SAY?
DO YOU HAVE TIME TO CHAT...?
ONCE HE FINDS OUT THAT I'M STILL IN HIGH SCHOOL...
WILL I STILL BE ABLE TO SEE HIM AGAIN...?

Cutie and the BEAST

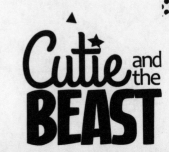

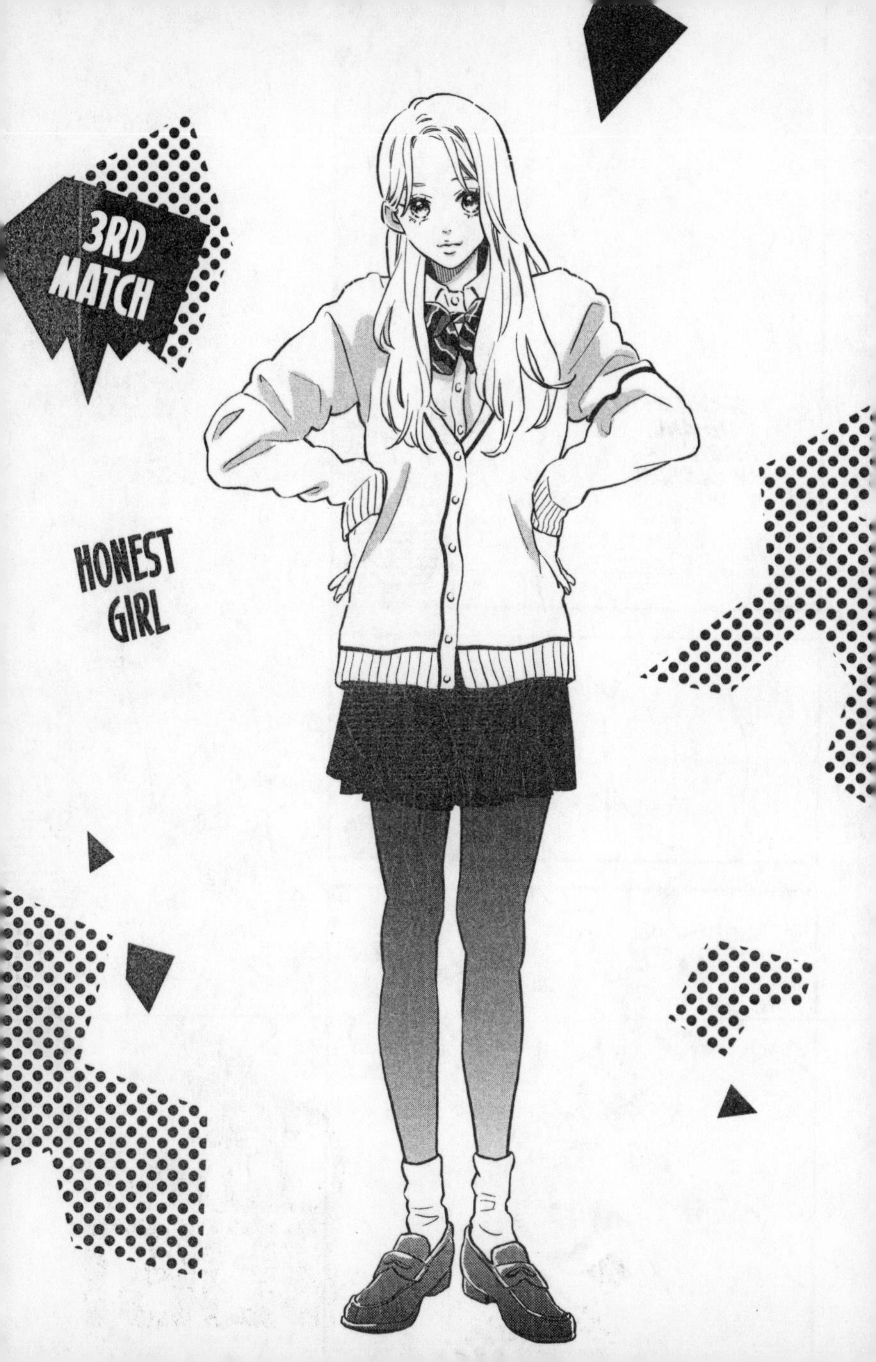
3RD MATCH
HONEST GIRL

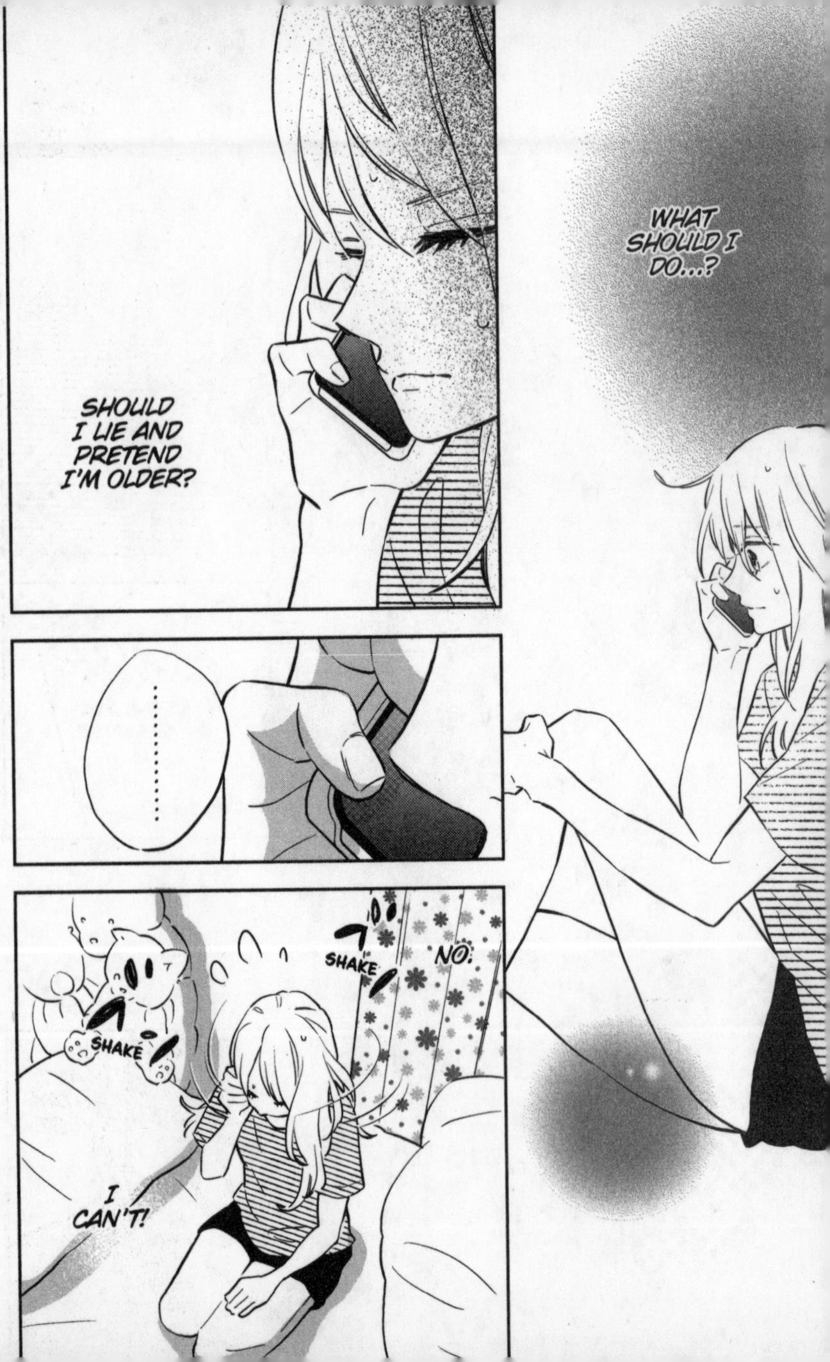
WHAT SHOULD I DO...?
SHOULD I LIE AND PRETEND I'M OLDER?
......
NO.
SHAKE
SHAKE
I CAN'T!

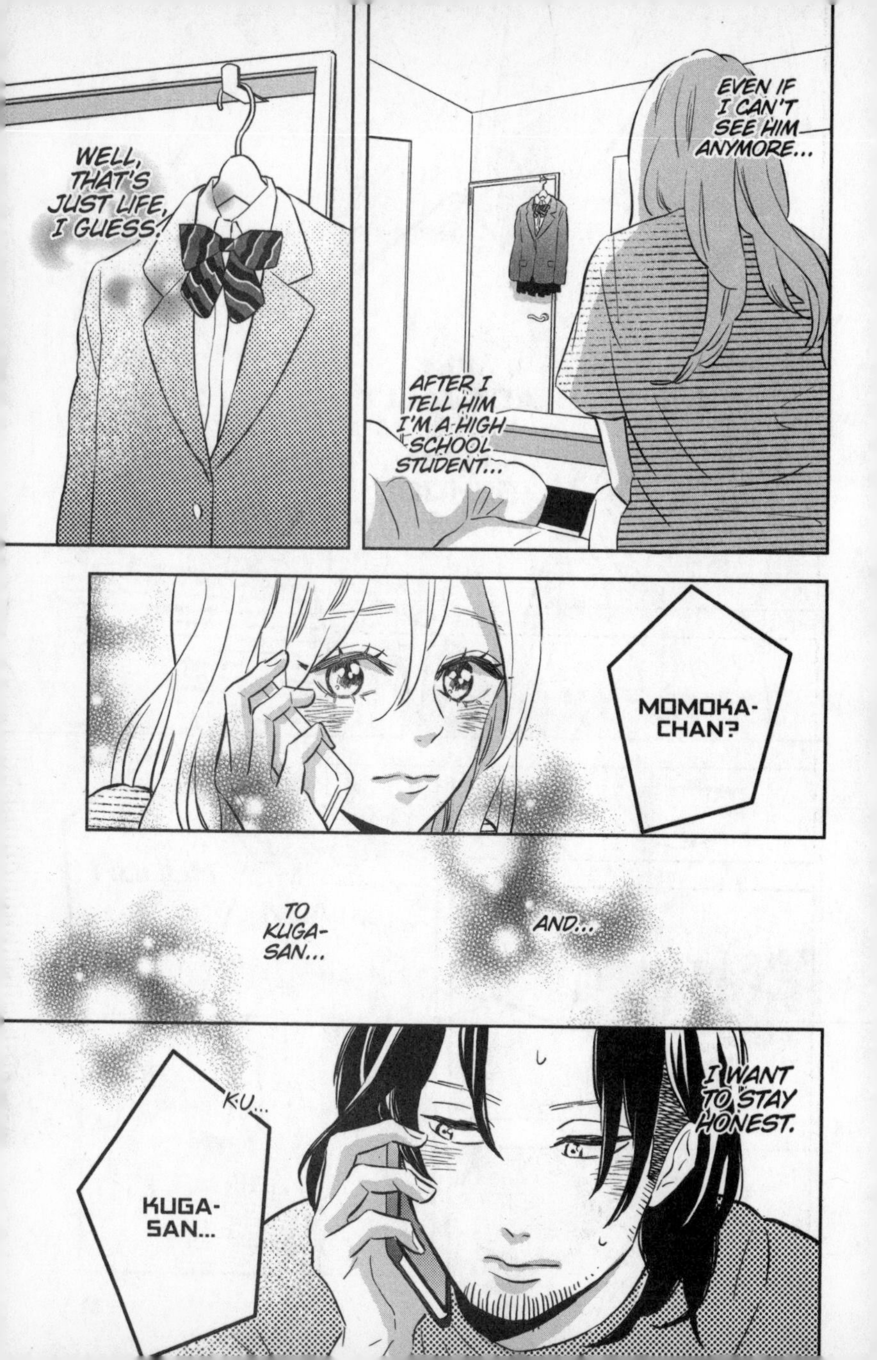
EVEN IF I CAN'T SEE HIM ANYMORE...
AFTER I TELL HIM I'M A HIGH SCHOOL STUDENT...
WELL, THAT'S JUST LIFE, I GUESS.
MOMOKA-CHAN?
TO KUGA-SAN...
AND...
I WANT TO STAY HONEST.
KU...
KUGA-SAN...

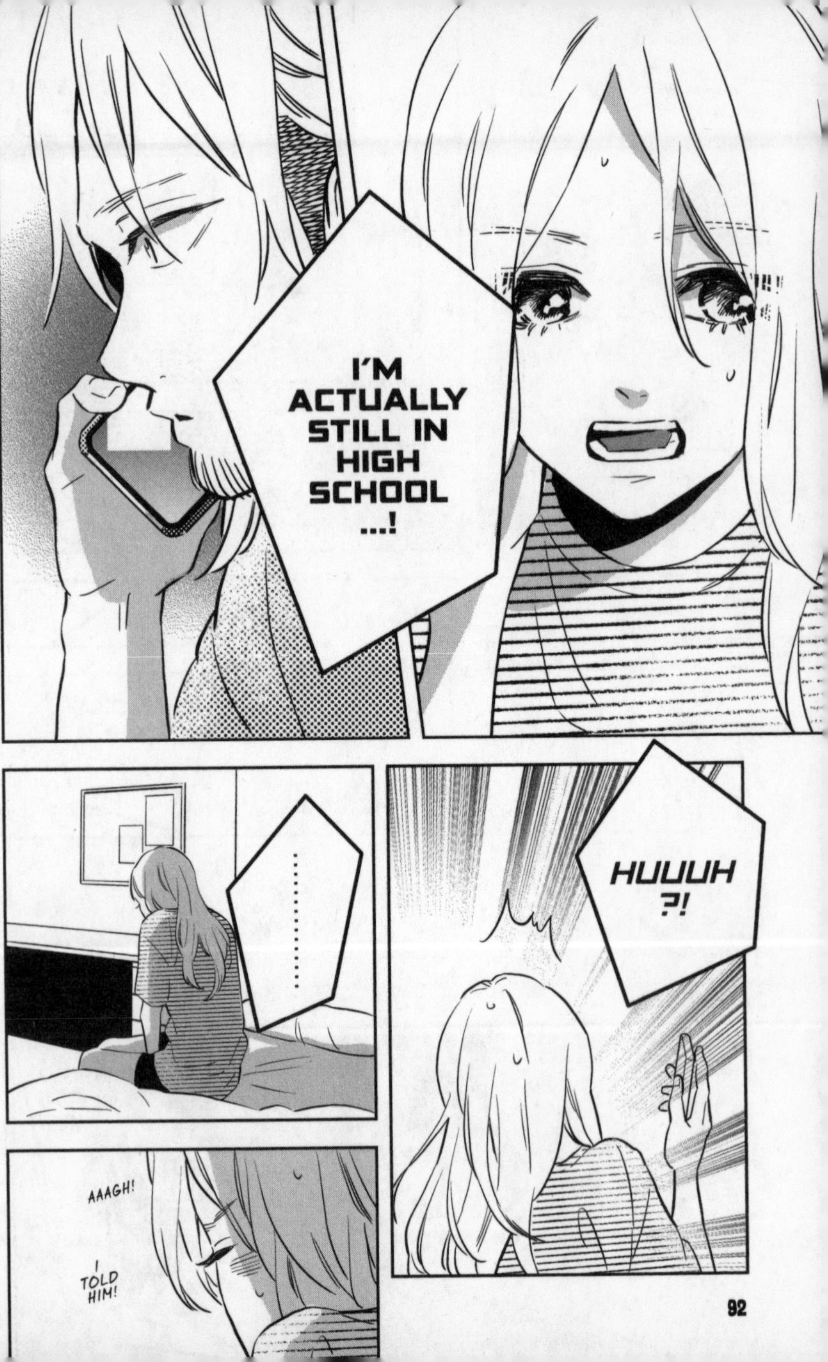
I'M ACTUALLY STILL IN HIGH SCHOOL ...!
HUUUH ?!
......
AAAGH!
I TOLD HIM!

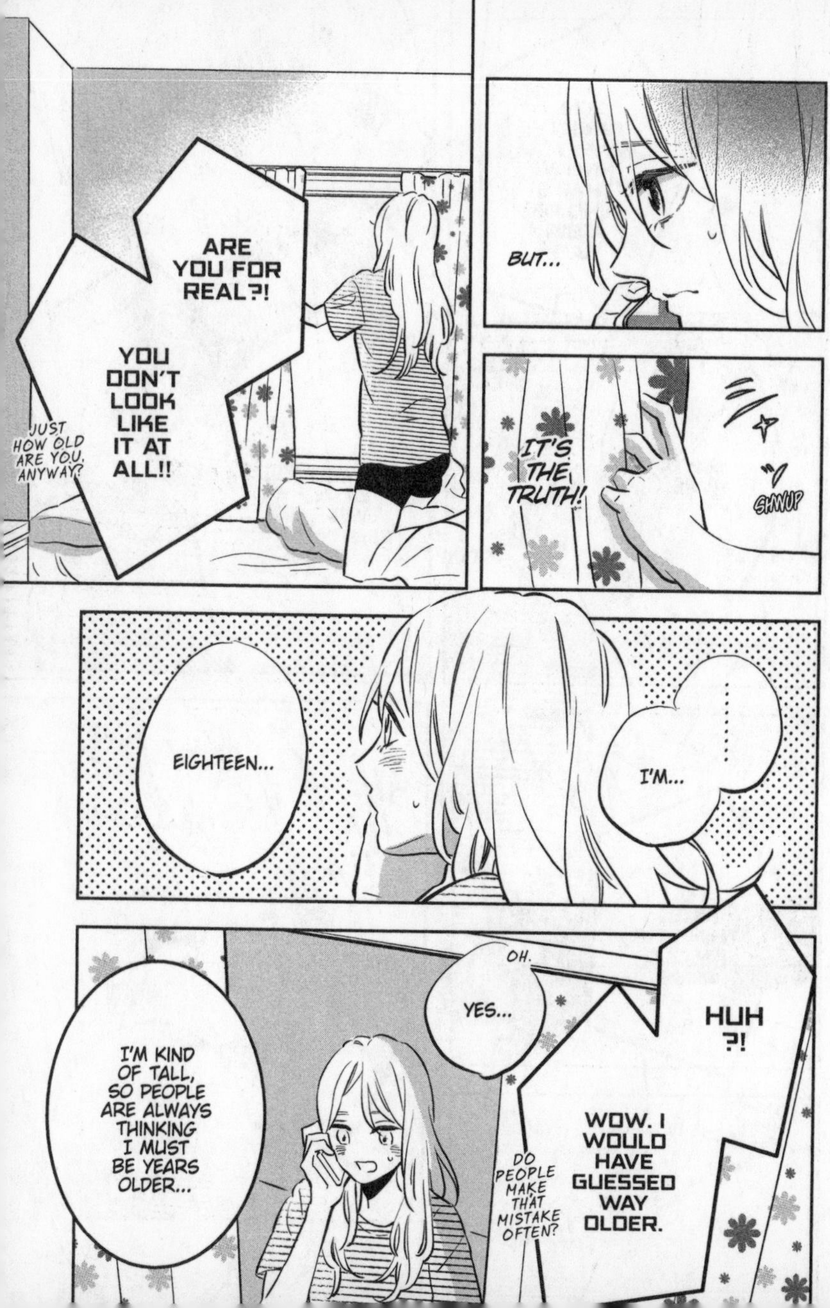
BUT...
IT'S THE TRUTH!
SHWUP
ARE YOU FOR REAL?!
YOU DON'T LOOK LIKE IT AT ALL!!
JUST HOW OLD ARE YOU, ANYWAY?
I'M......
EIGHTEEN...
HUH?!
OH.
YES...
WOW. I WOULD HAVE GUESSED WAY OLDER.
DO PEOPLE MAKE THAT MISTAKE OFTEN?
I'M KIND OF TALL, SO PEOPLE ARE ALWAYS THINKING I MUST BE YEARS OLDER...

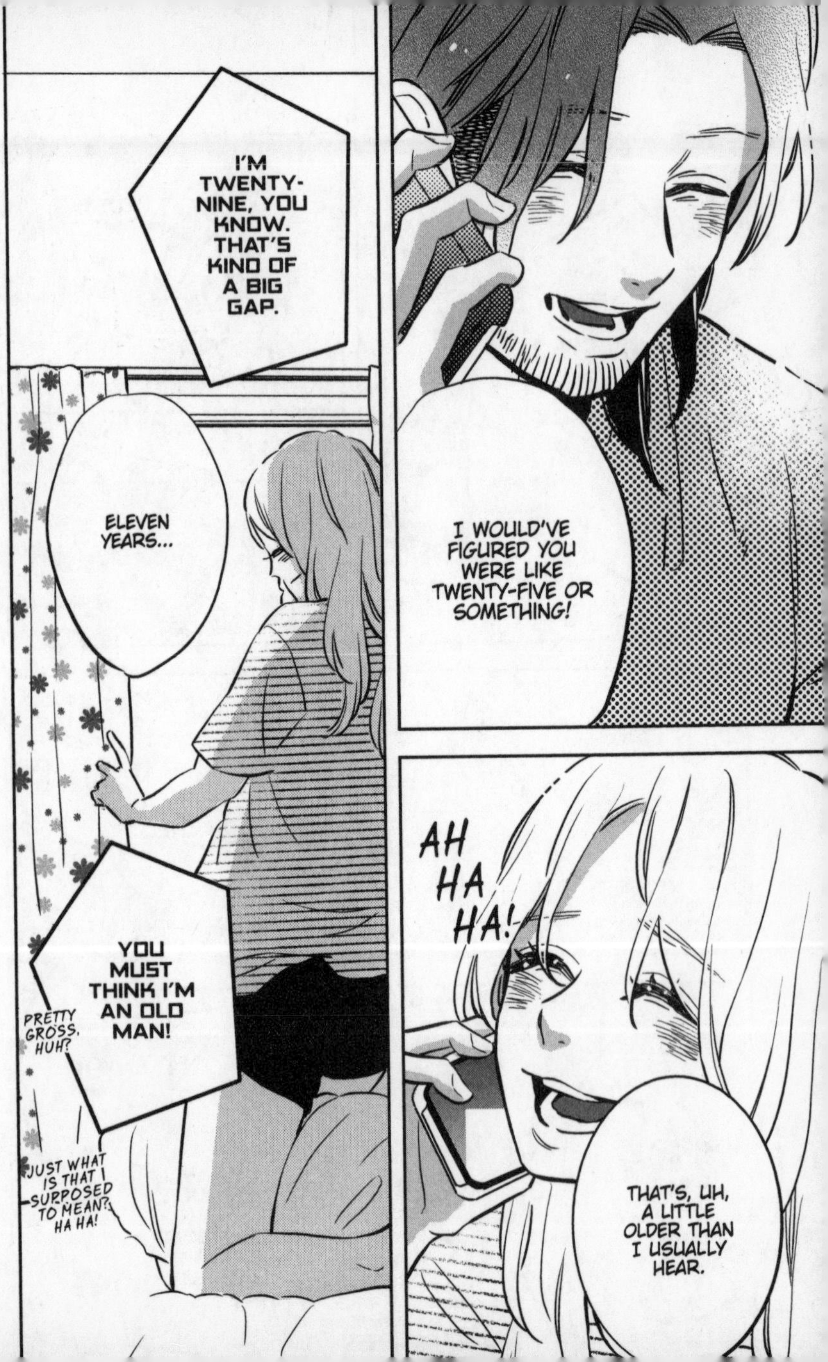
I WOULD'VE FIGURED YOU WERE LIKE TWENTY-FIVE OR SOMETHING!
AH HA HA!
THAT'S, UH, A LITTLE OLDER THAN I USUALLY HEAR.
I'M TWENTY-NINE, YOU KNOW. THAT'S KIND OF A BIG GAP.
ELEVEN YEARS...
YOU MUST THINK I'M AN OLD MAN!
PRETTY GROSS, HUH?
JUST WHAT IS THAT I SUPPOSED TO MEAN? HA HA!

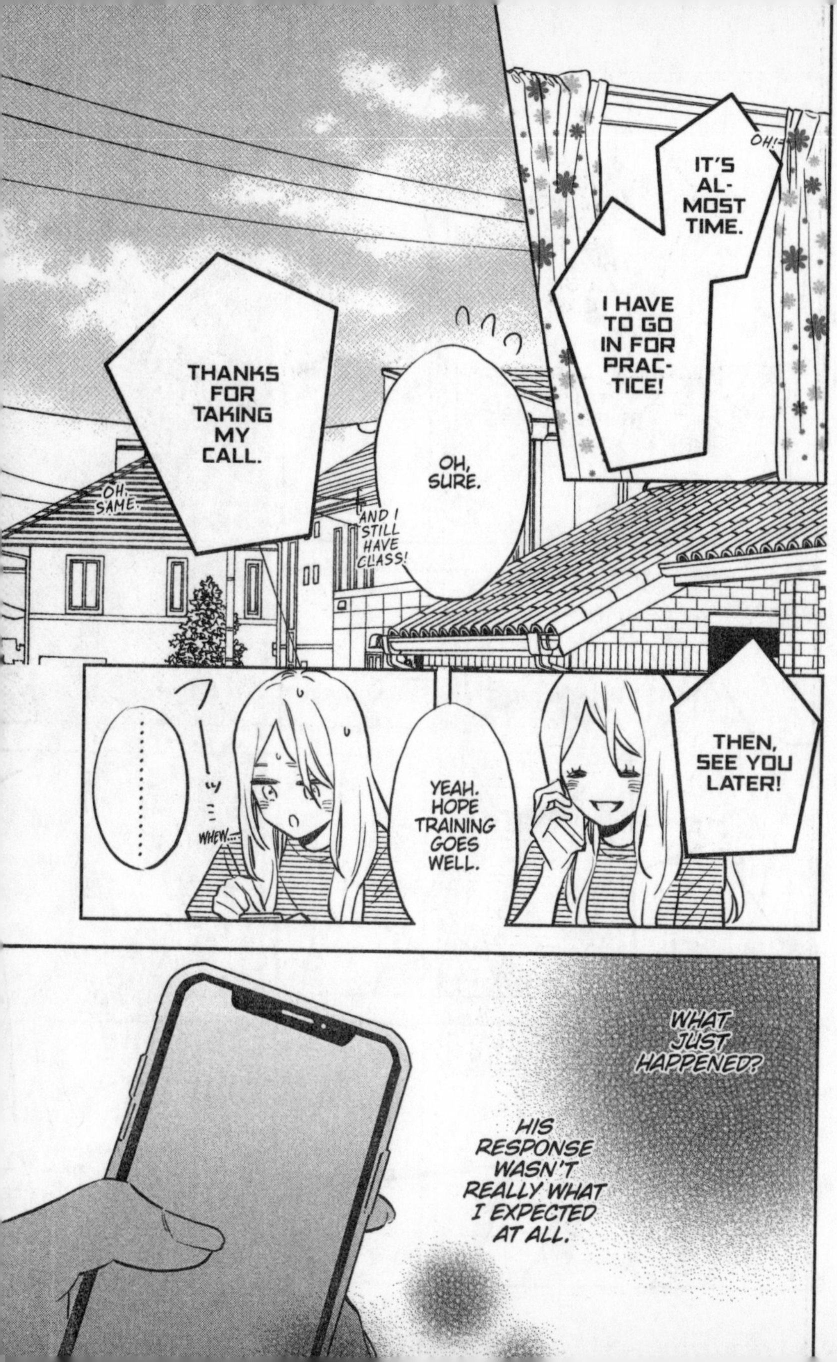
OH!
IT'S AL-MOST TIME.
I HAVE TO GO IN FOR PRAC-TICE!
OH, SURE.
AND I STILL HAVE CLASS!
THANKS FOR TAKING MY CALL.
OH, SAME.
THEN, SEE YOU LATER!
YEAH. HOPE TRAINING GOES WELL.
......
WHEW...
WHAT JUST HAPPENED?
HIS RESPONSE WASN'T REALLY WHAT I EXPECTED AT ALL.

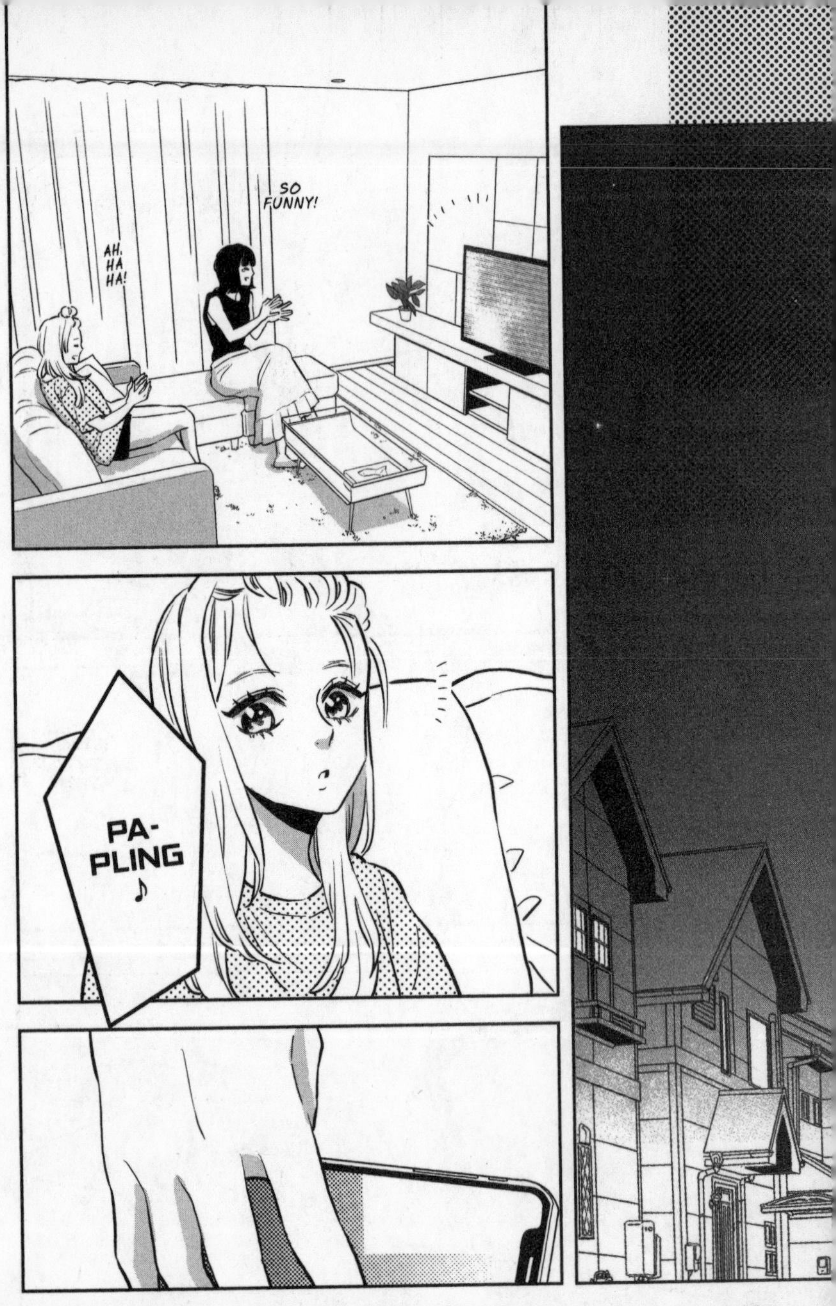
SO FUNNY!
AH, HA HA!
PA-PLING ♪

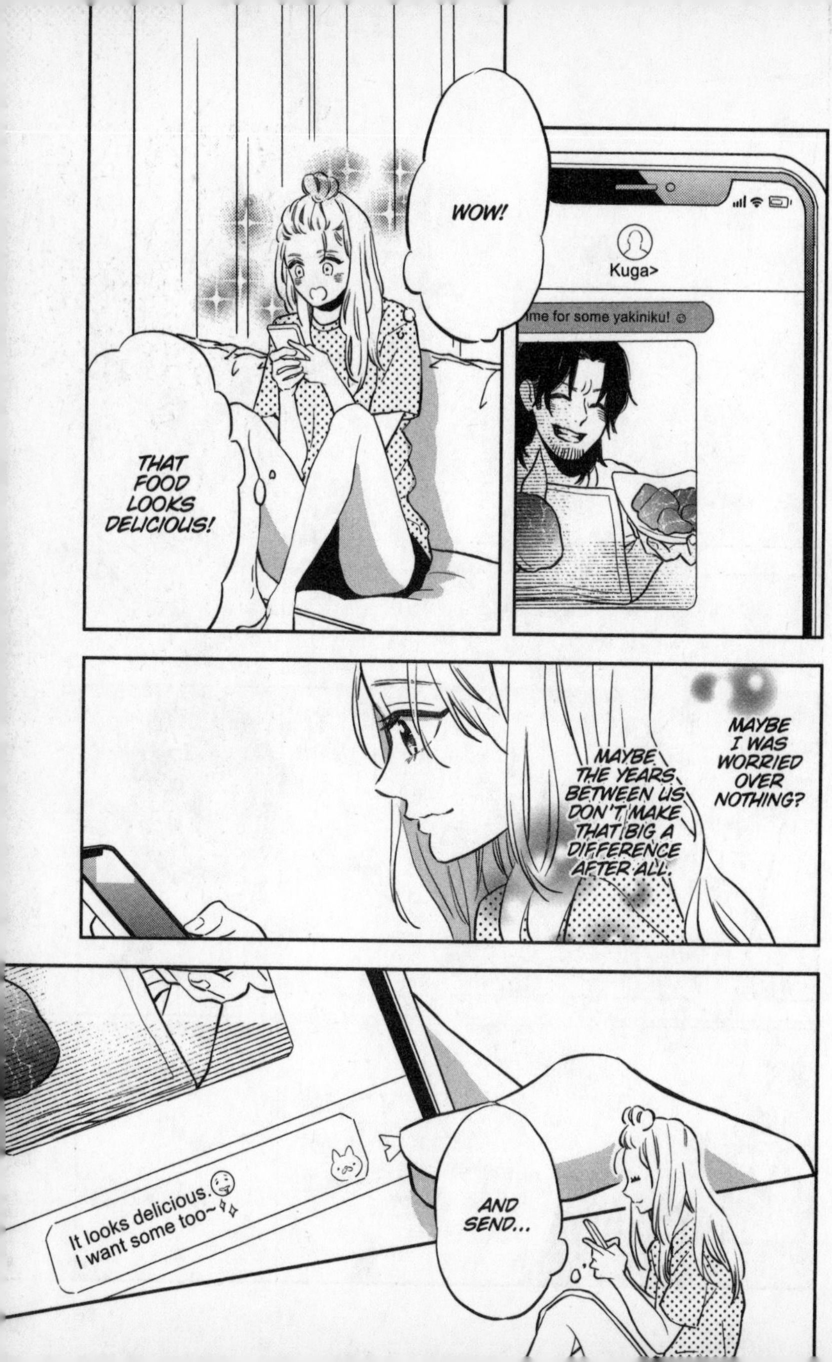
Kuga>
ime for some yakiniku!
WOW!
THAT FOOD LOOKS DELICIOUS!
MAYBE I WAS WORRIED OVER NOTHING?
MAYBE THE YEARS BETWEEN US DON'T MAKE THAT BIG A DIFFERENCE AFTER ALL.
AND SEND...
It looks delicious.
I want some too~

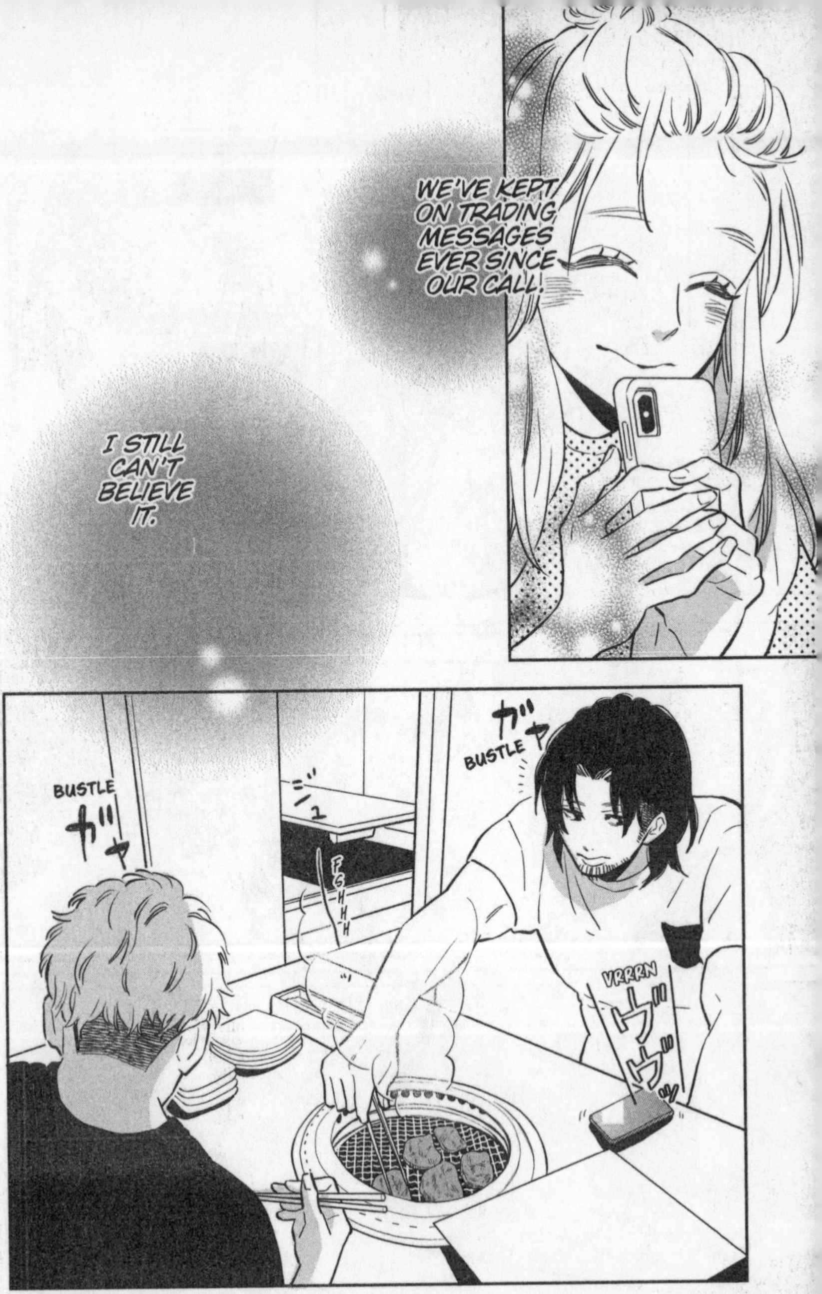
WE'VE KEPT ON TRADING MESSAGES EVER SINCE OUR CALL.
I STILL CAN'T BELIEVE IT.
BUSTLE
ガヤ
BUSTLE
ガヤ
ジュ
FSHHH
VRRRN
ヴヴヴッ

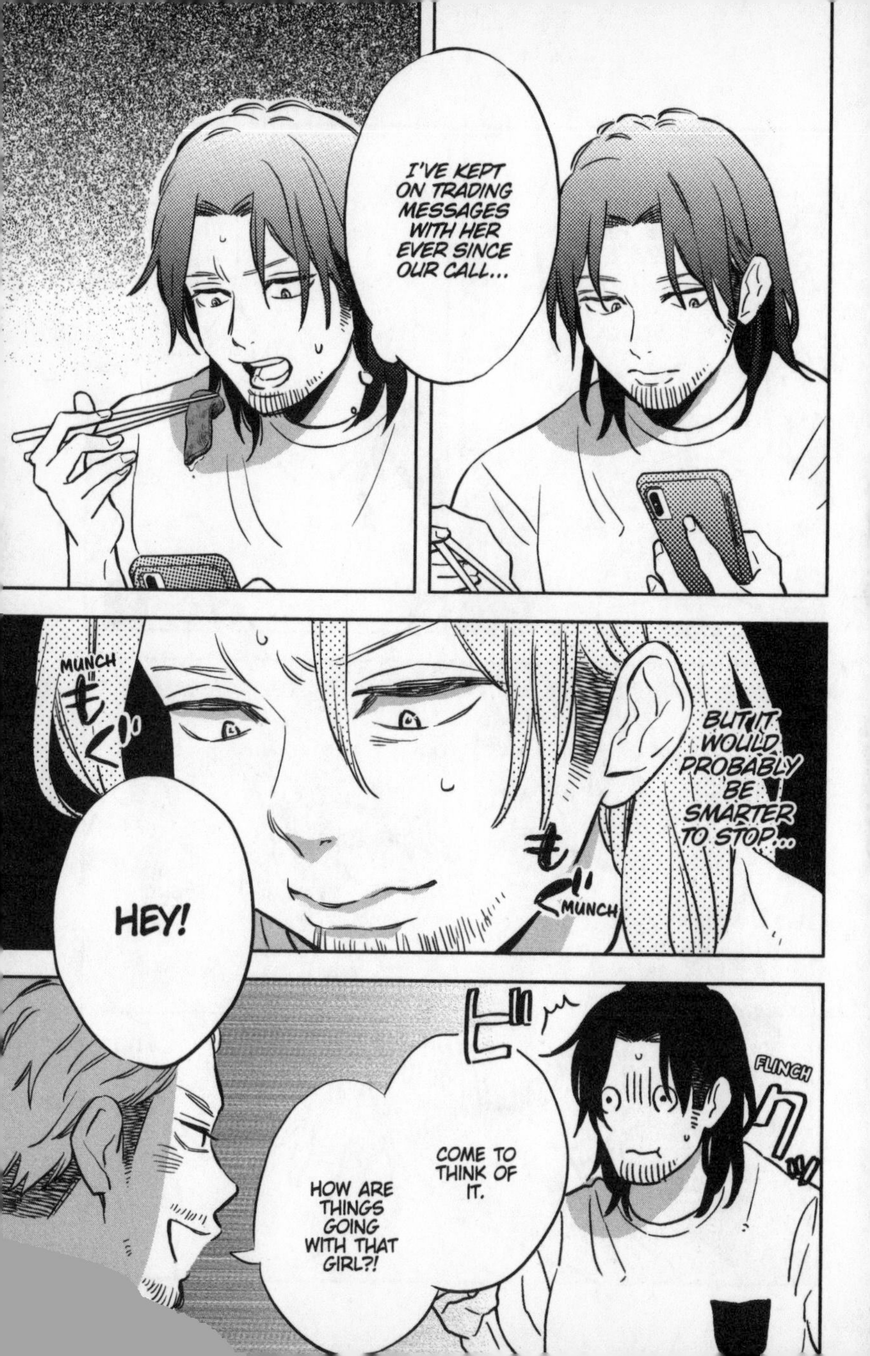
I'VE KEPT ON TRADING MESSAGES WITH HER EVER SINCE OUR CALL...
BUT IT WOULD PROBABLY BE SMARTER TO STOP...
MUNCH
MUNCH
HEY!
FLINCH
COME TO THINK OF IT.
HOW ARE THINGS GOING WITH THAT GIRL?!

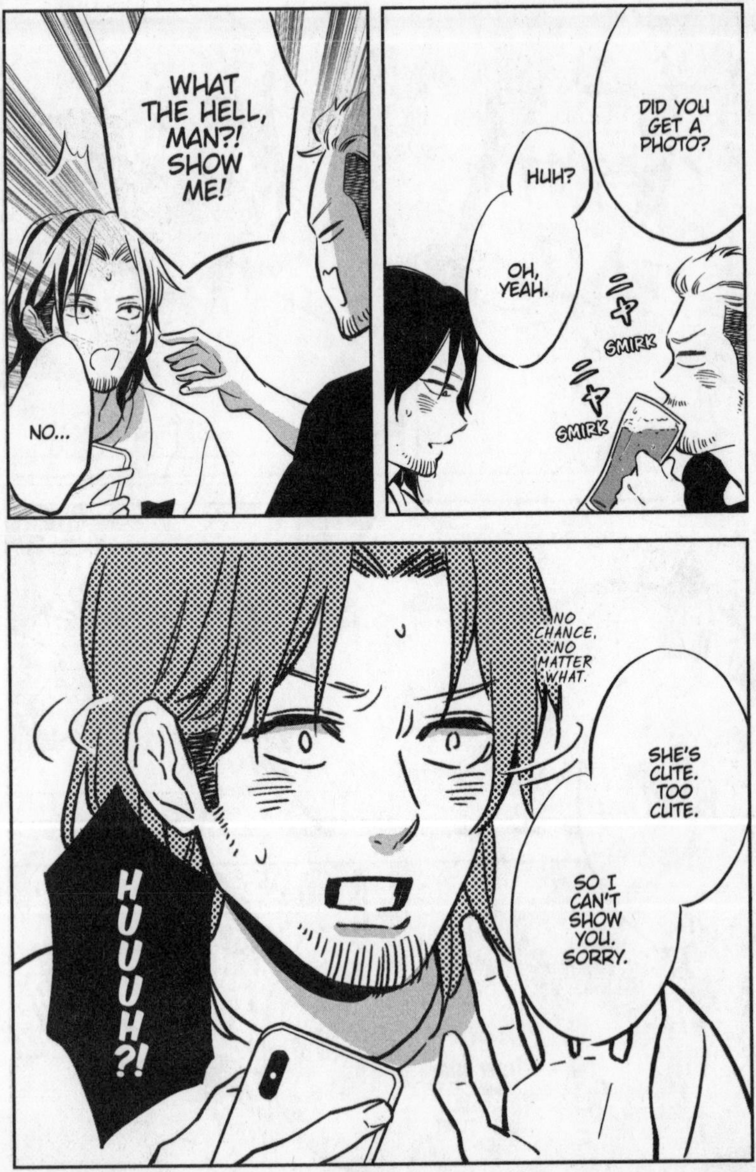
DID YOU GET A PHOTO?
HUH?
OH, YEAH.
SMIRK
SMIRK
WHAT THE HELL, MAN?! SHOW ME!
NO...
NO CHANCE, NO MATTER WHAT.
SHE'S CUTE. TOO CUTE.
SO I CAN'T SHOW YOU. SORRY.
HUUUUH?!

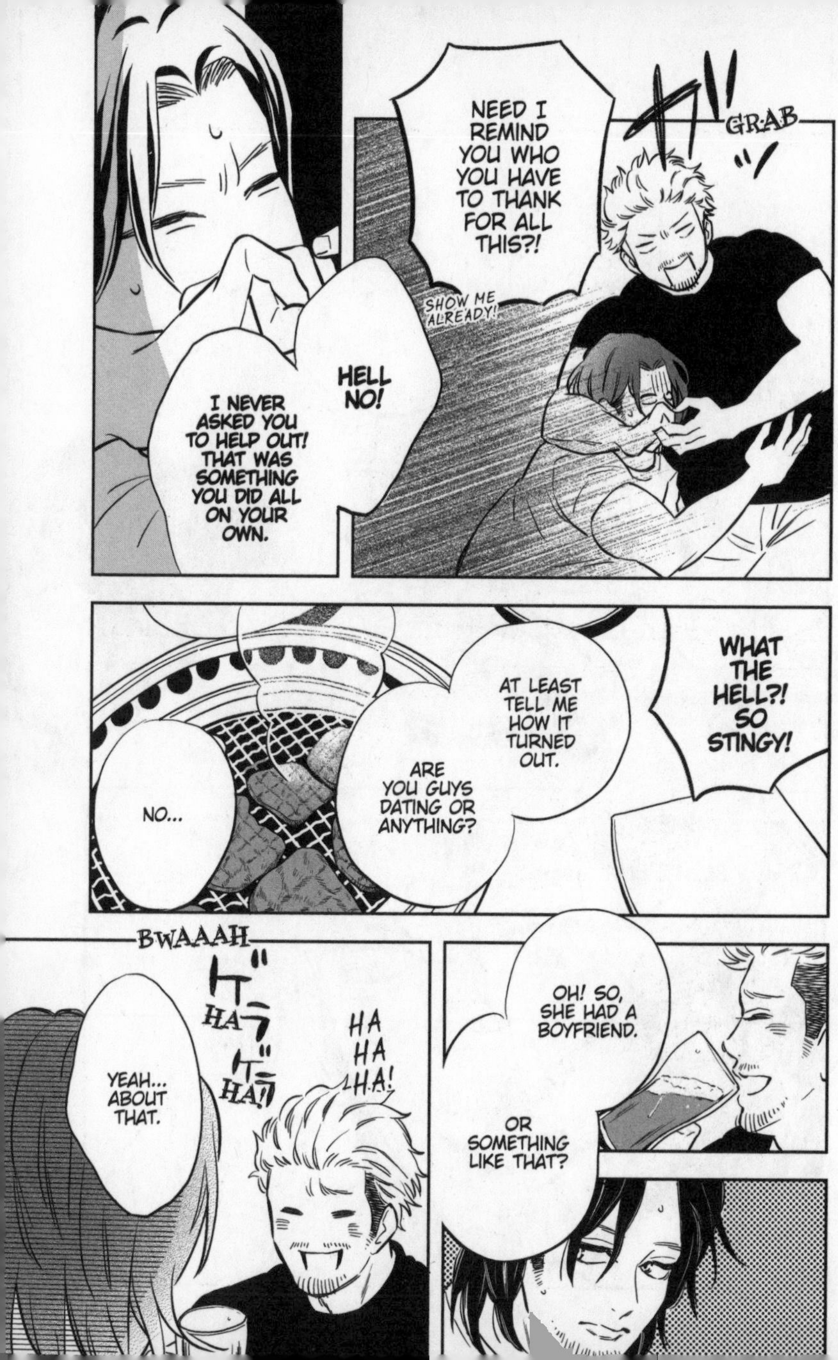
GRAB
NEED I REMIND YOU WHO YOU HAVE TO THANK FOR ALL THIS?!
SHOW ME ALREADY!
HELL NO!
I NEVER ASKED YOU TO HELP OUT! THAT WAS SOMETHING YOU DID ALL ON YOUR OWN.
WHAT THE HELL?! SO STINGY!
AT LEAST TELL ME HOW IT TURNED OUT.
ARE YOU GUYS DATING OR ANYTHING?
NO...
OH! SO, SHE HAD A BOYFRIEND.
OR SOMETHING LIKE THAT?
BWAAAH
HA
HA!
YEAH... ABOUT THAT.
HA HA HA!

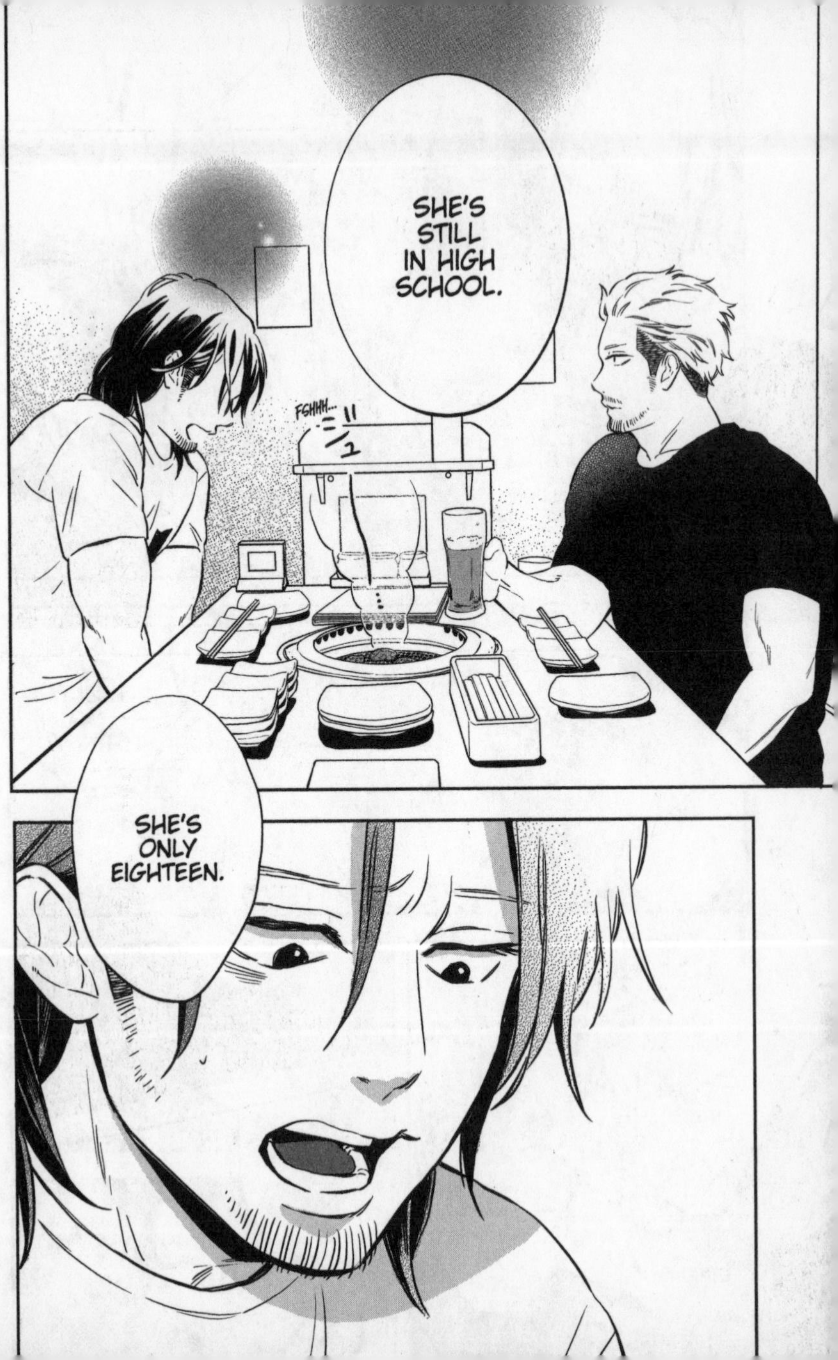
SHE'S STILL IN HIGH SCHOOL.
FSHHH...
SHE'S ONLY EIGHTEEN.

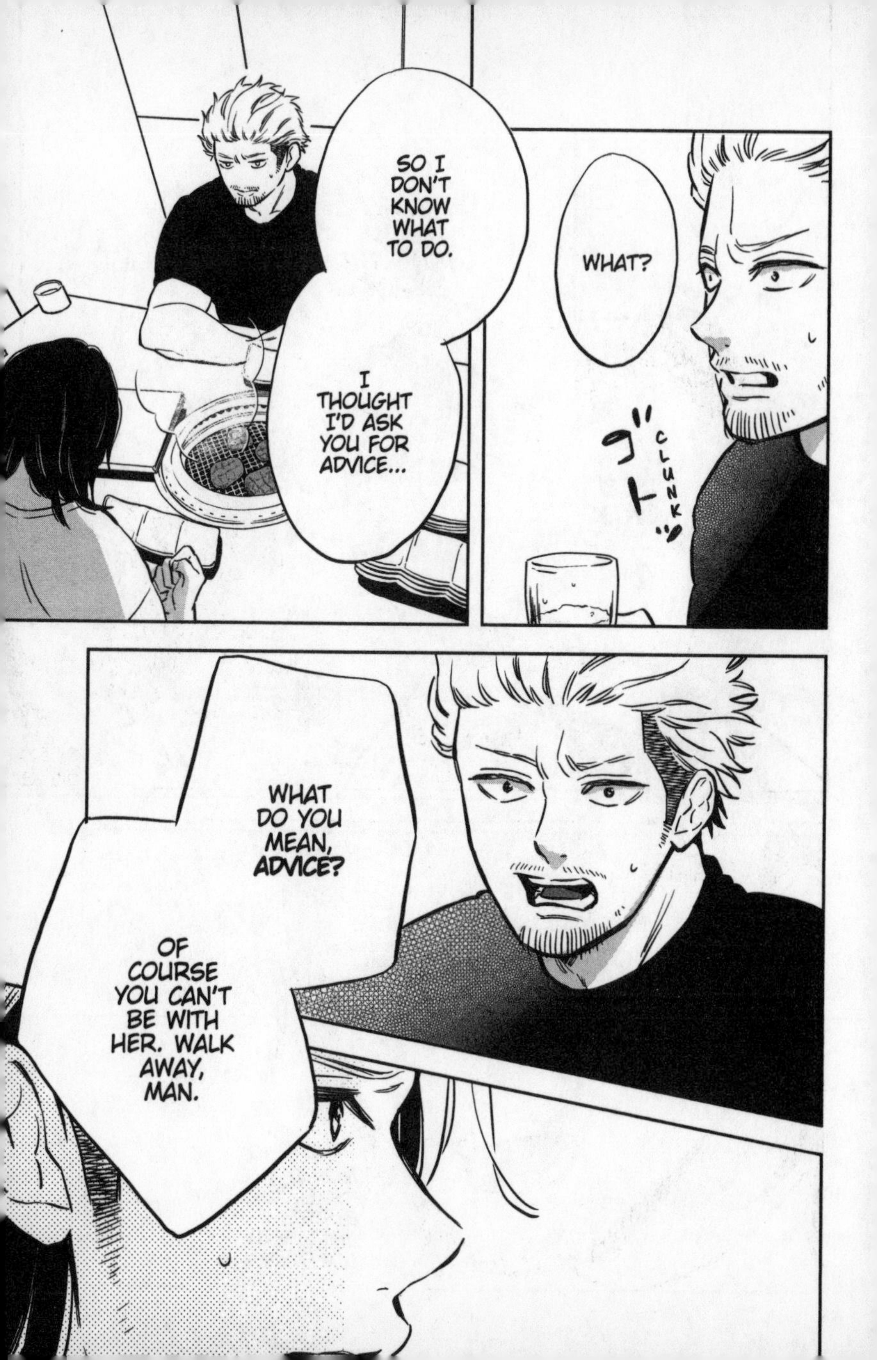
WHAT?
ゴト
CLUNK
SO I DON'T KNOW WHAT TO DO.
I THOUGHT I'D ASK YOU FOR ADVICE...
WHAT DO YOU MEAN, ADVICE?
OF COURSE YOU CAN'T BE WITH HER. WALK AWAY, MAN.

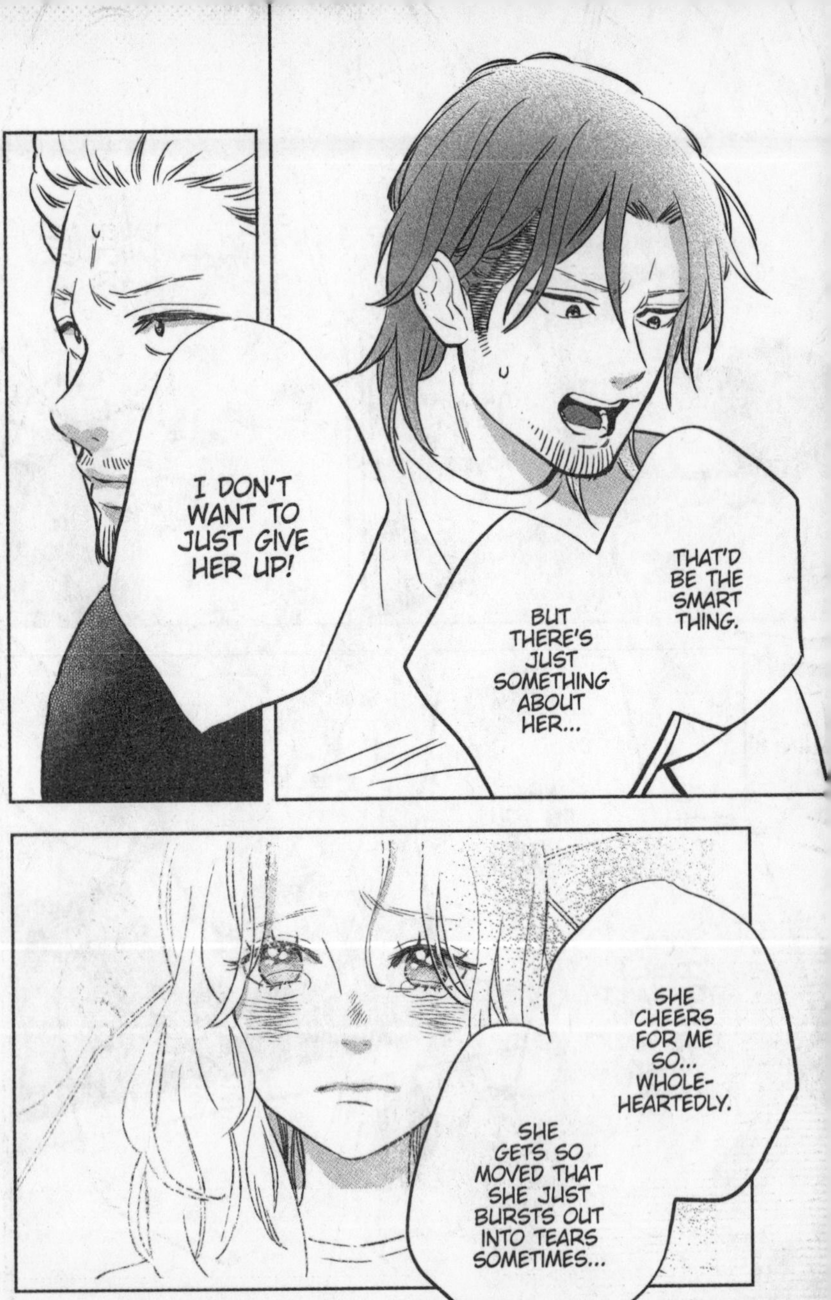
THAT'D BE THE SMART THING.
BUT THERE'S JUST SOMETHING ABOUT HER...
I DON'T WANT TO JUST GIVE HER UP!
SHE CHEERS FOR ME SO... WHOLE-HEARTEDLY.
SHE GETS SO MOVED THAT SHE JUST BURSTS OUT INTO TEARS SOMETIMES...

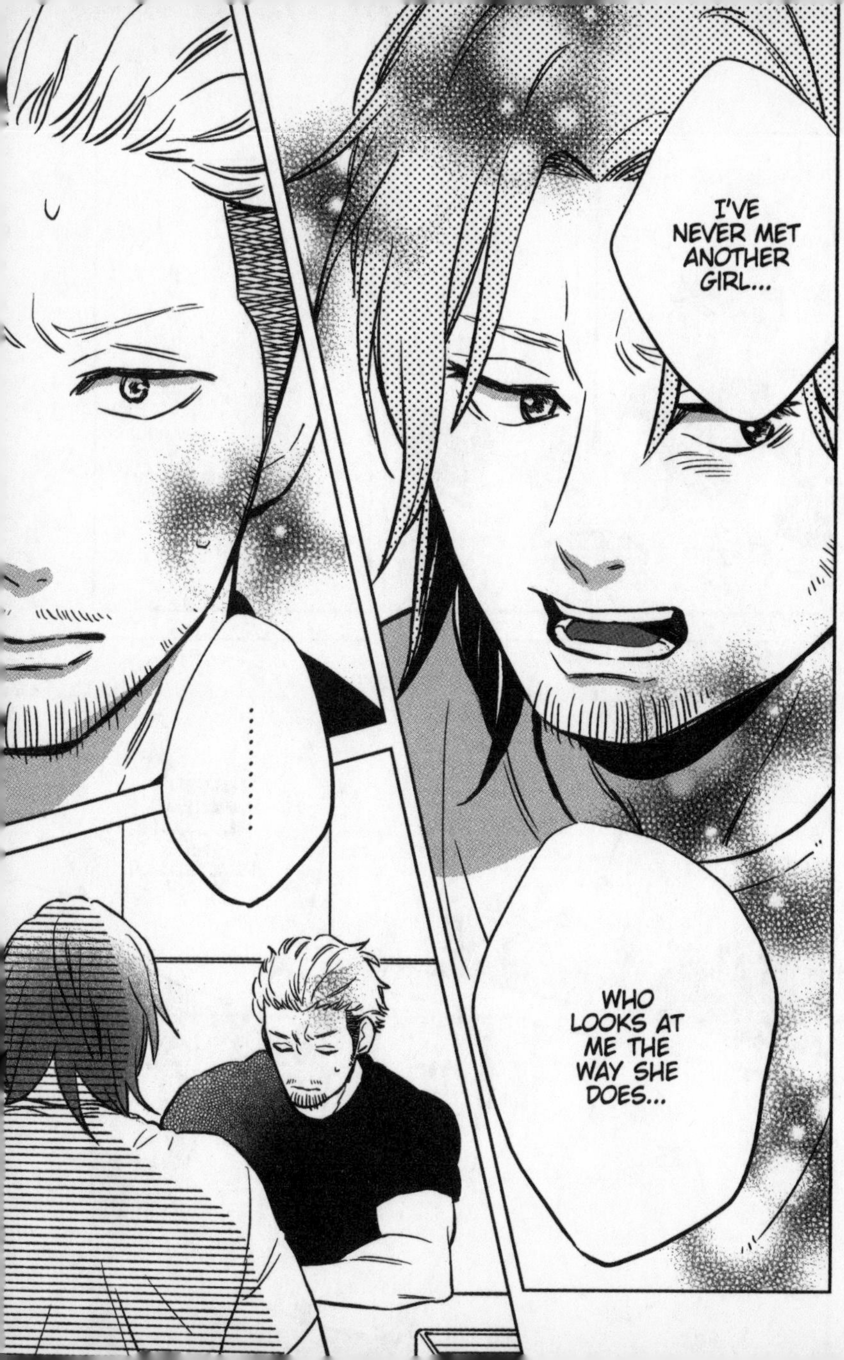
I'VE NEVER MET ANOTHER GIRL...
WHO LOOKS AT ME THE WAY SHE DOES...
......

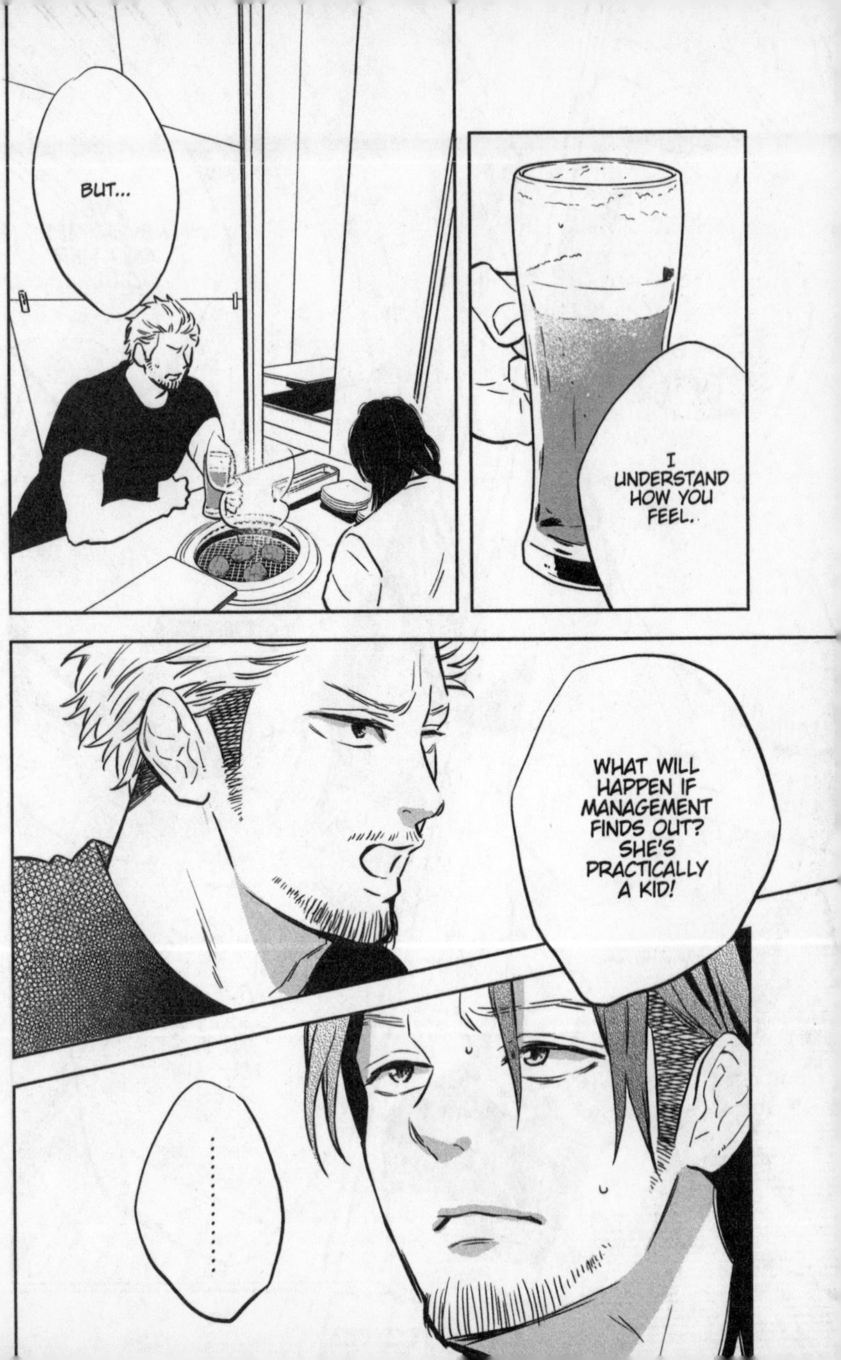
I UNDERSTAND HOW YOU FEEL.
BUT...
WHAT WILL HAPPEN IF MANAGEMENT FINDS OUT? SHE'S PRACTICALLY A KID!
......

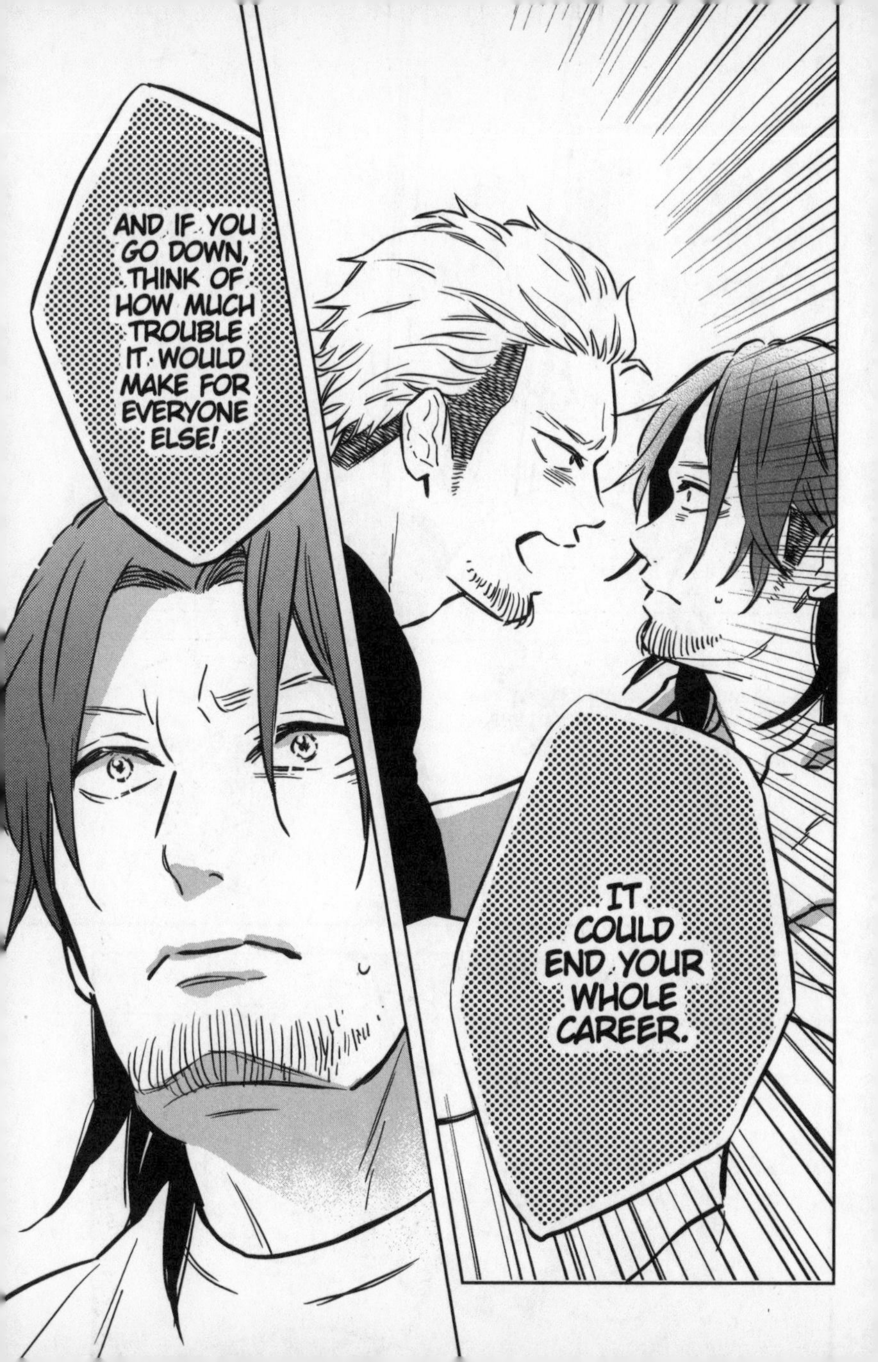
IT COULD END YOUR WHOLE CAREER.
AND IF YOU GO DOWN, THINK OF HOW MUCH TROUBLE IT WOULD MAKE FOR EVERYONE ELSE!

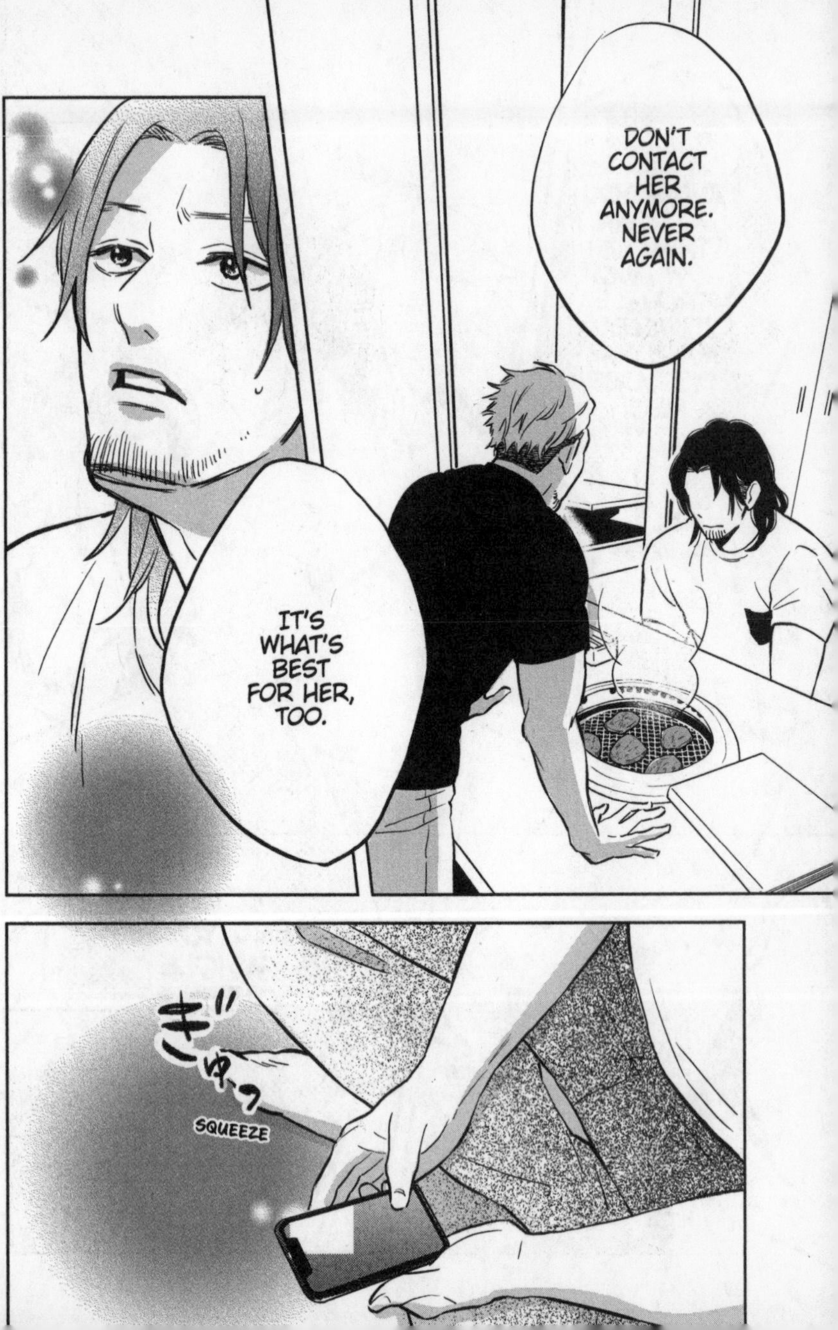
DON'T CONTACT HER ANYMORE. NEVER AGAIN.
IT'S WHAT'S BEST FOR HER, TOO.
ぎゅっ
SQUEEZE

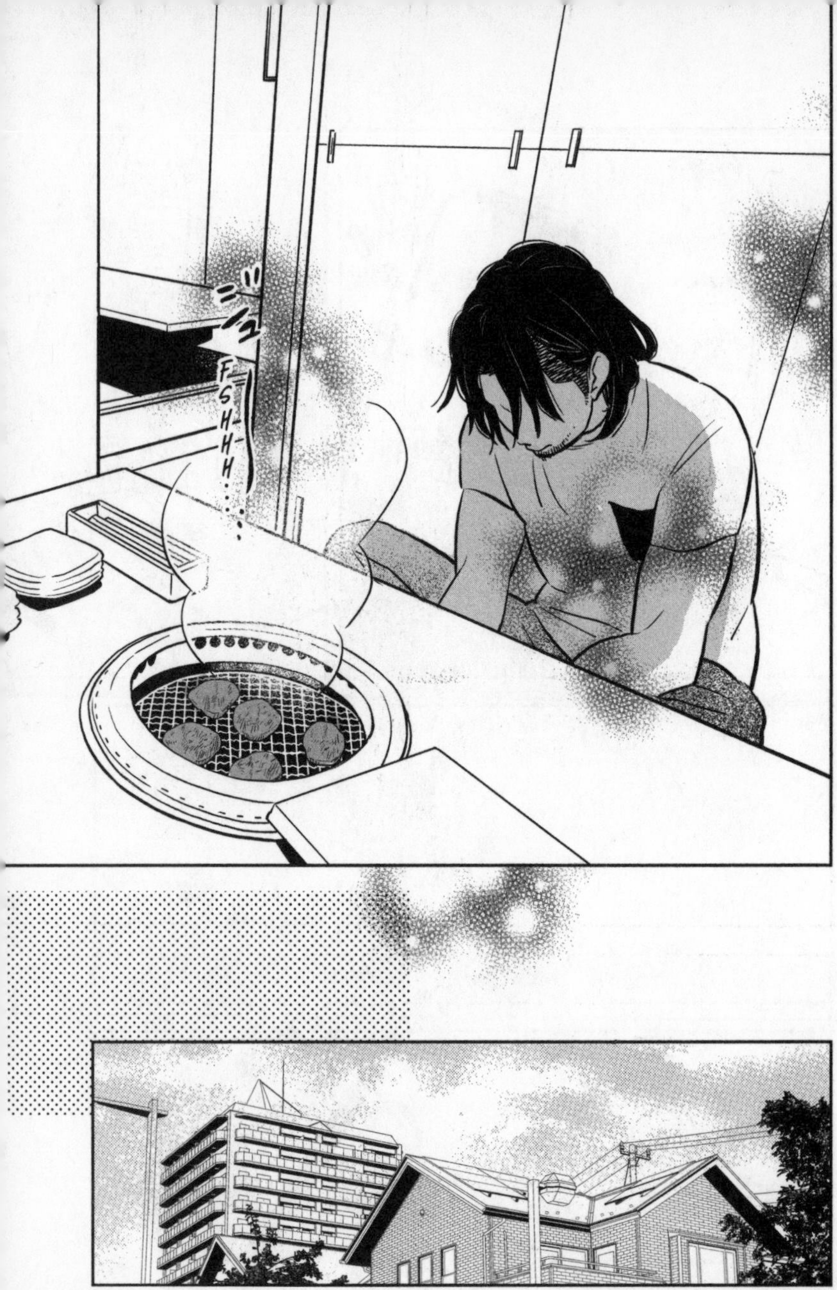
ジュ
FSHHH...

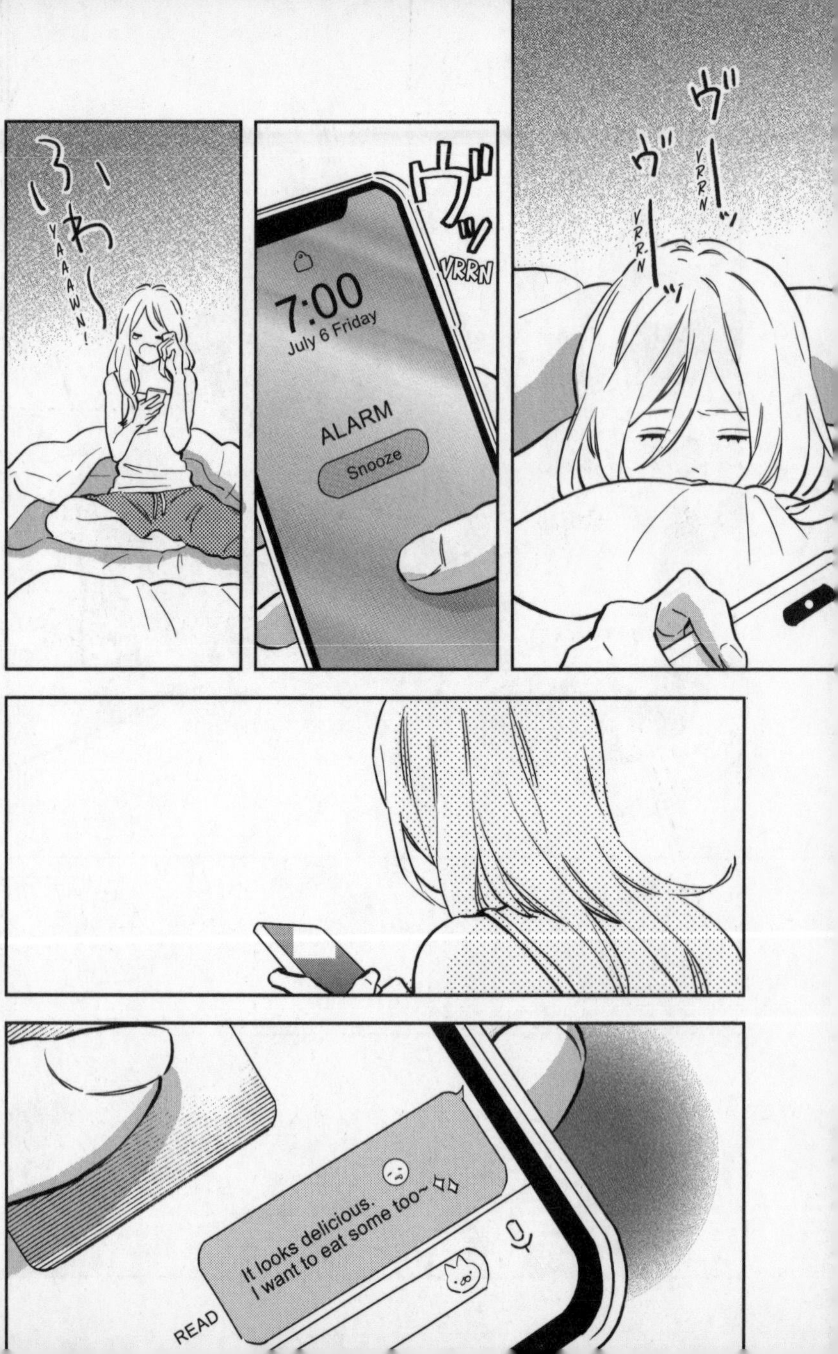
ヴーッ
VRRN
ヴーッ
VRRN
ヴッ
VRRN
7:00
July 6 Friday
ALARM
Snooze
ふわ
YAAAAWN!
It looks delicious.
I want to eat some too~
READ

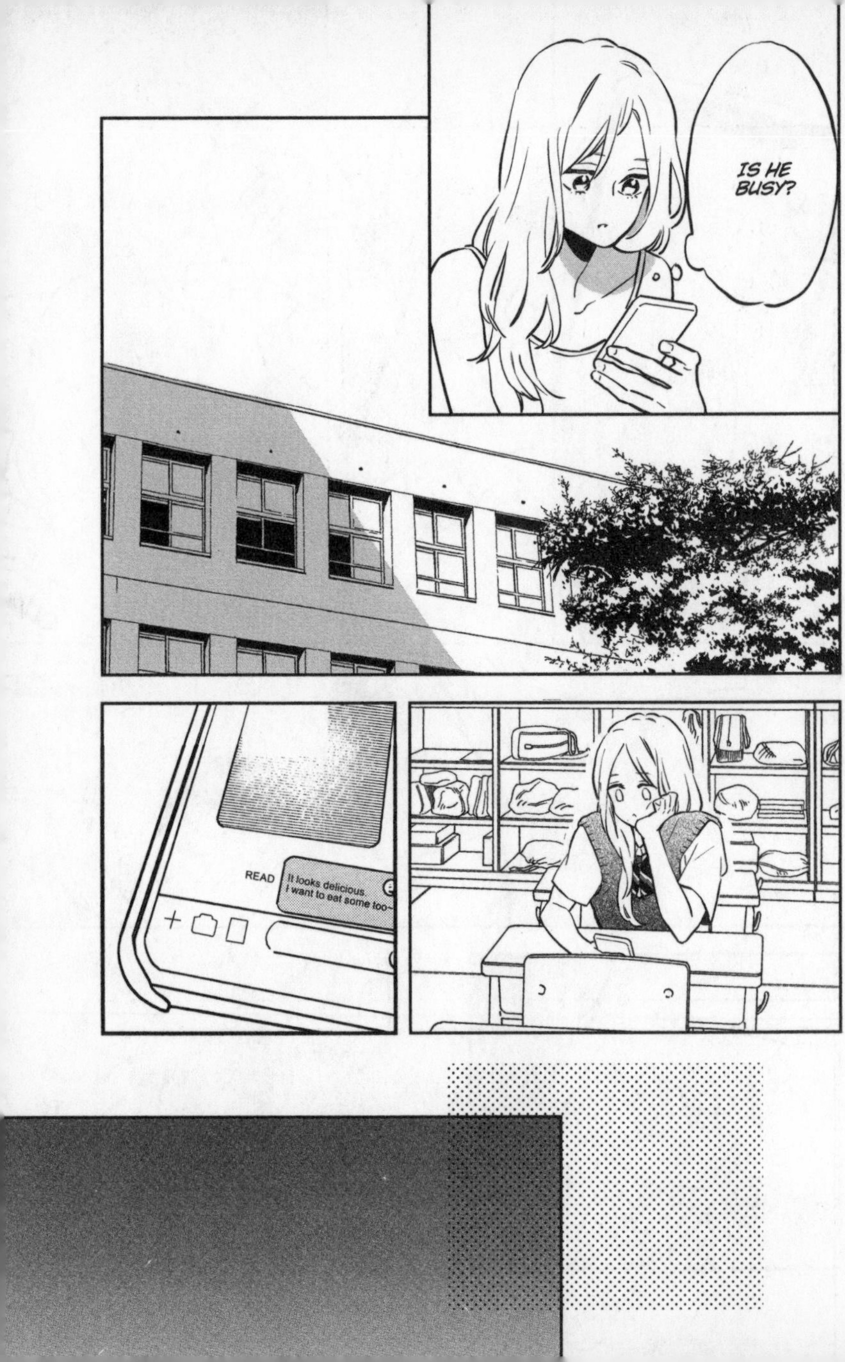
IS HE BUSY?
READ
It looks delicious.
I want to eat some too~

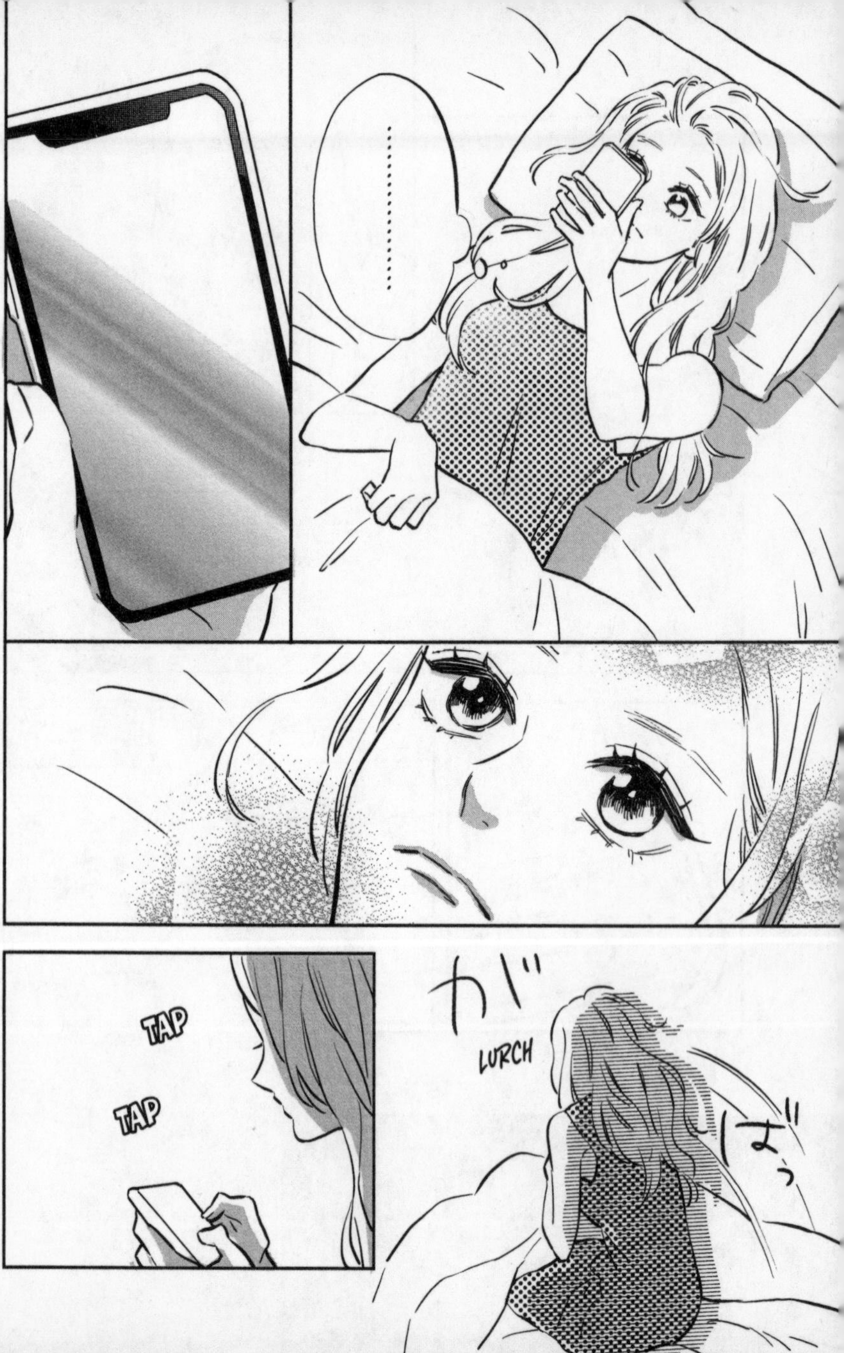

……
LURCH
が
ばっ
TAP
TAP

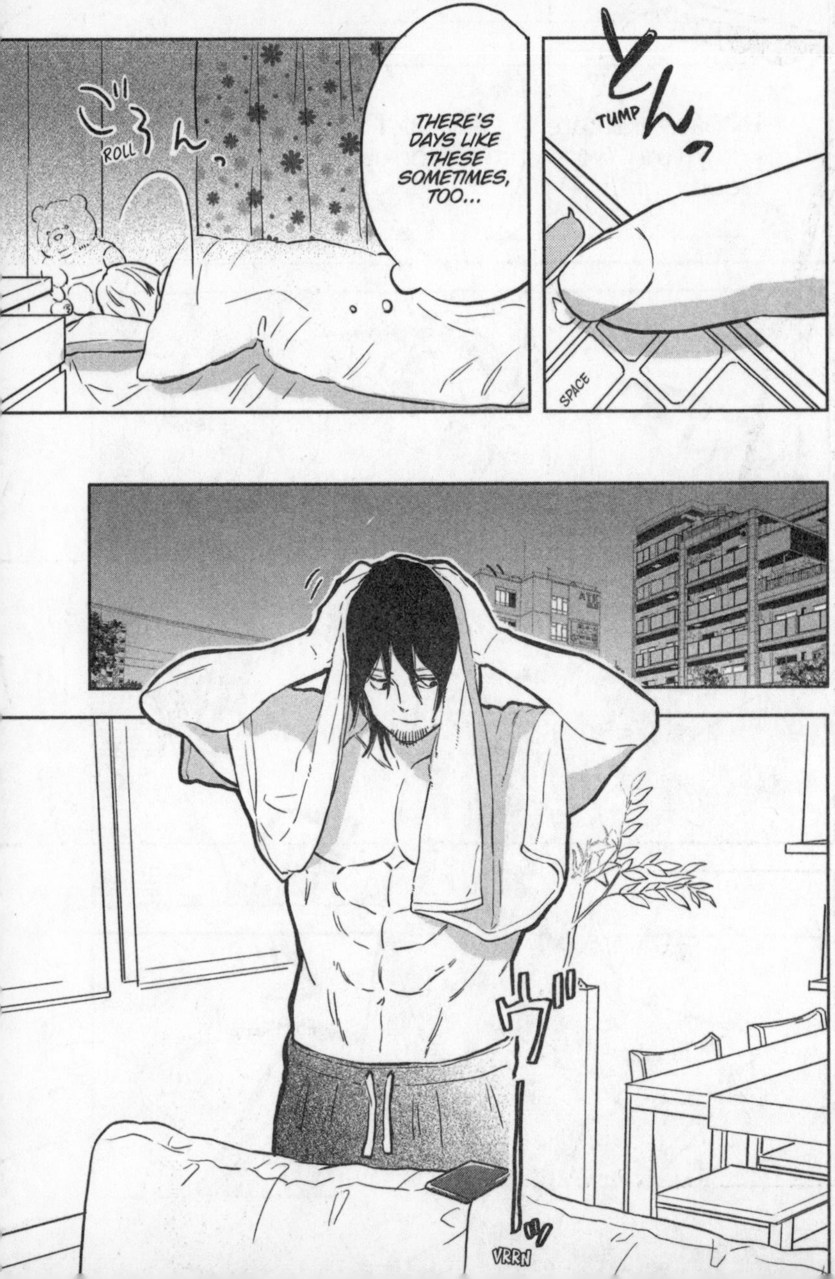
とん
TUMP
SPACE
ごろん
ROLL
THERE'S DAYS LIKE THESE SOMETIMES, TOO...
VRRN

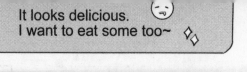

It looks delicious.
I want to eat some too~

Please take care of yourself. I know you'll work hard tomorrow. Good night.

SIGH...

CLENCH

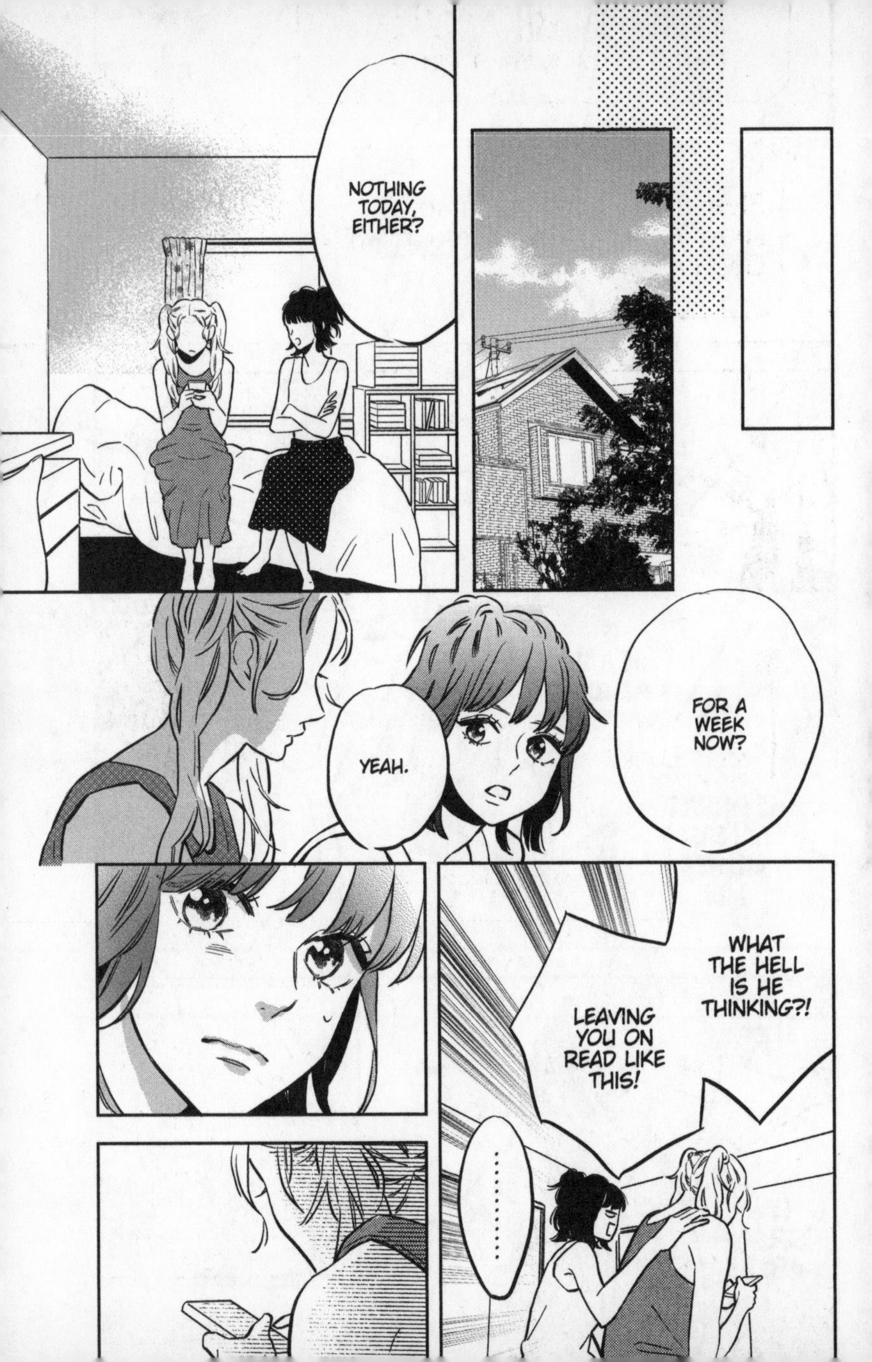
NOTHING TODAY, EITHER?
FOR A WEEK NOW?
YEAH.
WHAT THE HELL IS HE THINKING?!
LEAVING YOU ON READ LIKE THIS!
......

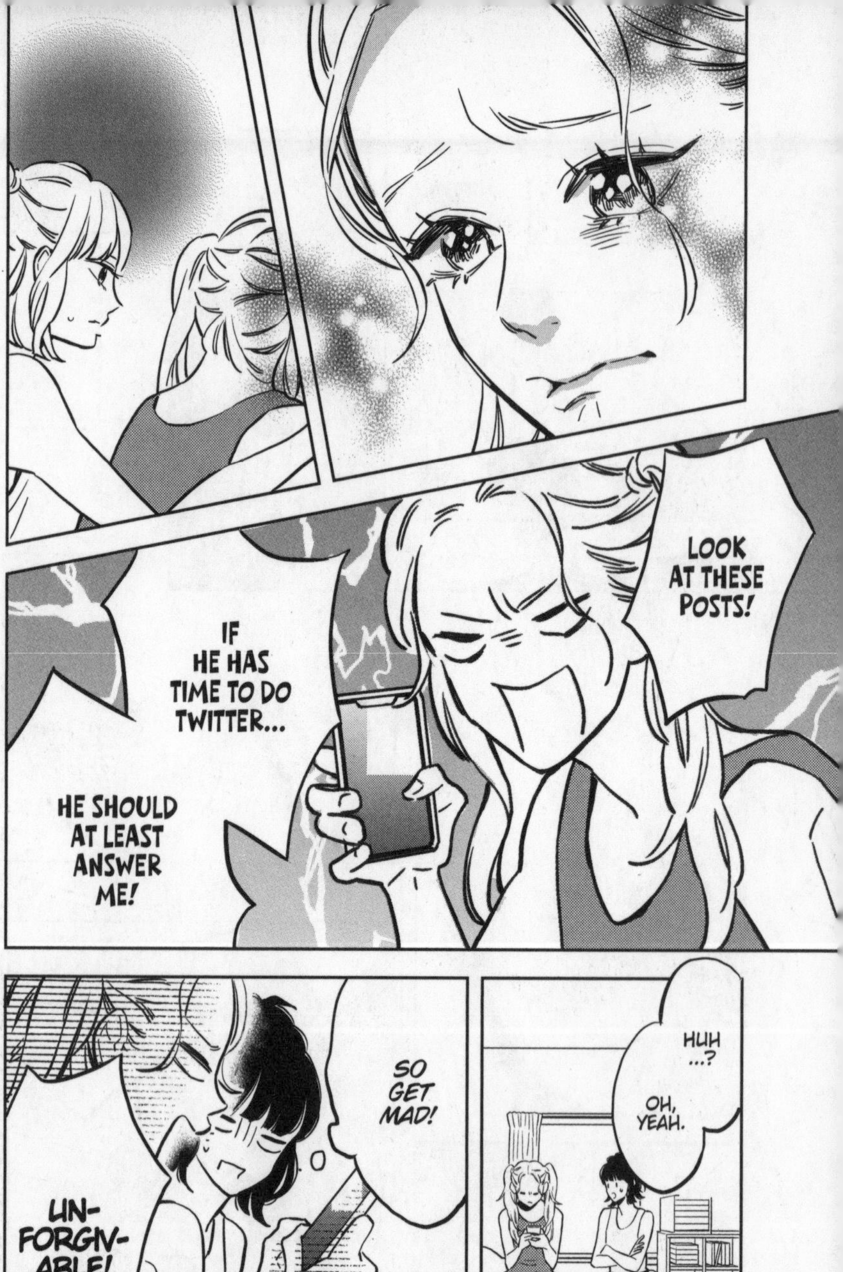
LOOK AT THESE POSTS!
IF HE HAS TIME TO DO TWITTER...
HE SHOULD AT LEAST ANSWER ME!
HUH ...?
OH, YEAH.
SO GET MAD!
UN-FORGIV-ABLE!

I'M GIVING UP.

Please take care of yourself. I know you'll work hard tomorrow. Good night.

READ

Please contact me when you have time.

IF HE LEAVES THIS ON READ...

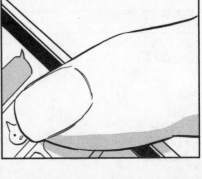

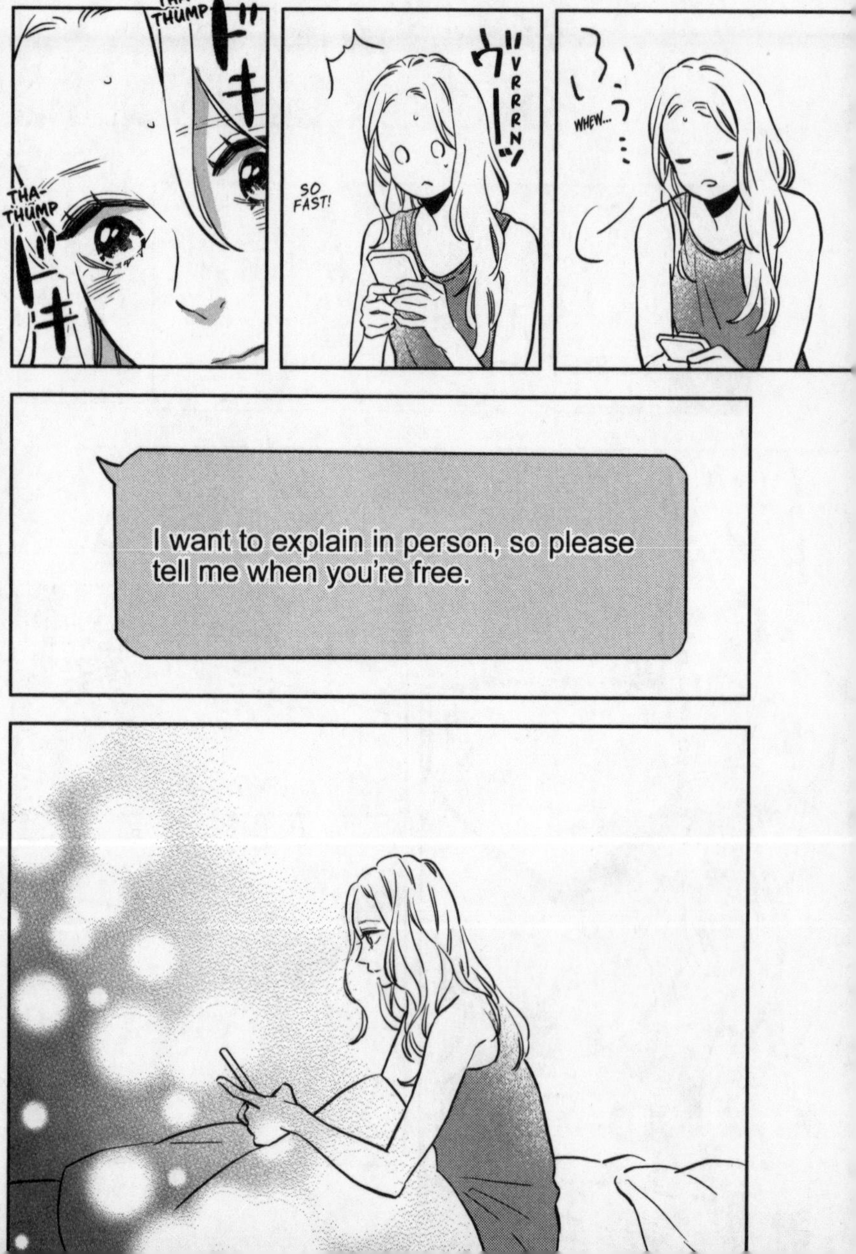
WHEW...
VRRRRN
SO FAST!
THA-THUMP
THA-THUMP
I want to explain in person, so please tell me when you're free.

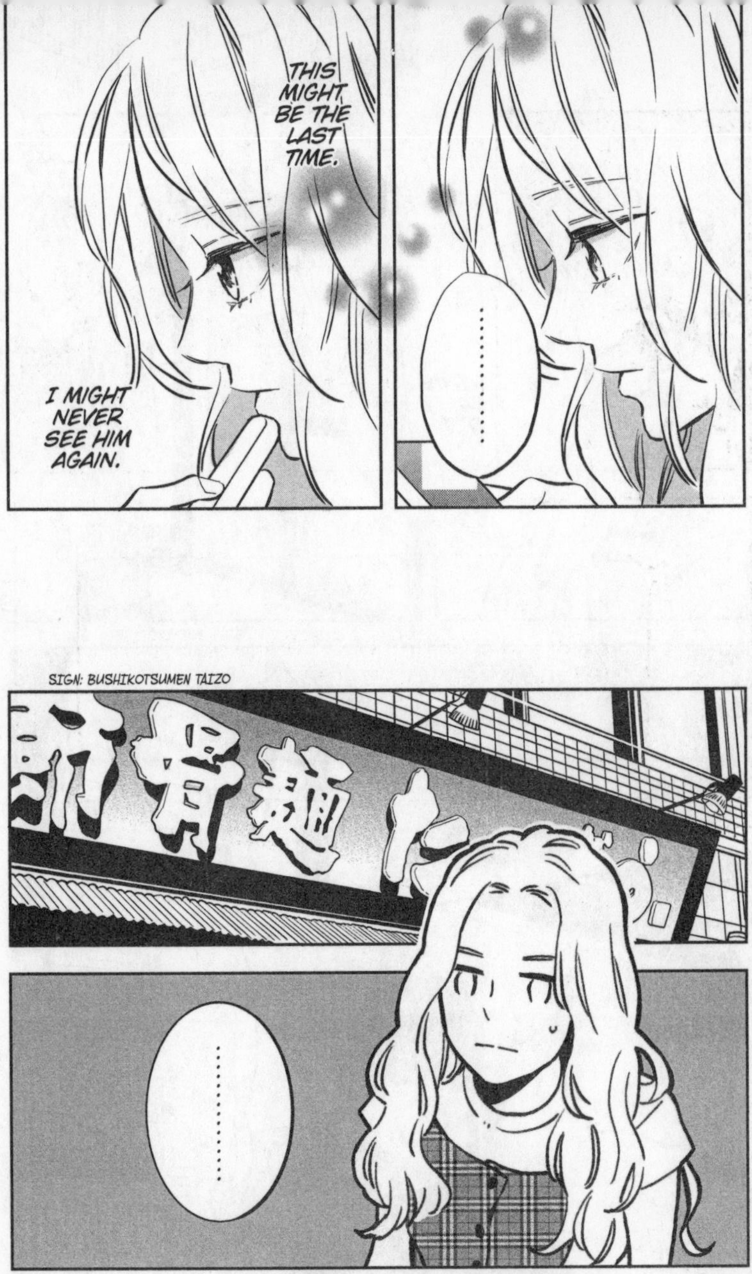
……
THIS MIGHT BE THE LAST TIME.
I MIGHT NEVER SEE HIM AGAIN.
SIGN: BUSHIKOTSUMEN TAIZO
……

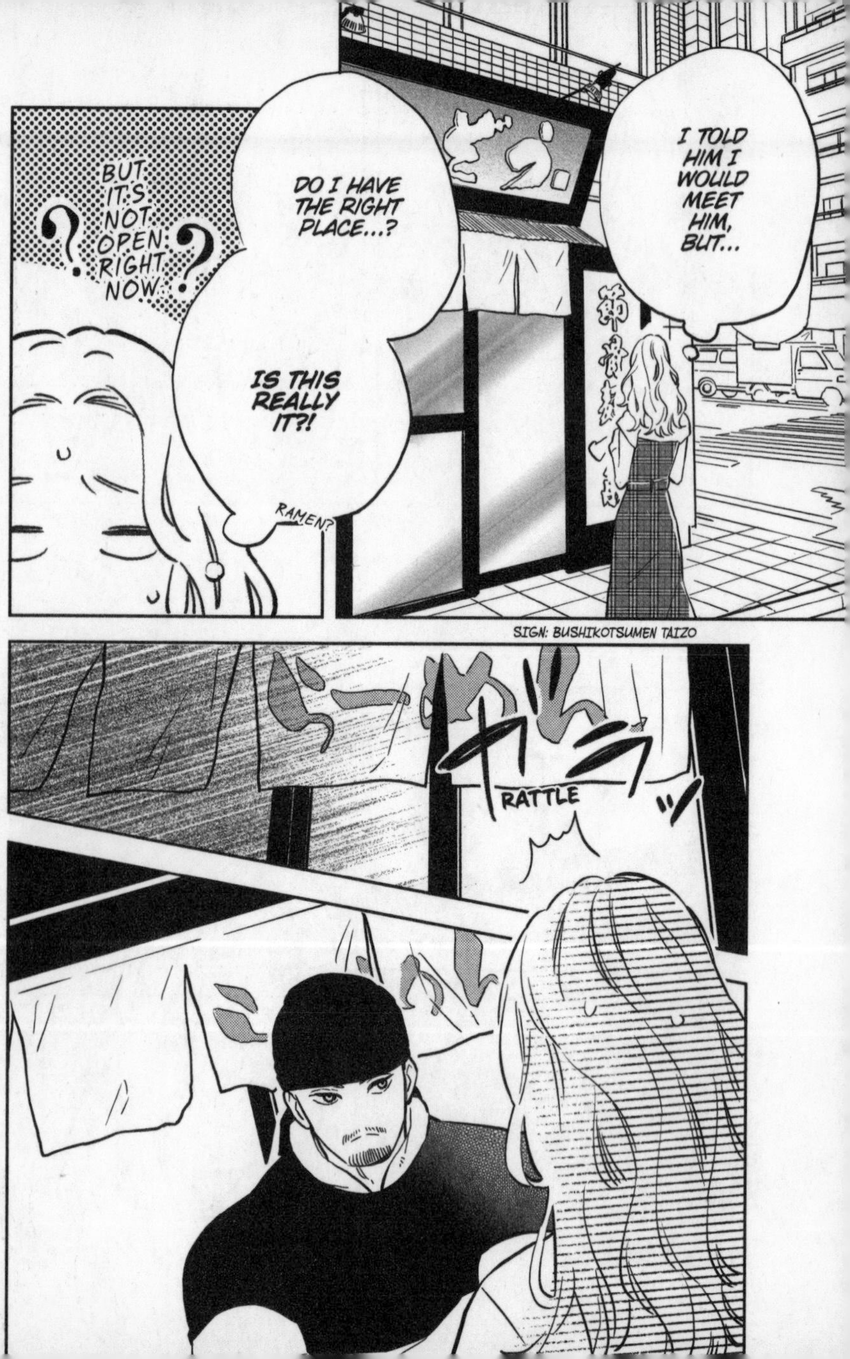
I TOLD HIM I WOULD MEET HIM, BUT...
DO I HAVE THE RIGHT PLACE...?
IS THIS REALLY IT?!
RAMEN?
BUT IT'S NOT OPEN RIGHT NOW
SIGN: BUSHIKOTSUMEN TAIZO
RATTLE

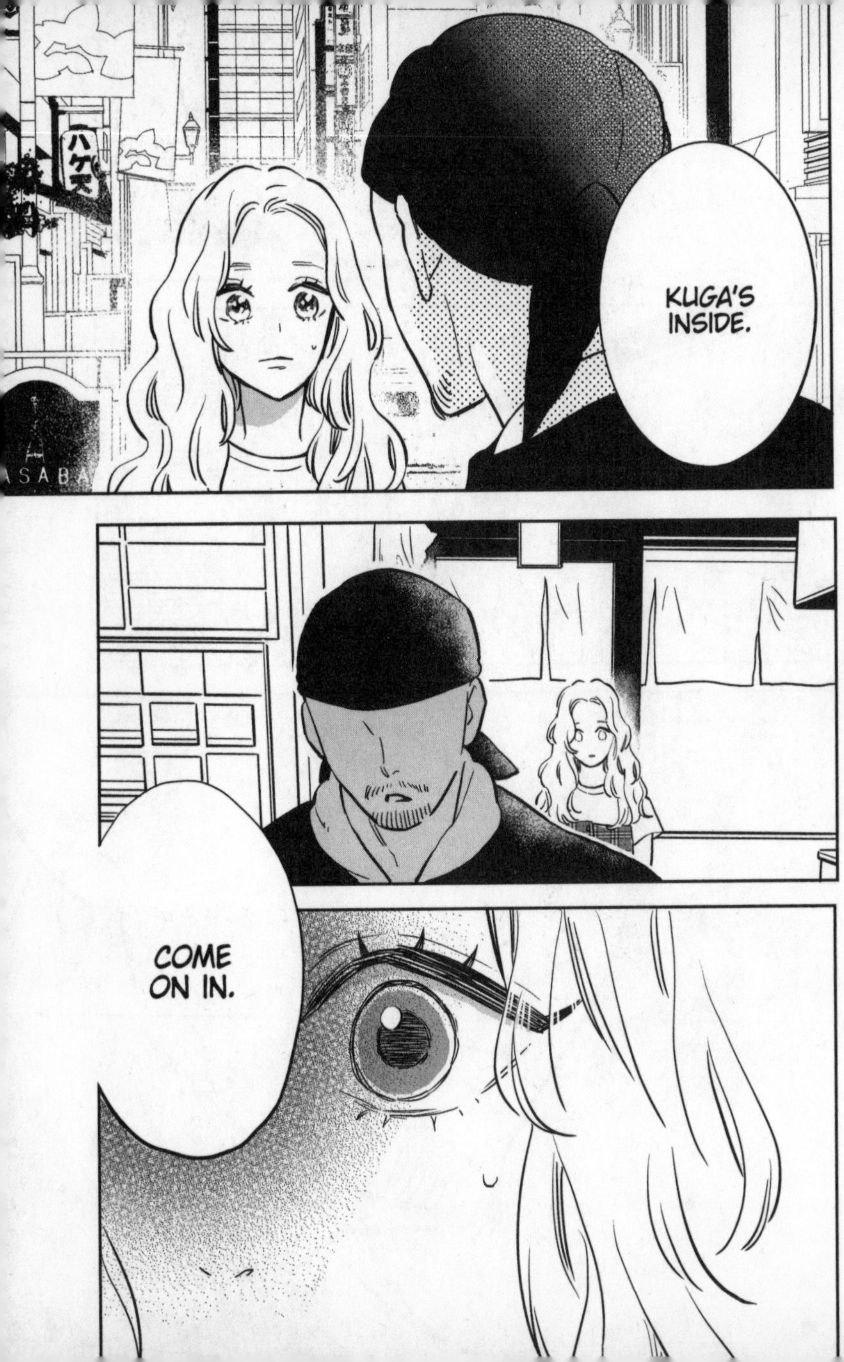
KUGA'S INSIDE.
COME ON IN.

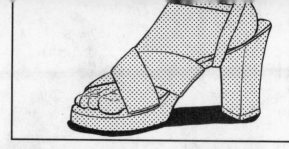

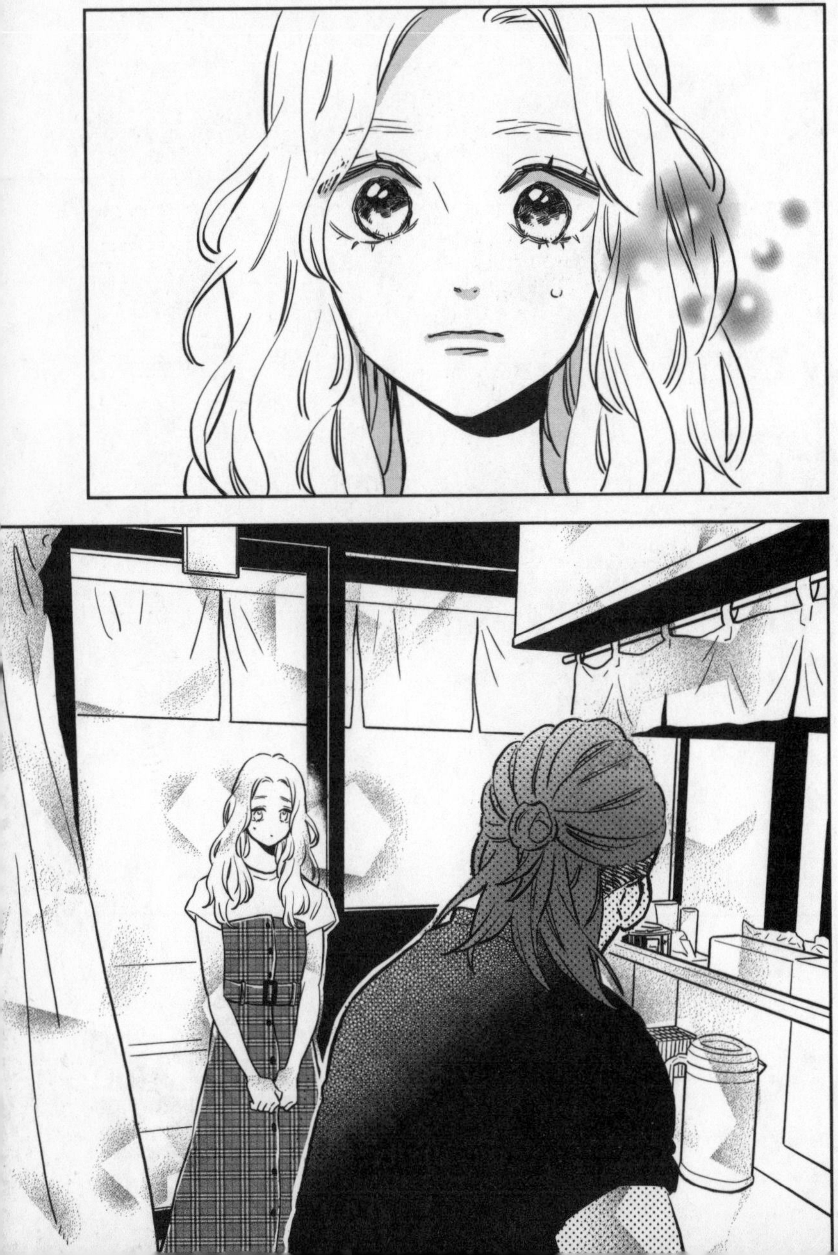

Cutie and the BEAST

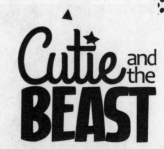

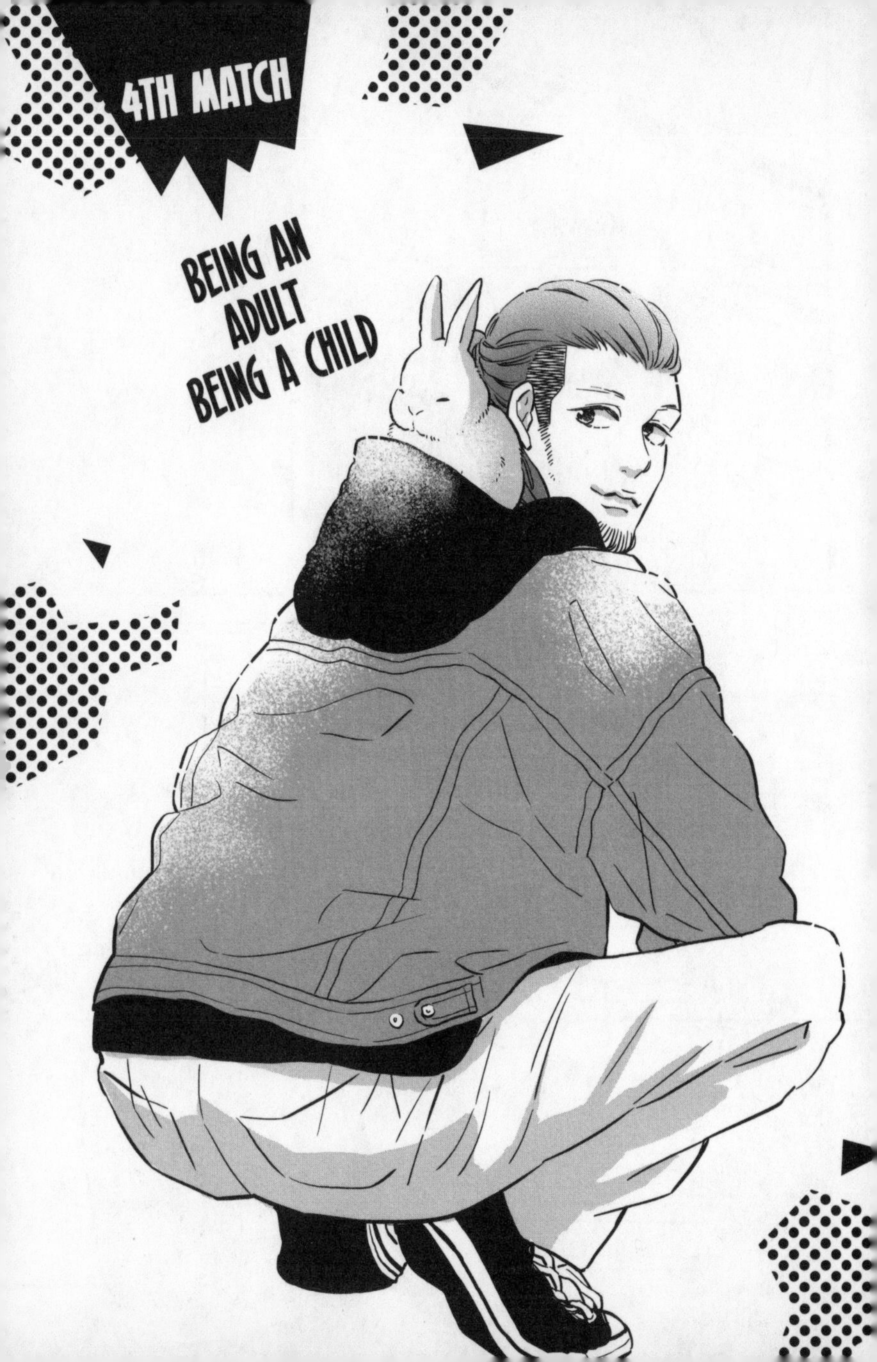
4TH MATCH
BEING AN ADULT BEING A CHILD

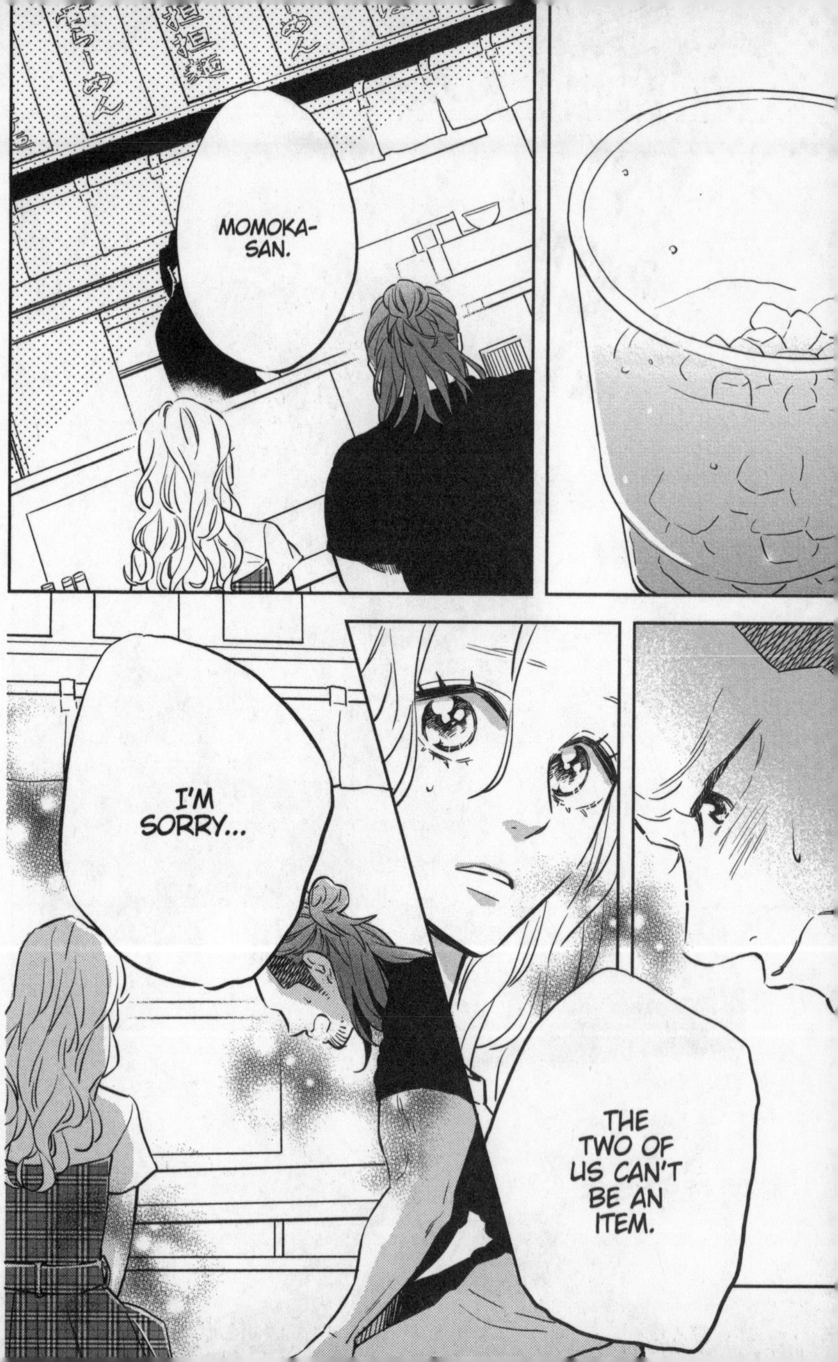
MOMOKA-SAN.
I'M SORRY...
THE TWO OF US CAN'T BE AN ITEM.

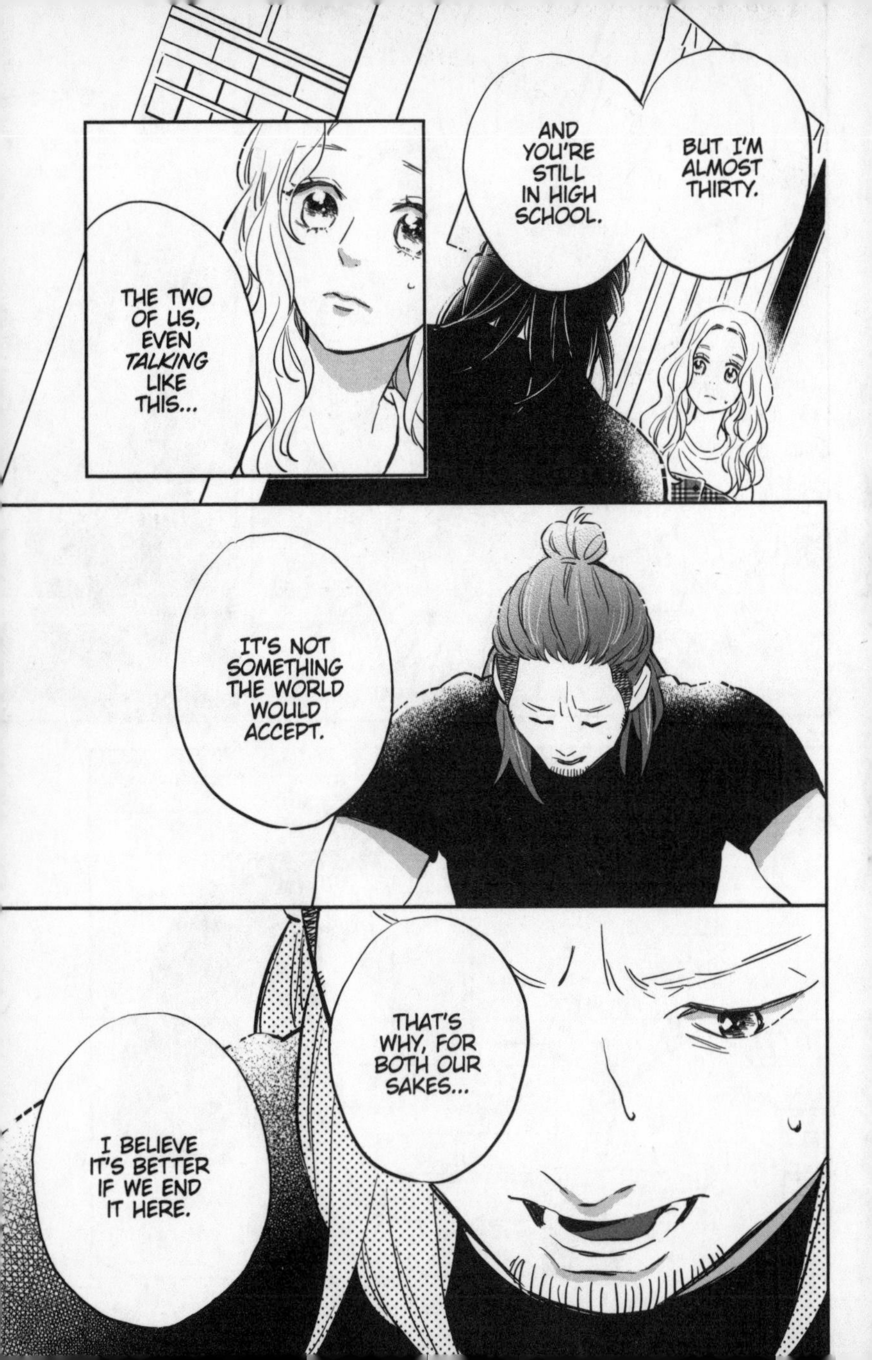
BUT I'M ALMOST THIRTY.
AND YOU'RE STILL IN HIGH SCHOOL.
THE TWO OF US, EVEN *TALKING* LIKE THIS...
IT'S NOT SOMETHING THE WORLD WOULD ACCEPT.
THAT'S WHY, FOR BOTH OUR SAKES...
I BELIEVE IT'S BETTER IF WE END IT HERE.

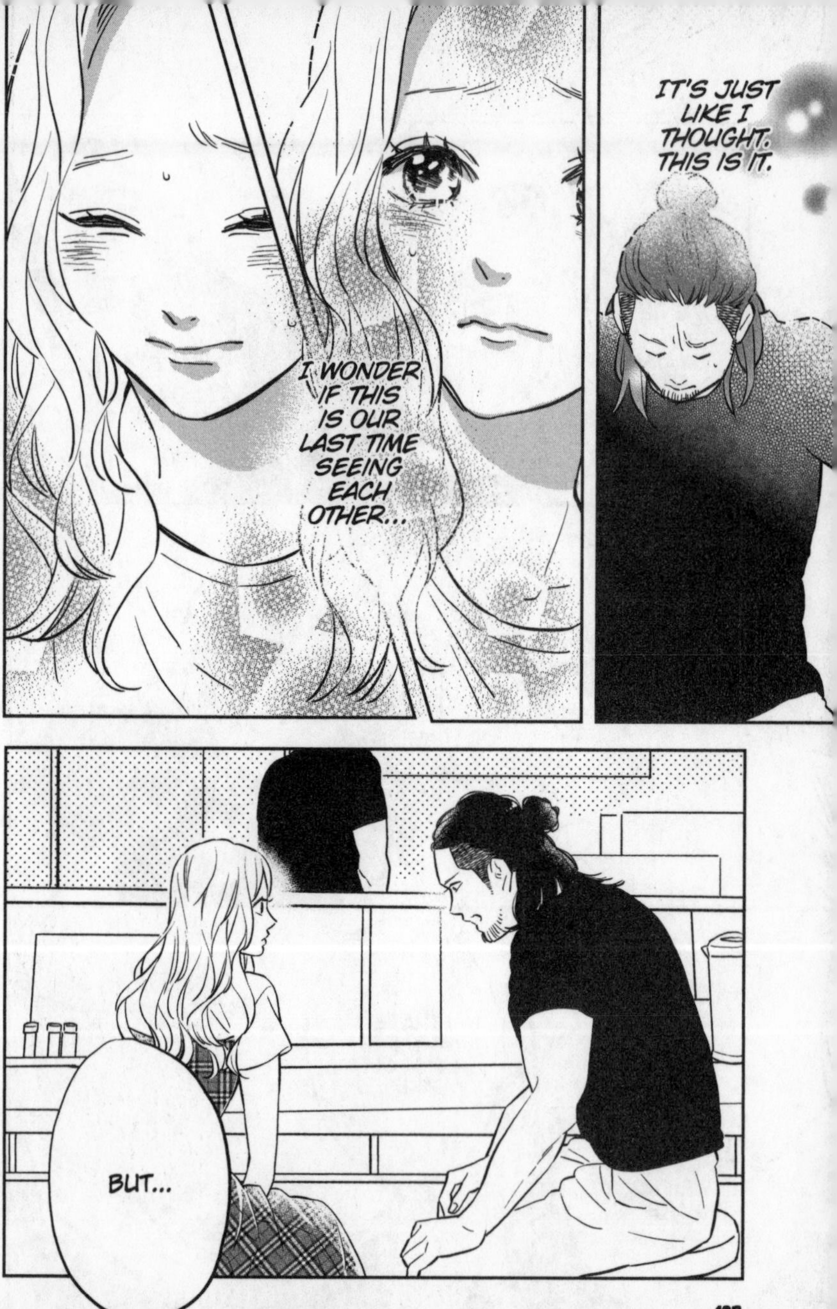
IT'S JUST LIKE I THOUGHT. THIS IS IT.
I WONDER IF THIS IS OUR LAST TIME SEEING EACH OTHER...
BUT...

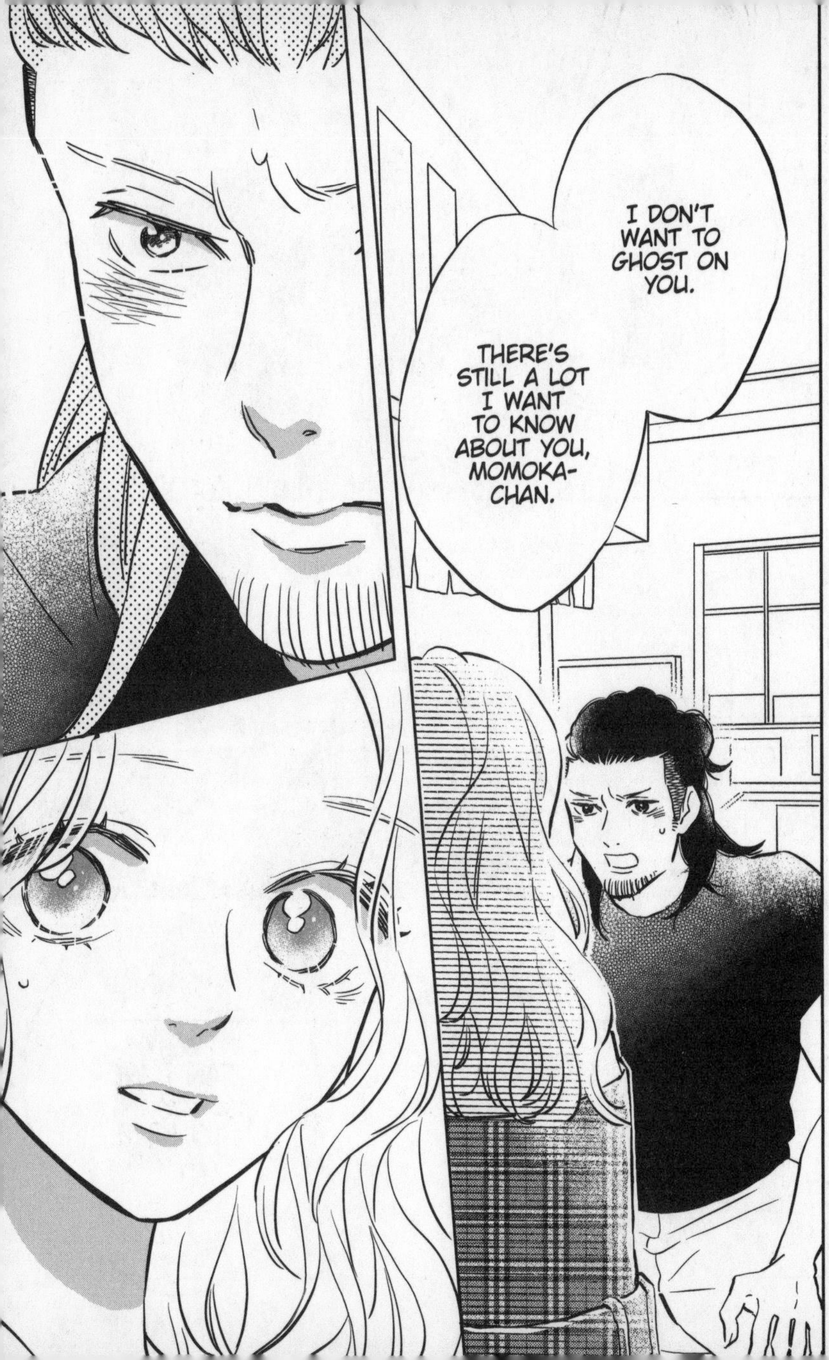
I DON'T WANT TO GHOST ON YOU.
THERE'S STILL A LOT I WANT TO KNOW ABOUT YOU, MOMOKA-CHAN.

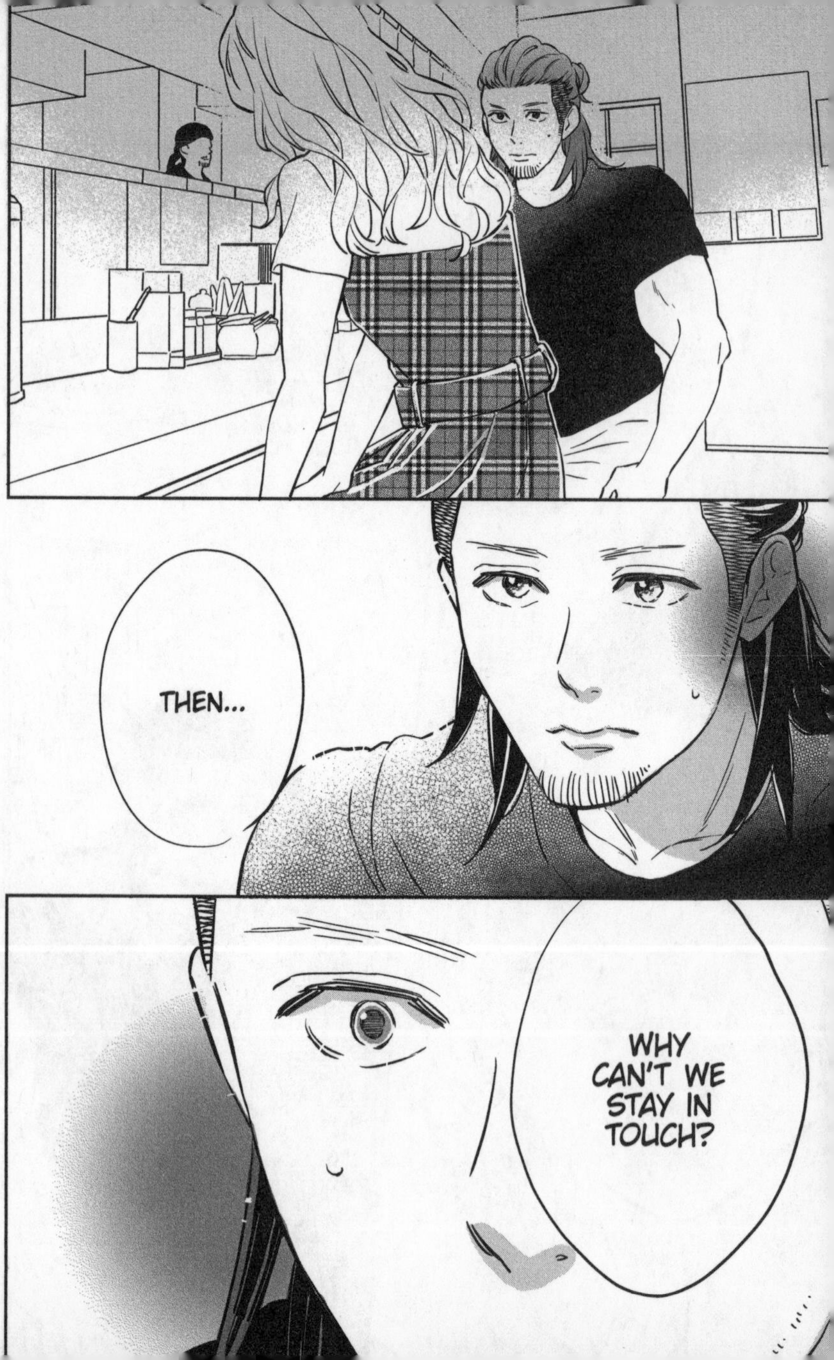
THEN...
WHY CAN'T WE STAY IN TOUCH?

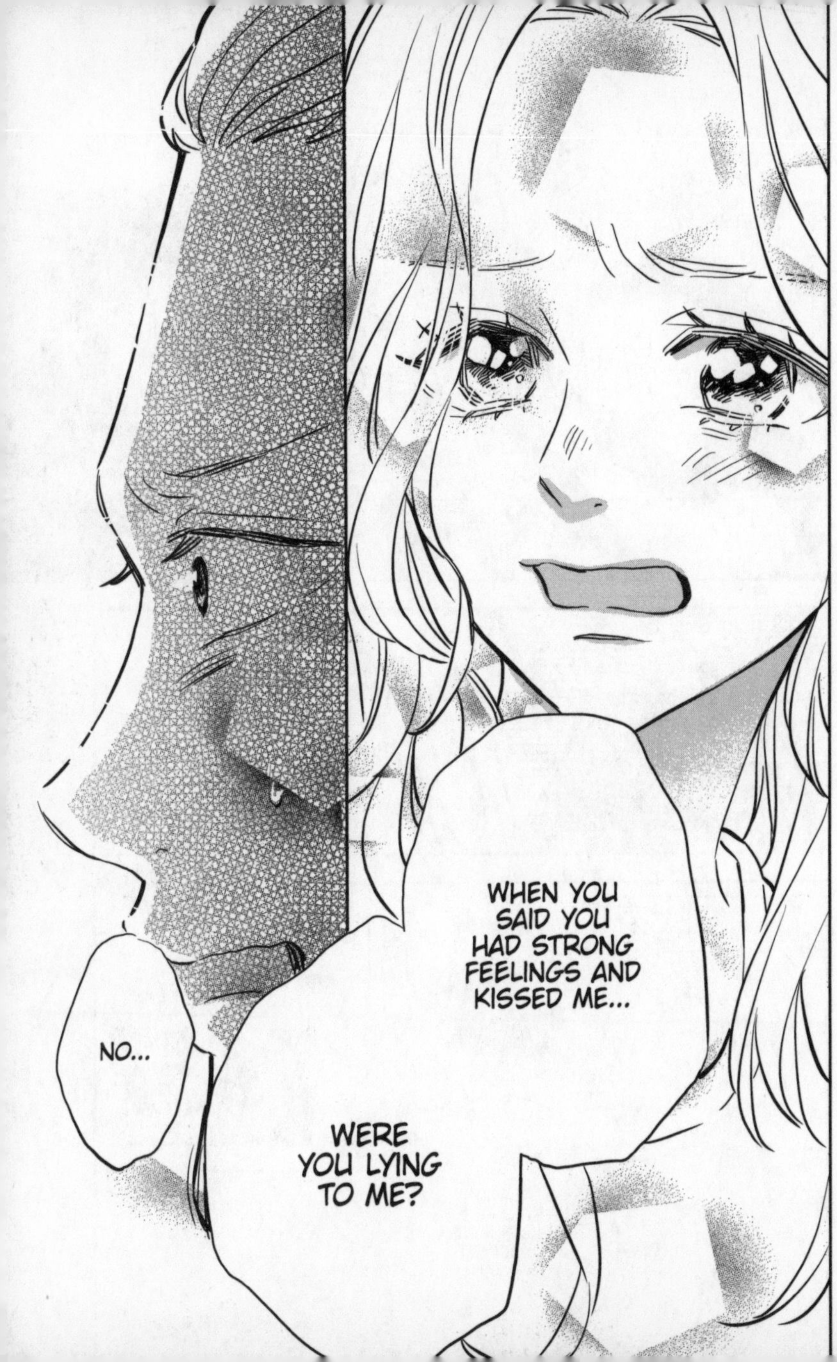
WHEN YOU SAID YOU HAD STRONG FEELINGS AND KISSED ME...
WERE YOU LYING TO ME?
NO...

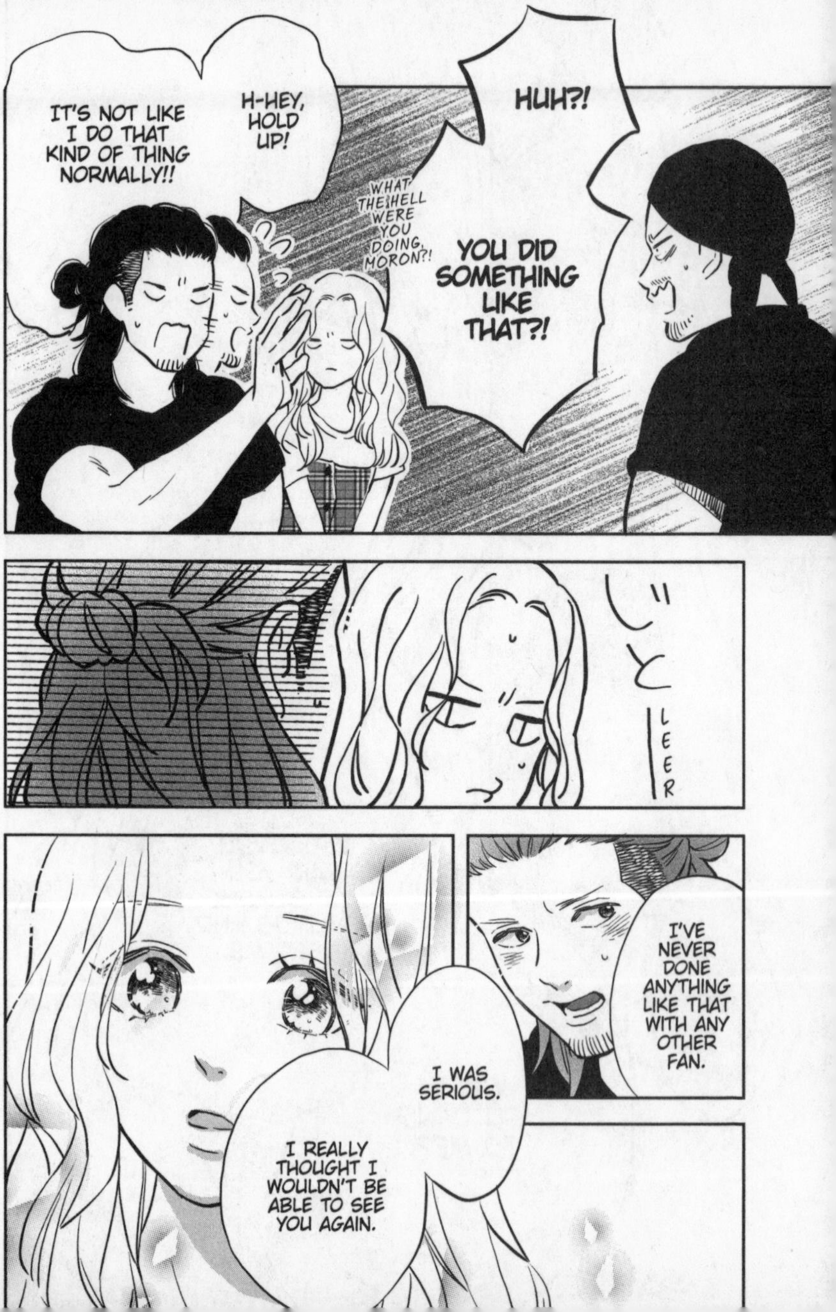
HUH?!
YOU DID SOMETHING LIKE THAT?!
WHAT THE HELL WERE YOU DOING, MORON?!
H-HEY, HOLD UP!
IT'S NOT LIKE I DO THAT KIND OF THING NORMALLY!!
じと
LEER
I'VE NEVER DONE ANYTHING LIKE THAT WITH ANY OTHER FAN.
I WAS SERIOUS.
I REALLY THOUGHT I WOULDN'T BE ABLE TO SEE YOU AGAIN.

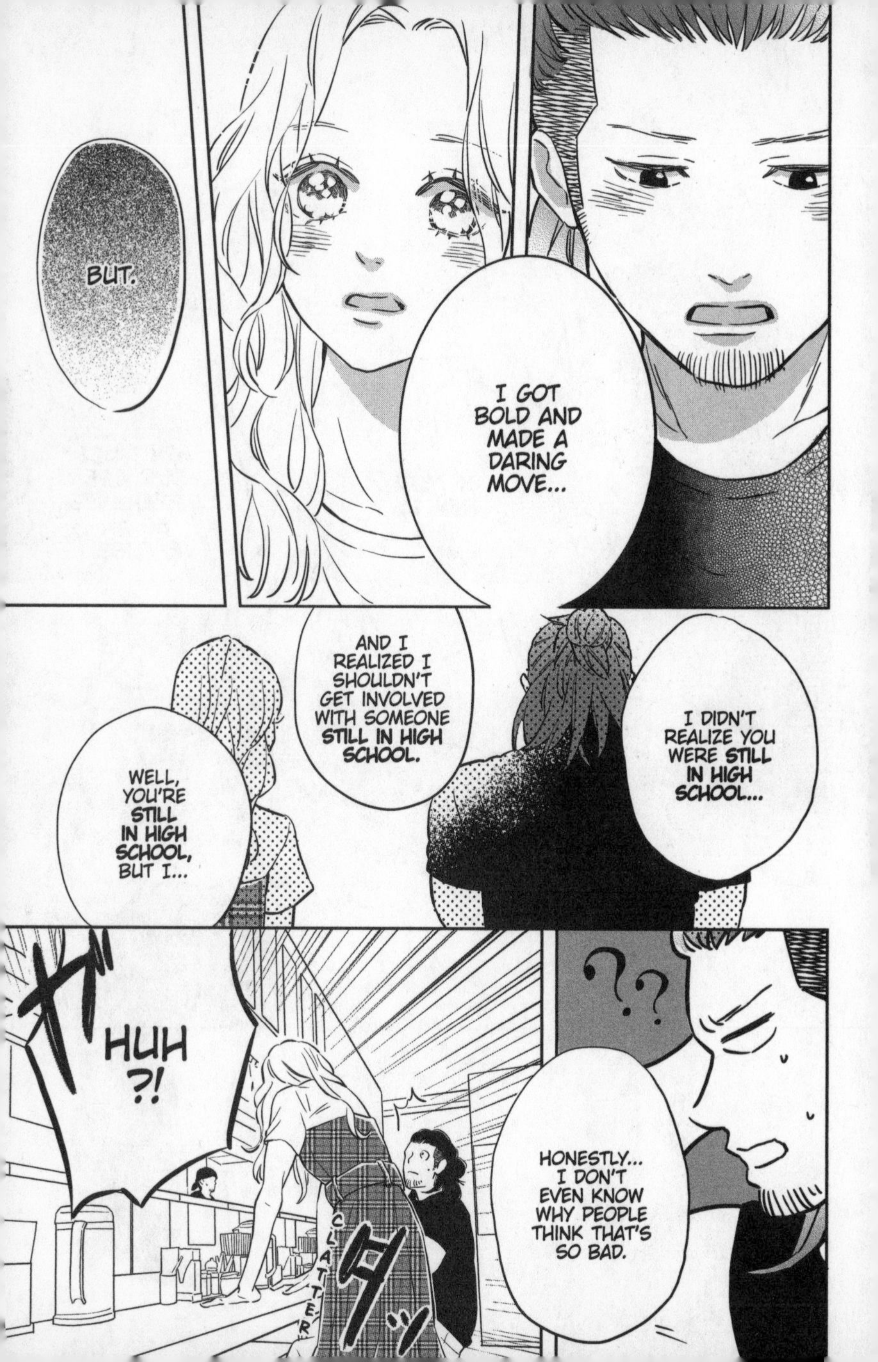
I GOT BOLD AND MADE A DARING MOVE...
BUT.
I DIDN'T REALIZE YOU WERE STILL IN HIGH SCHOOL...
AND I REALIZED I SHOULDN'T GET INVOLVED WITH SOMEONE STILL IN HIGH SCHOOL.
WELL, YOU'RE STILL IN HIGH SCHOOL, BUT I...
HONESTLY... I DON'T EVEN KNOW WHY PEOPLE THINK THAT'S SO BAD.
HUH ?!
CLATTER

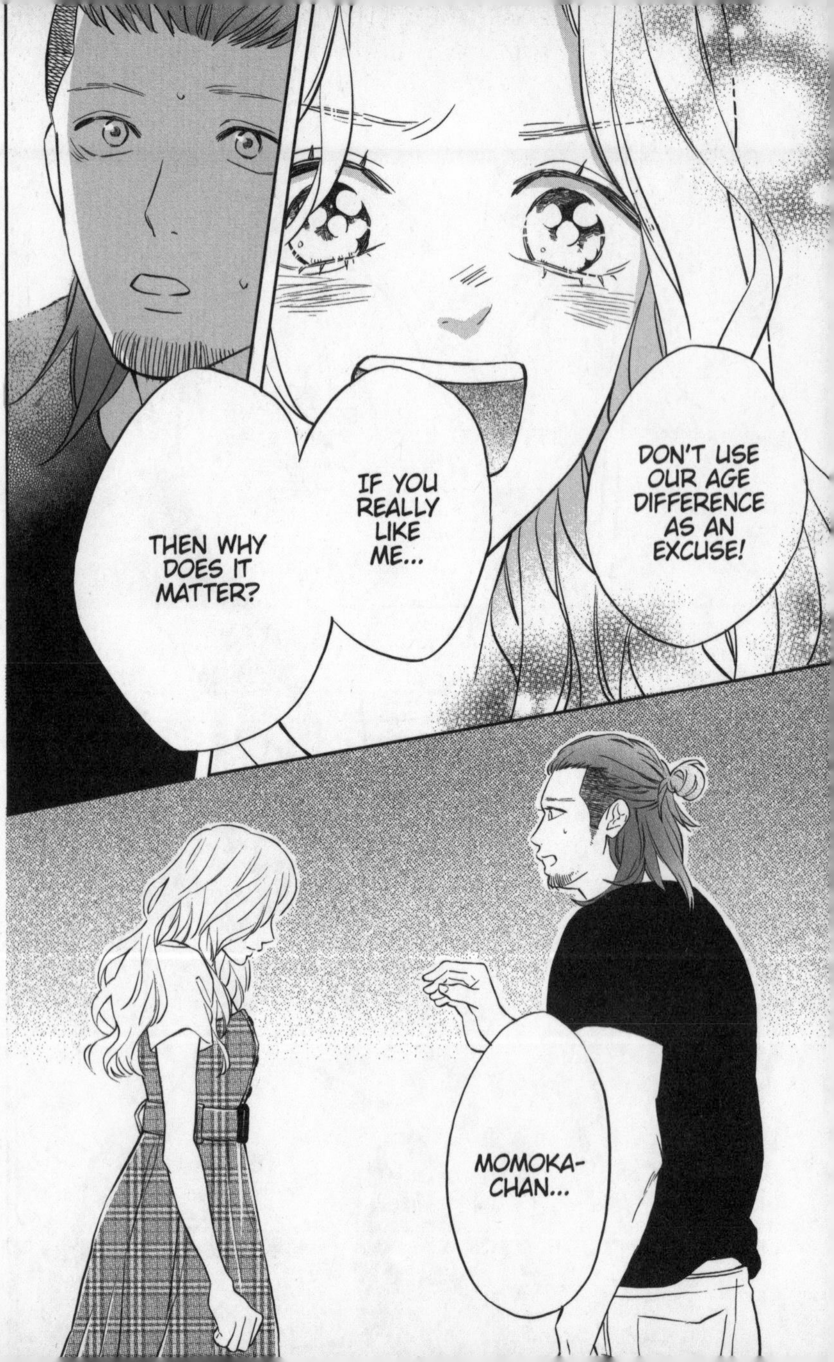
DON'T USE OUR AGE DIFFERENCE AS AN EXCUSE!
IF YOU REALLY LIKE ME...
THEN WHY DOES IT MATTER?
MOMOKA-CHAN...

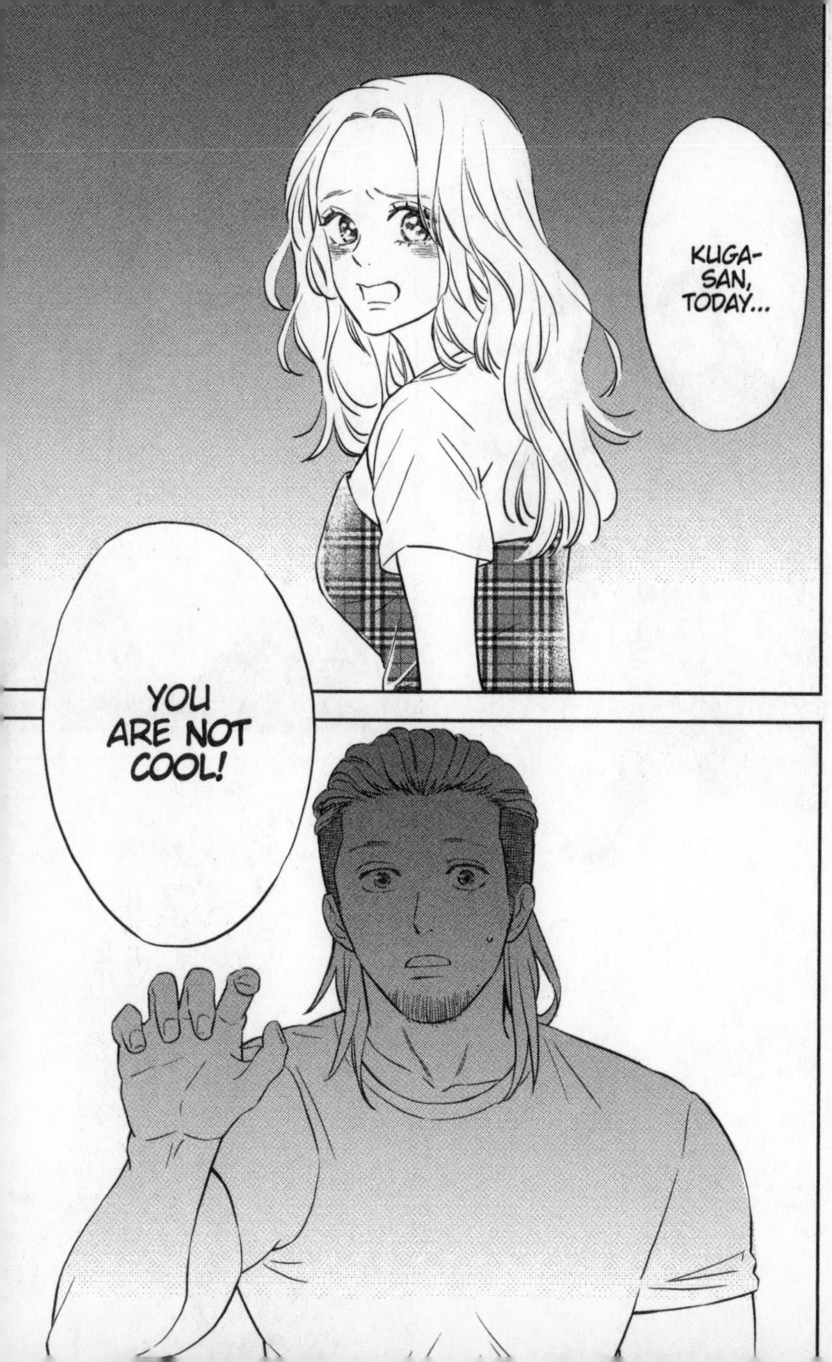
KUGA-SAN, TODAY...
YOU ARE NOT COOL!

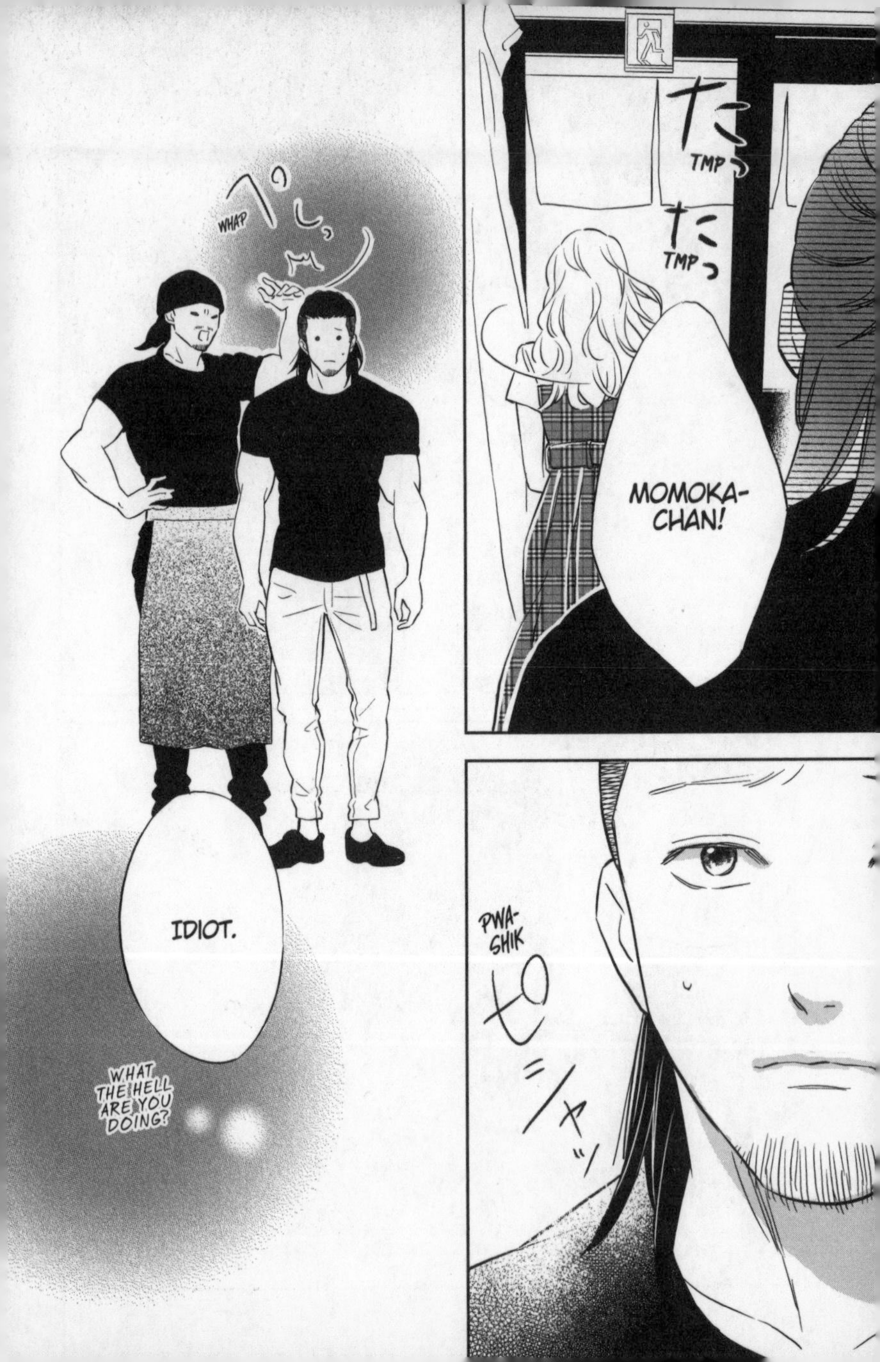
TMP
TMP
MOMOKA-CHAN!
PWA-SHIK
WHAP
IDIOT.
WHAT THE HELL ARE YOU DOING?

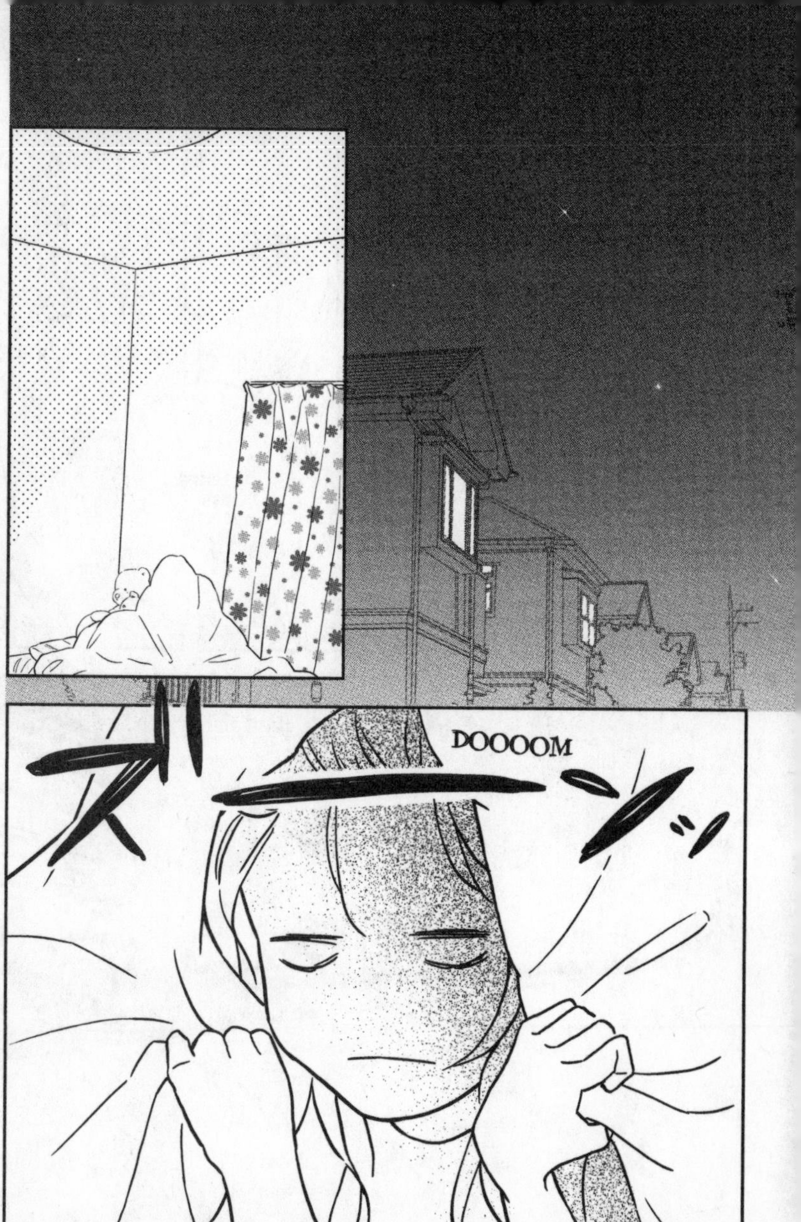
DOOOOM

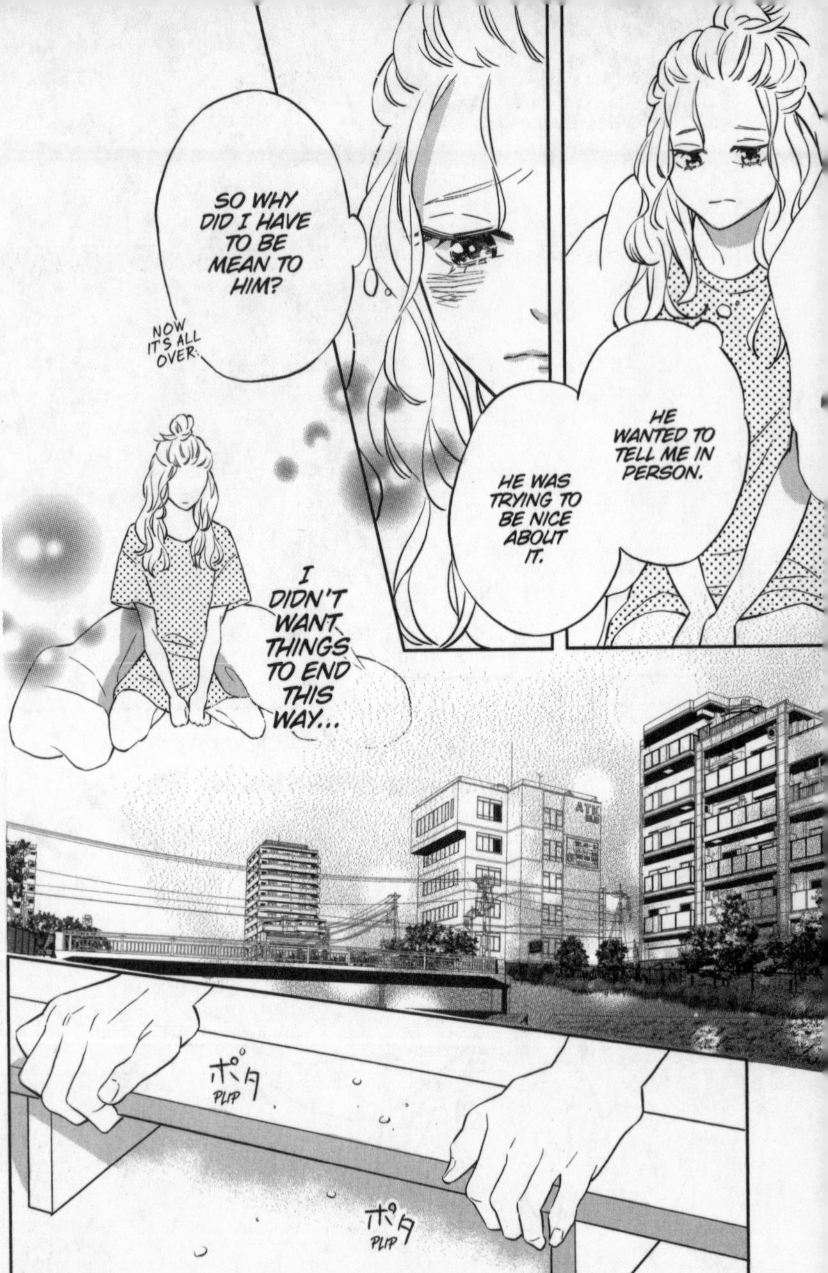
HE WANTED TO TELL ME IN PERSON.
HE WAS TRYING TO BE NICE ABOUT IT.
SO WHY DID I HAVE TO BE MEAN TO HIM?
NOW IT'S ALL OVER.
I DIDN'T WANT THINGS TO END THIS WAY...
ポタ PLIP
ポタ PLIP

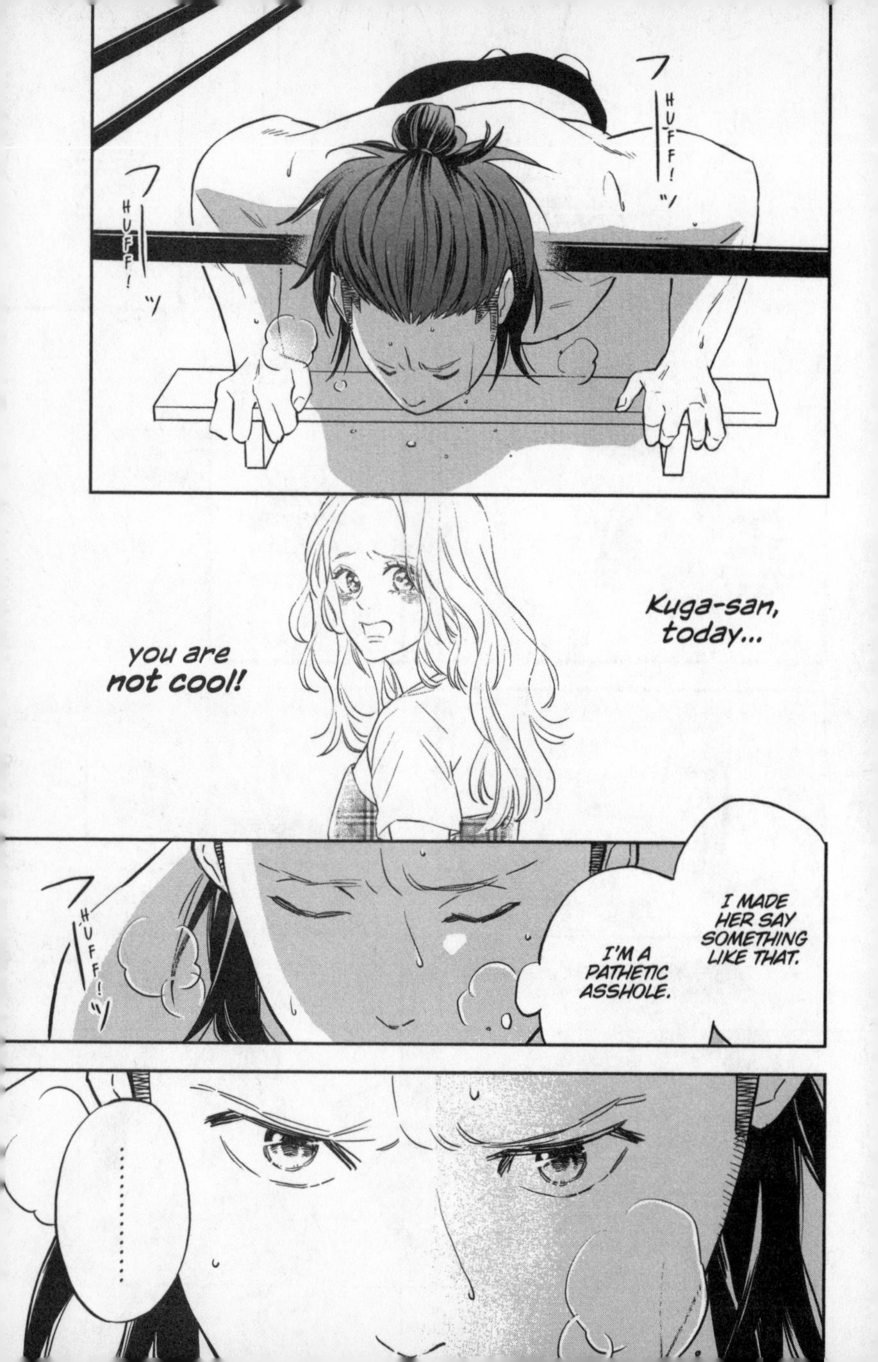
HUFF!
HUFF!
Kuga-san, today...
you are not cool!
I MADE HER SAY SOMETHING LIKE THAT.
I'M A PATHETIC ASSHOLE.
HUFF!
......

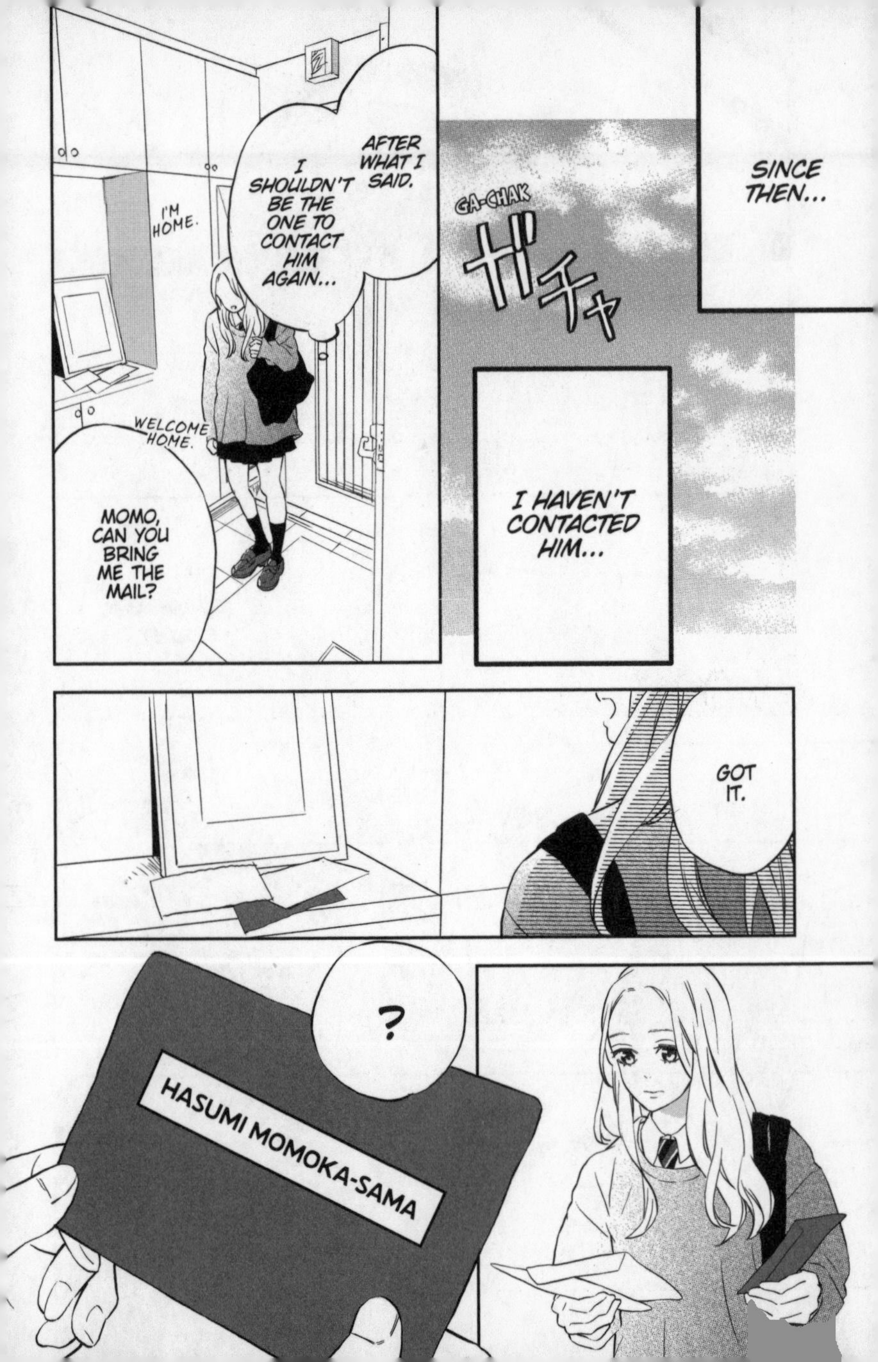
SINCE THEN...
GA-CHAK
ガチャ
I HAVEN'T CONTACTED HIM...
AFTER WHAT I SAID.
I SHOULDN'T BE THE ONE TO CONTACT HIM AGAIN...
I'M HOME.
WELCOME HOME.
MOMO, CAN YOU BRING ME THE MAIL?
GOT IT.
?
HASUMI MOMOKA-SAMA

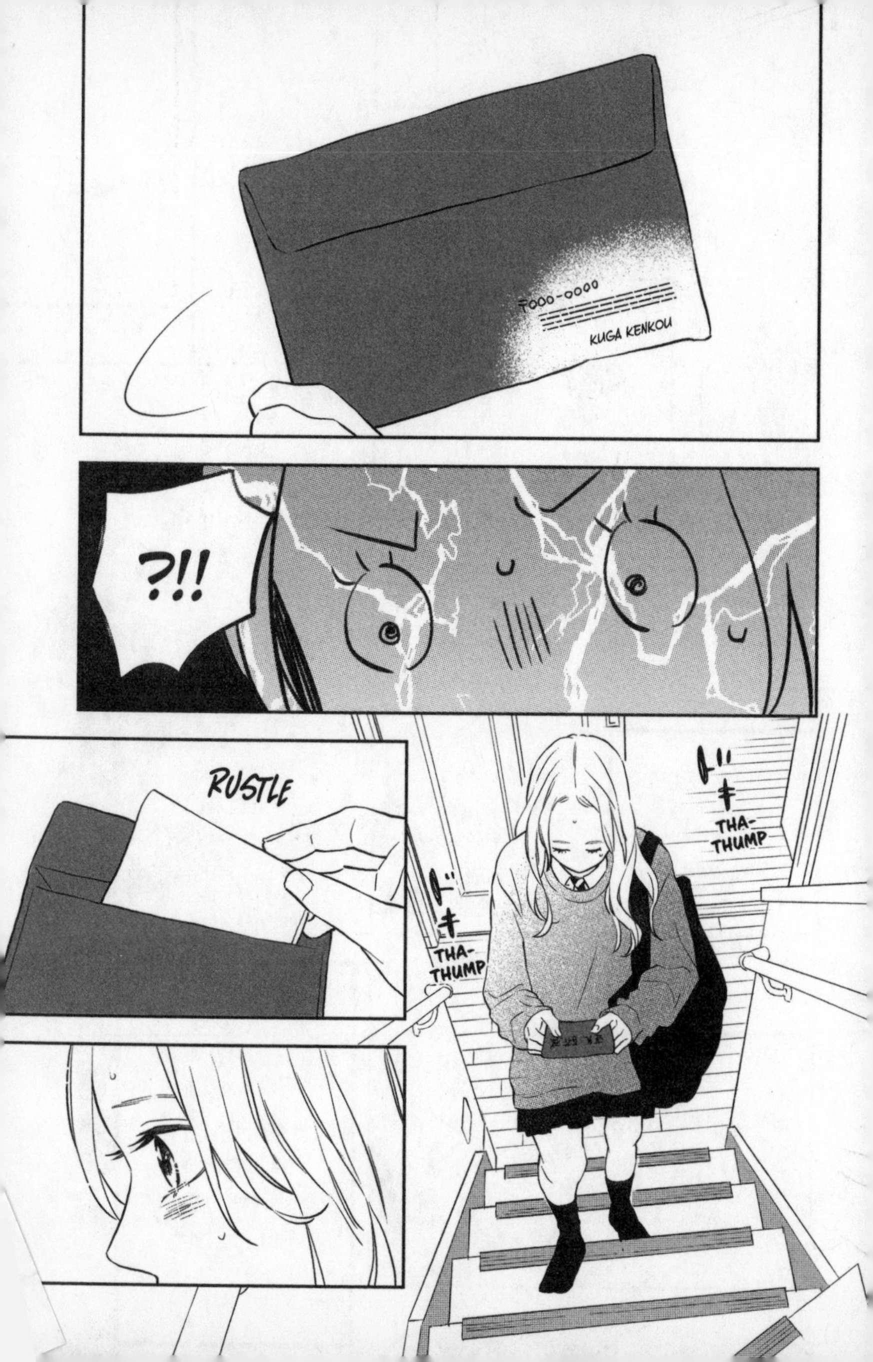
〒000-0000
KUGA KENKOU
?!!
ドキ
THA-THUMP
ドキ
THA-THUMP
RUSTLE

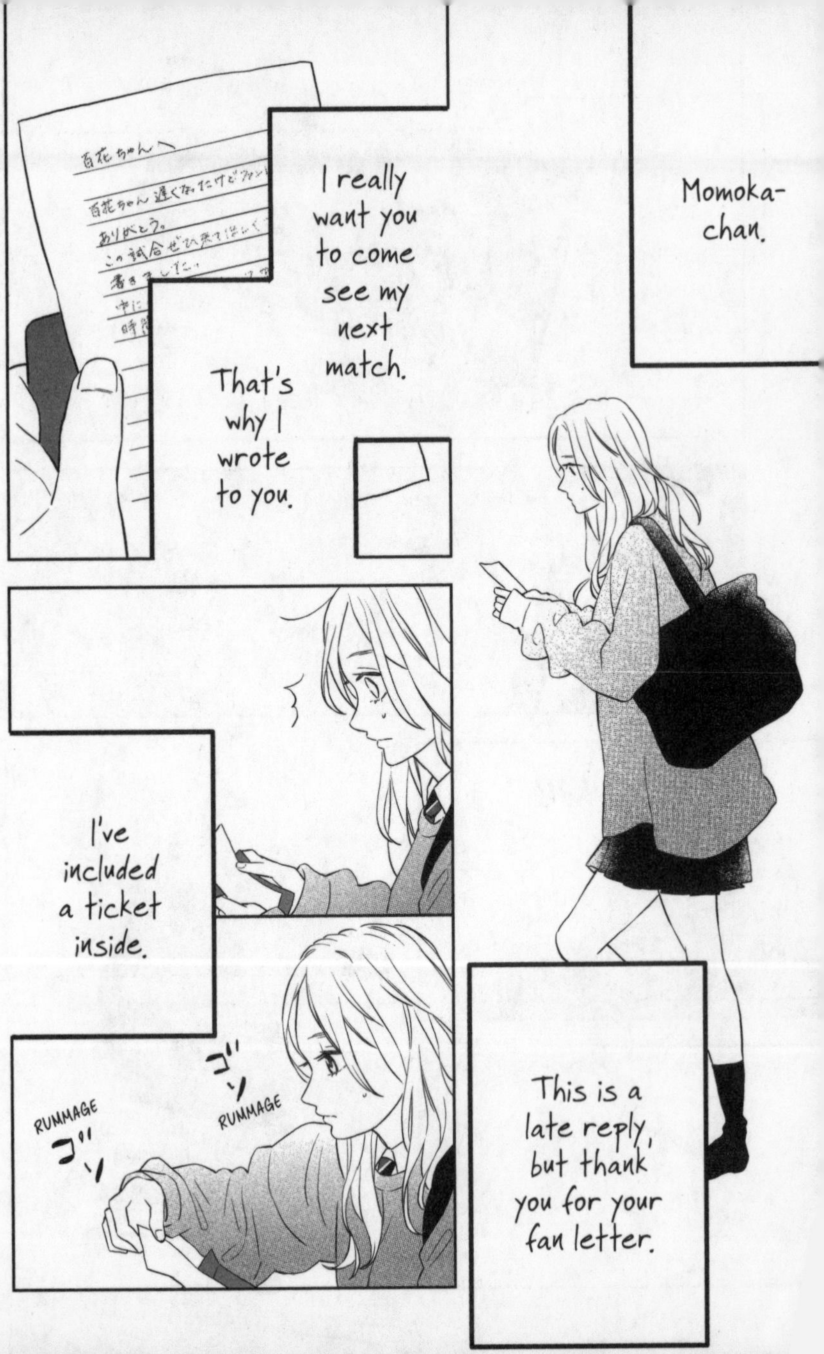
Momoka-chan.
This is a late reply, but thank you for your fan letter.
百花ちゃんへ
百花ちゃん 遅くなったけどファン
ありがとう。
この試合ぜひ来て欲しくて
書きました。
中に
I really want you to come see my next match.
That's why I wrote to you.
I've included a ticket inside.
ゴソ
RUMMAGE
ゴソ
RUMMAGE

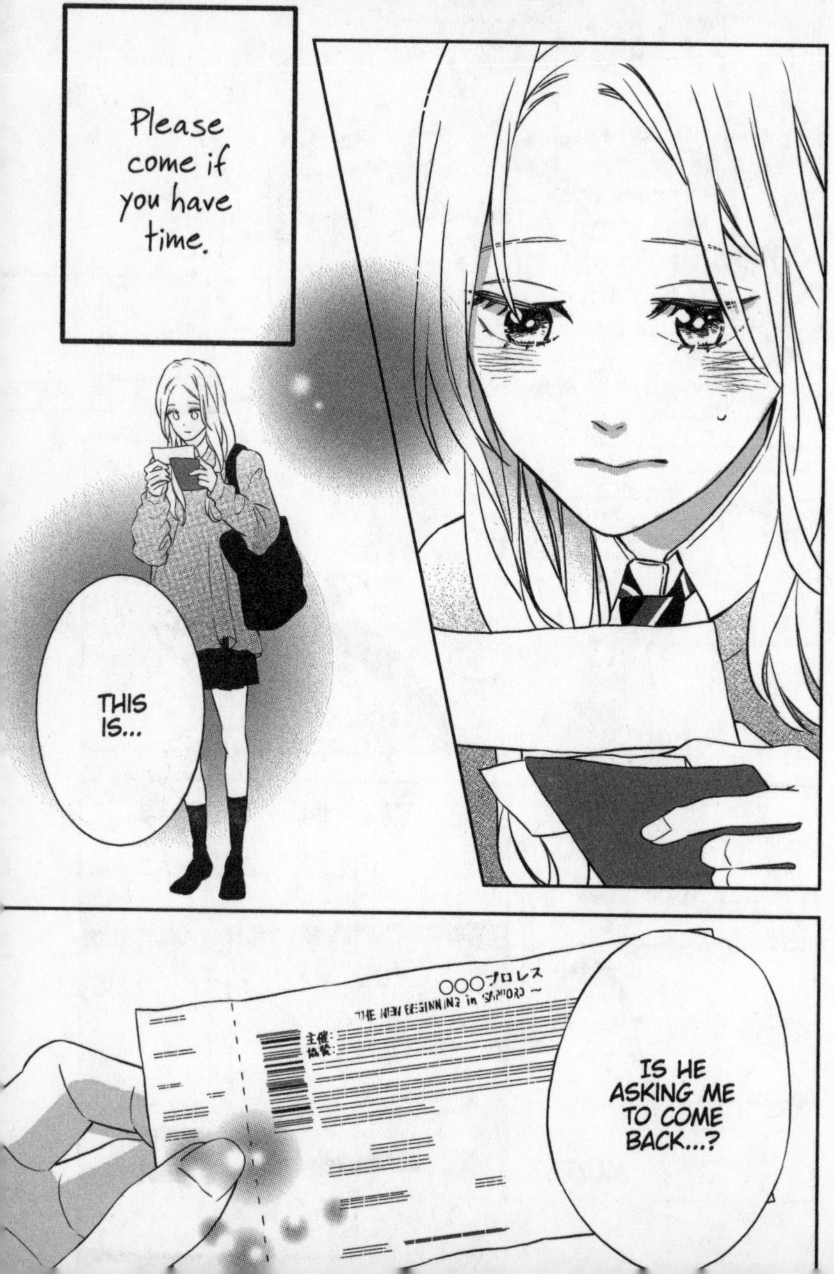
Please come if you have time.
THIS IS...
○○○プロレス
THE NEW BEGINNING in SAPPORO ~
主催:
協賛:
IS HE ASKING ME TO COME BACK...?

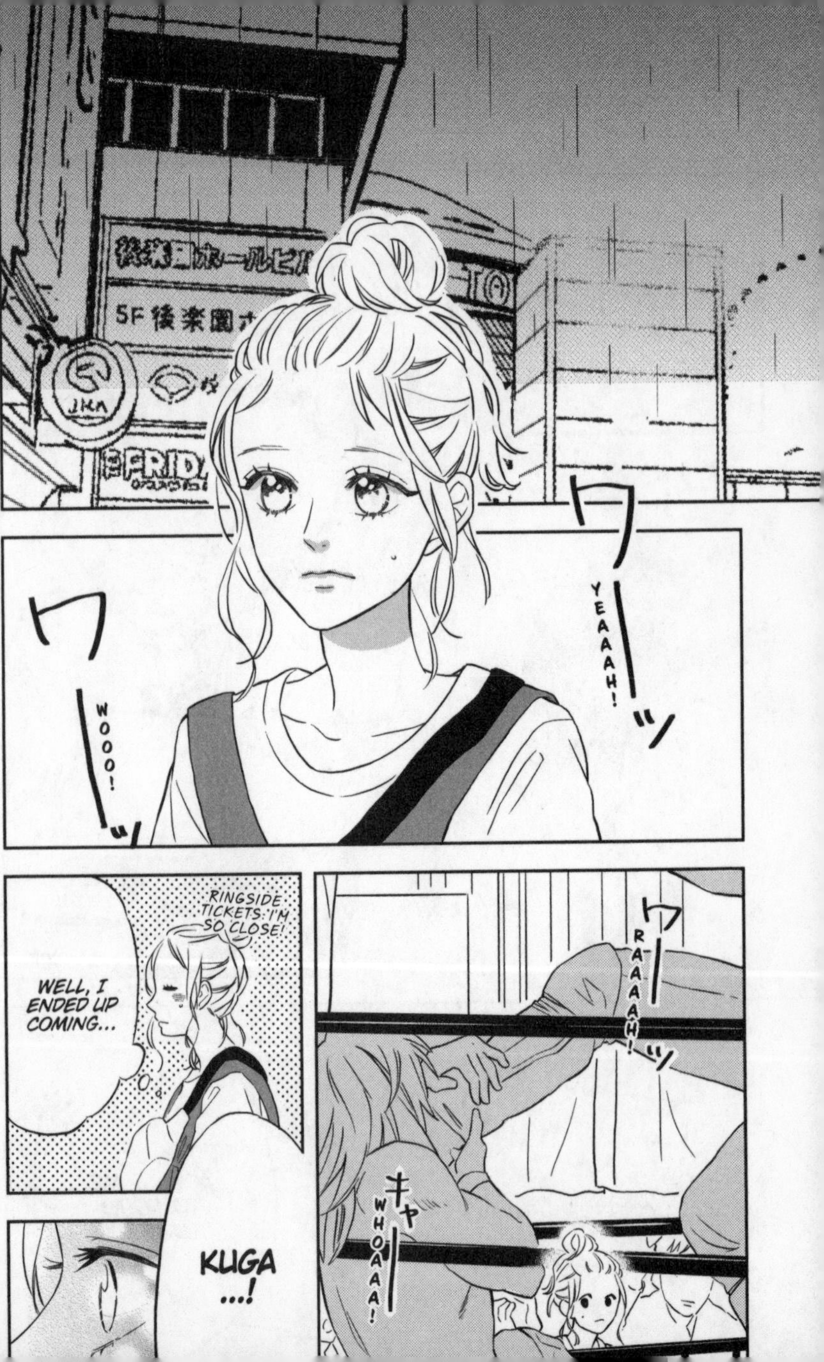
ワーッ
YEAAAAH!
ワーッ
WOOOO!
ワーッ
RAAAAAH!
キャー
WHOAAAA!
RINGSIDE TICKETS. I'M SO CLOSE!
WELL, I ENDED UP COMING...
KUGA ...!

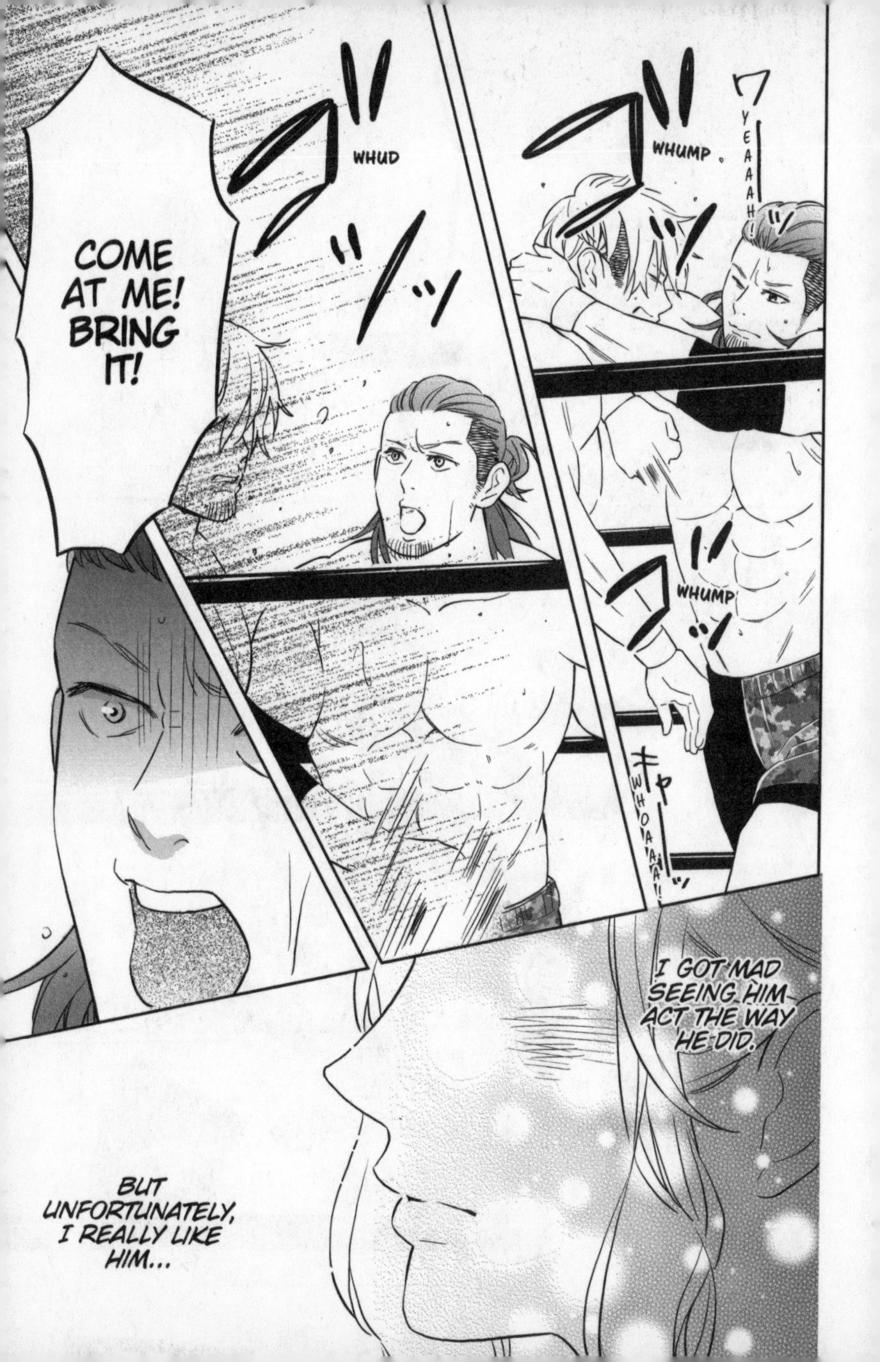
YEAAAAH!!
WHUMP
WHUMP
WHOAAAA!!
WHUD
COME AT ME! BRING IT!
I GOT MAD SEEING HIM ACT THE WAY HE DID.
BUT UNFORTUNATELY, I REALLY LIKE HIM...

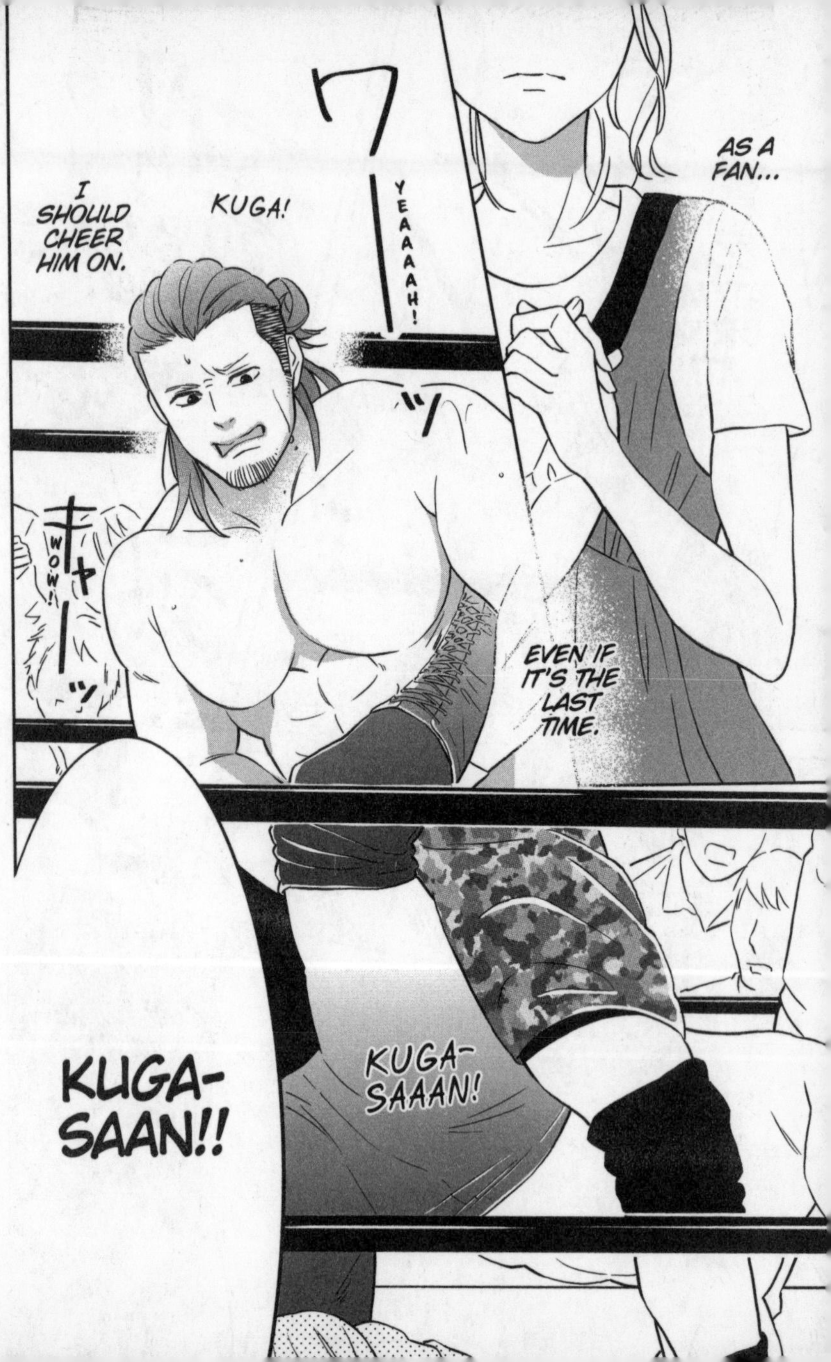
AS A FAN...
EVEN IF IT'S THE LAST TIME.
YEAAAAH!
KUGA!
I SHOULD CHEER HIM ON.
WOW!
KUGA-SAAAN!
KUGA-SAAN!!

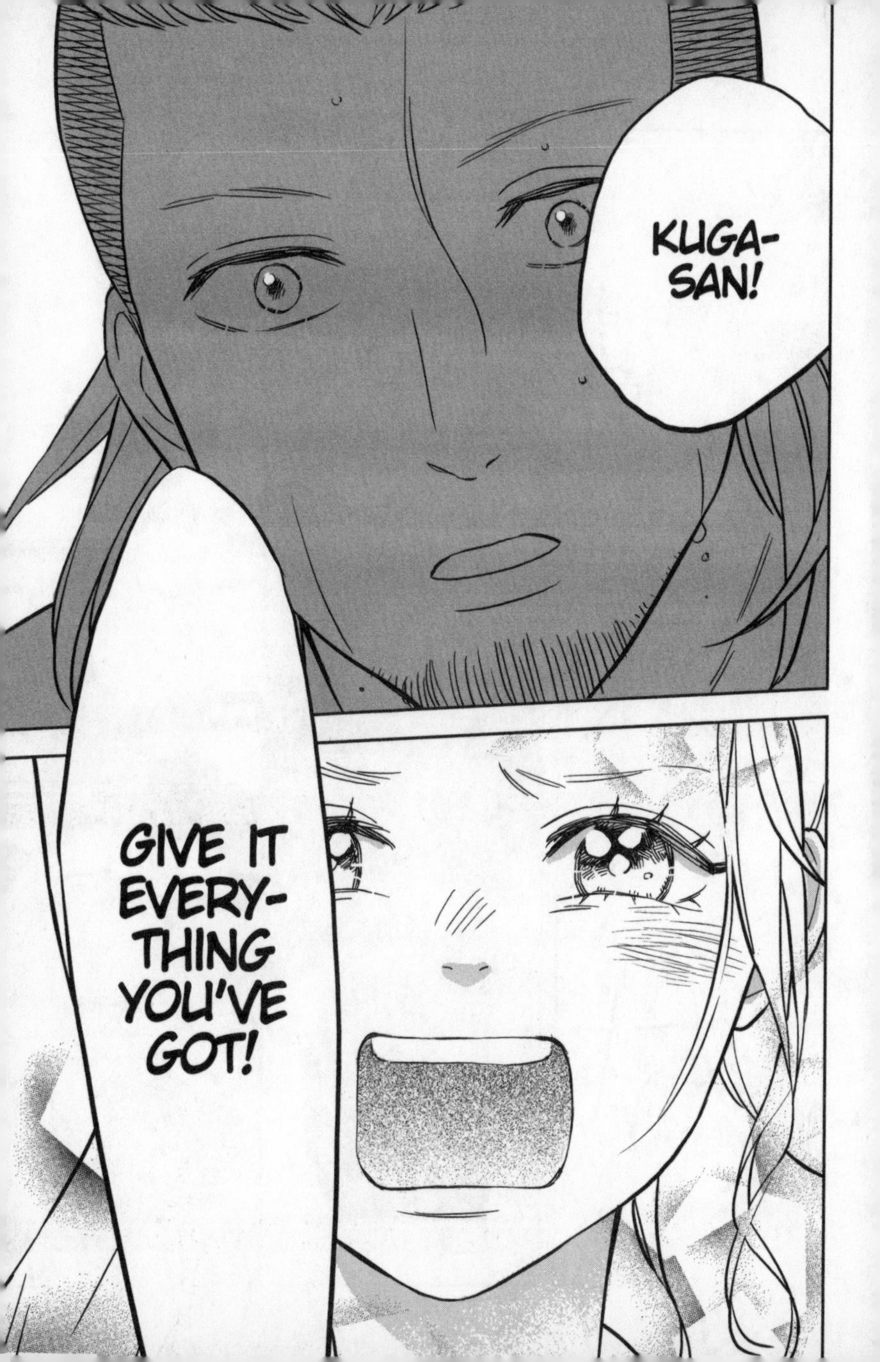
KUGA-SAN!
GIVE IT EVERY-THING YOU'VE GOT!

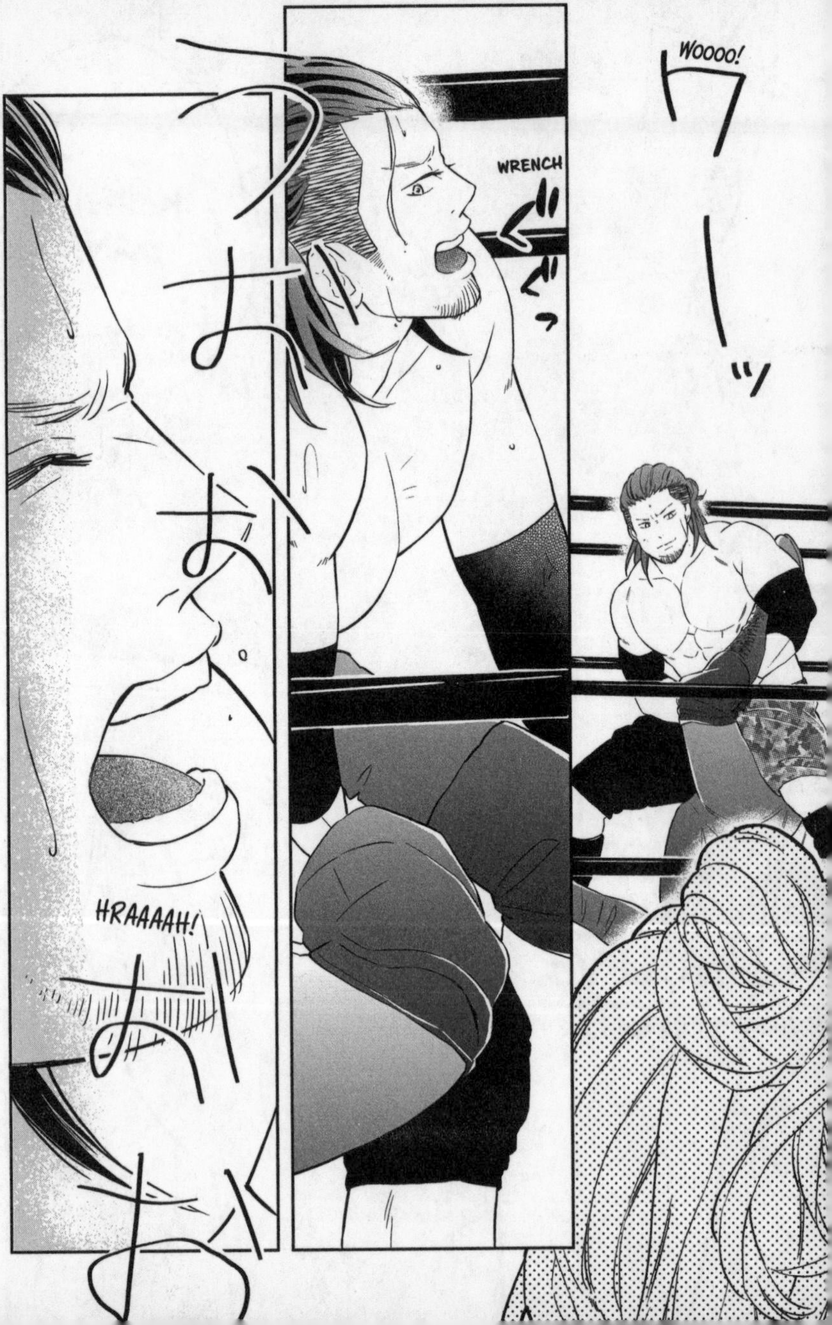
WOOOO!
WRENCH
HRAAAAH!

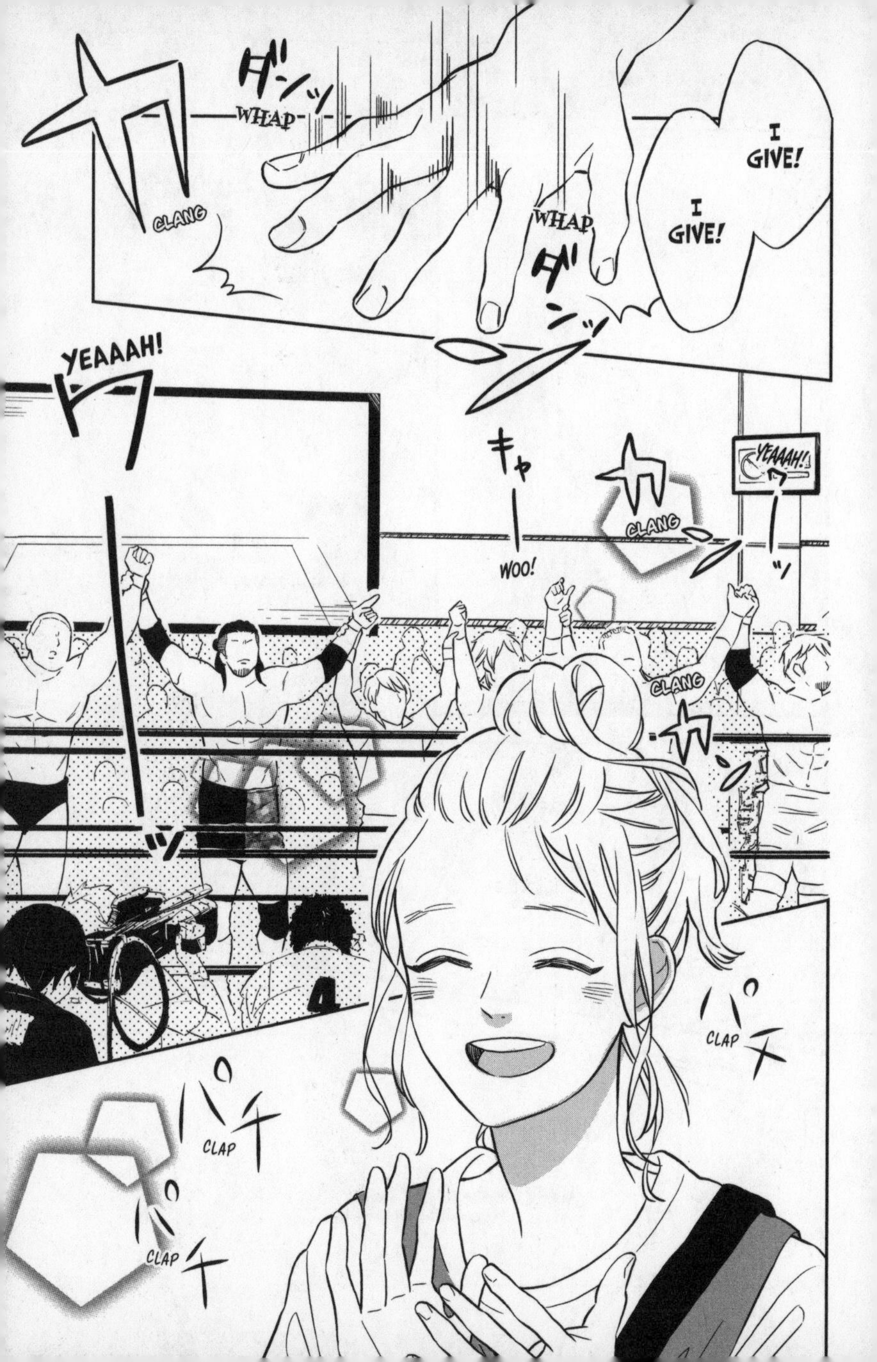
I GIVE!
I GIVE!
WHAP
WHAP
CLANG
YEAAAH!
YEAAAH!
CLANG
WOO!
CLANG
CLAP
CLAP
CLAP

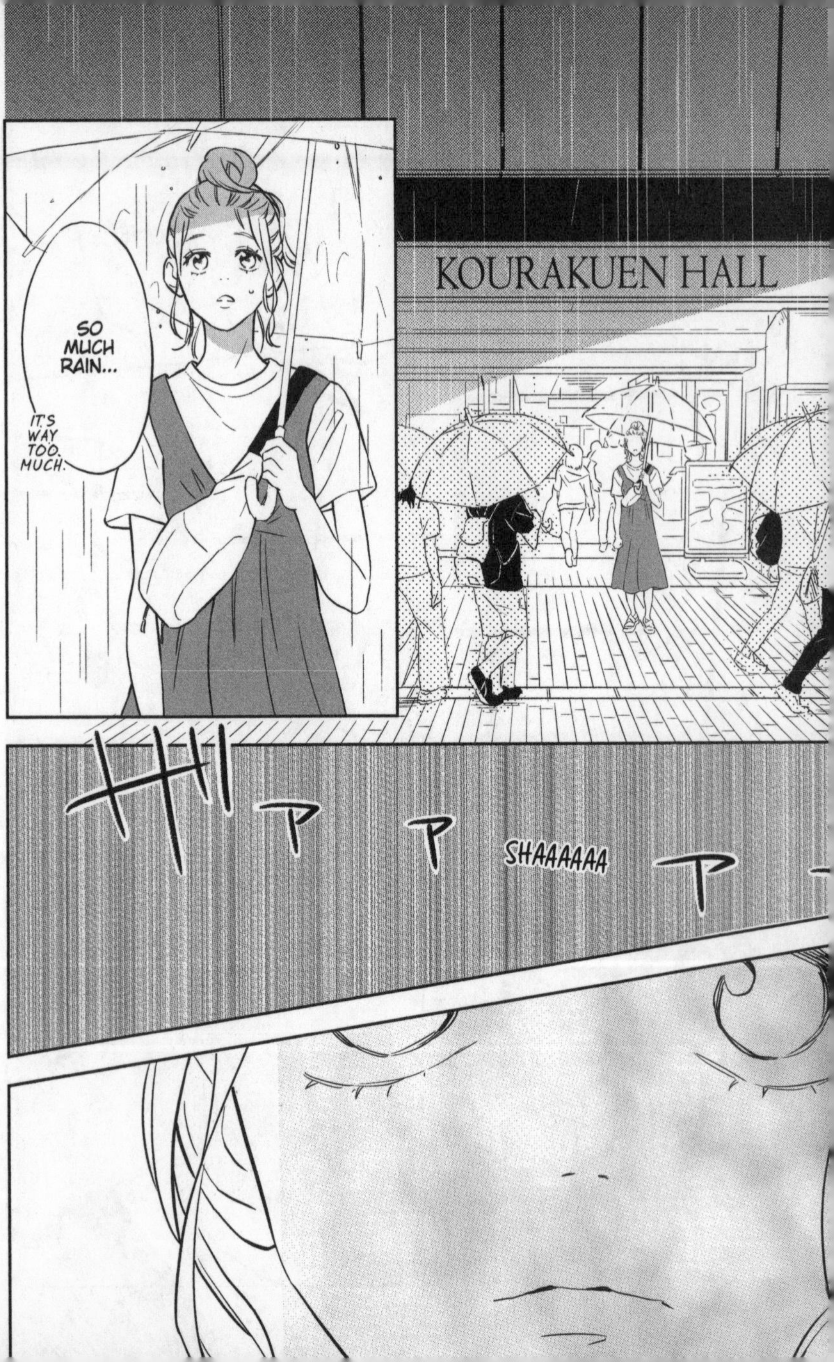
KOURAKUEN HALL
SO MUCH RAIN...
IT'S WAY TOO. MUCH.
SHAAAAAA

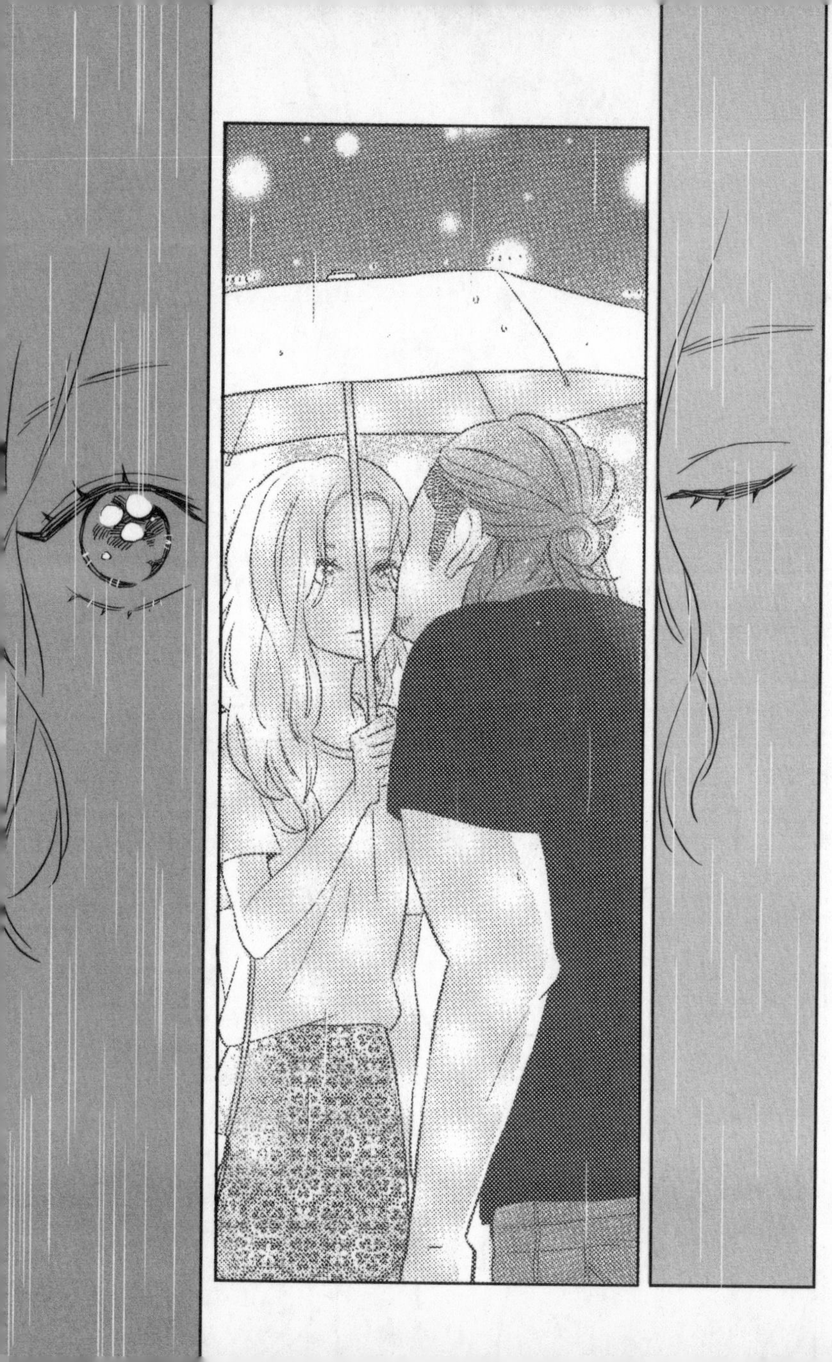

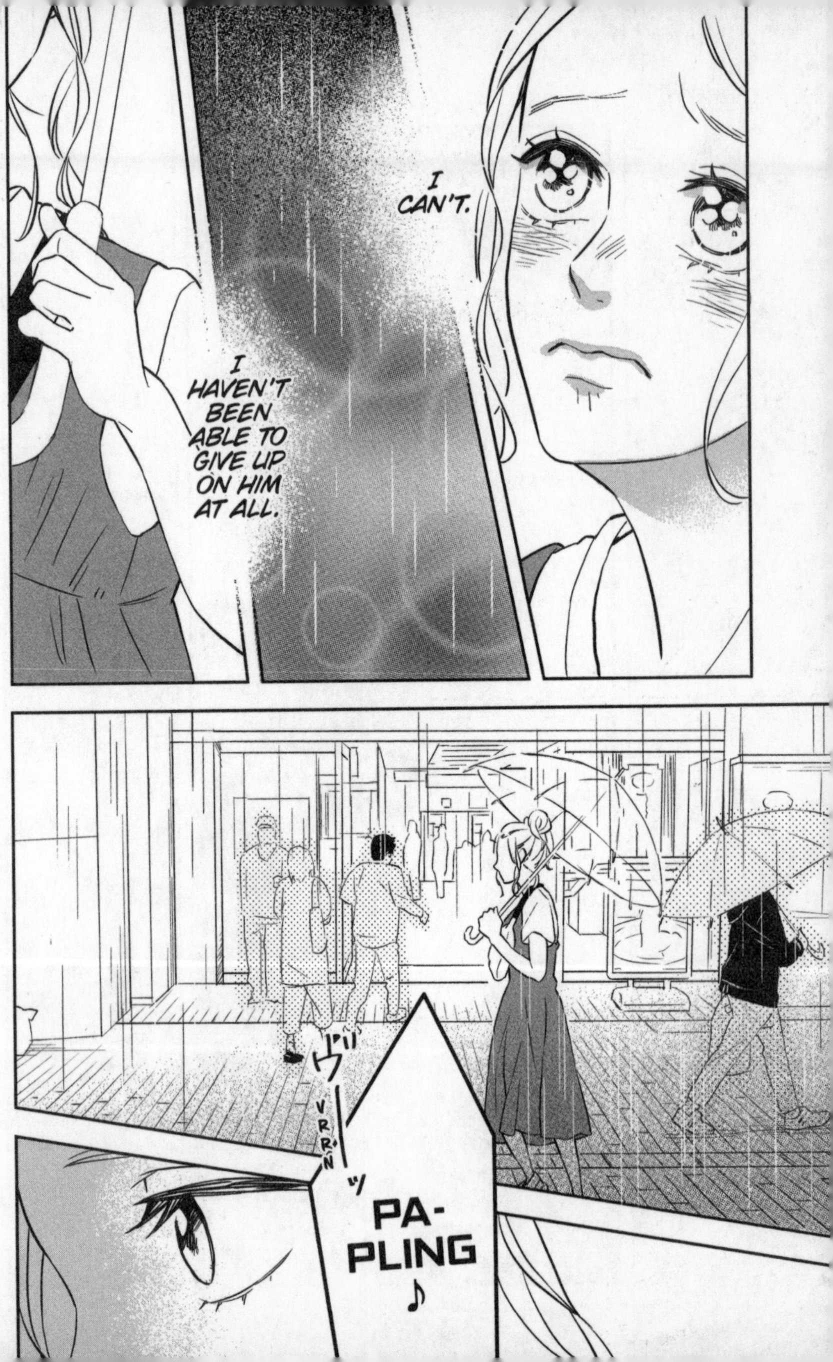
I CAN'T.
I HAVEN'T BEEN ABLE TO GIVE UP ON HIM AT ALL.
VRRRN
PA-PLING ♪

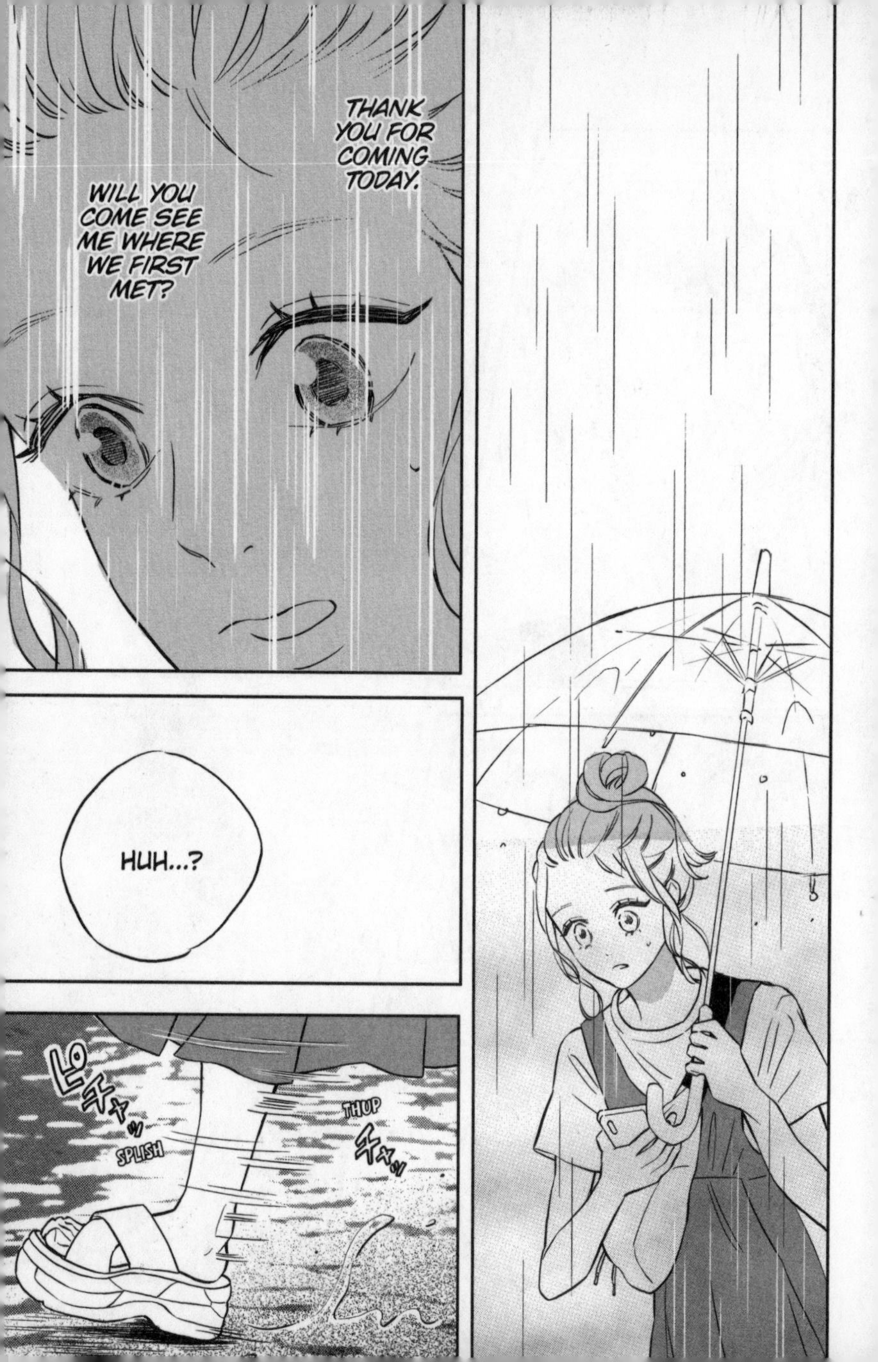
THANK YOU FOR COMING TODAY.
WILL YOU COME SEE ME WHERE WE FIRST MET?
HUH...?
チャッ
THUP
ピチャッ
SPLISH

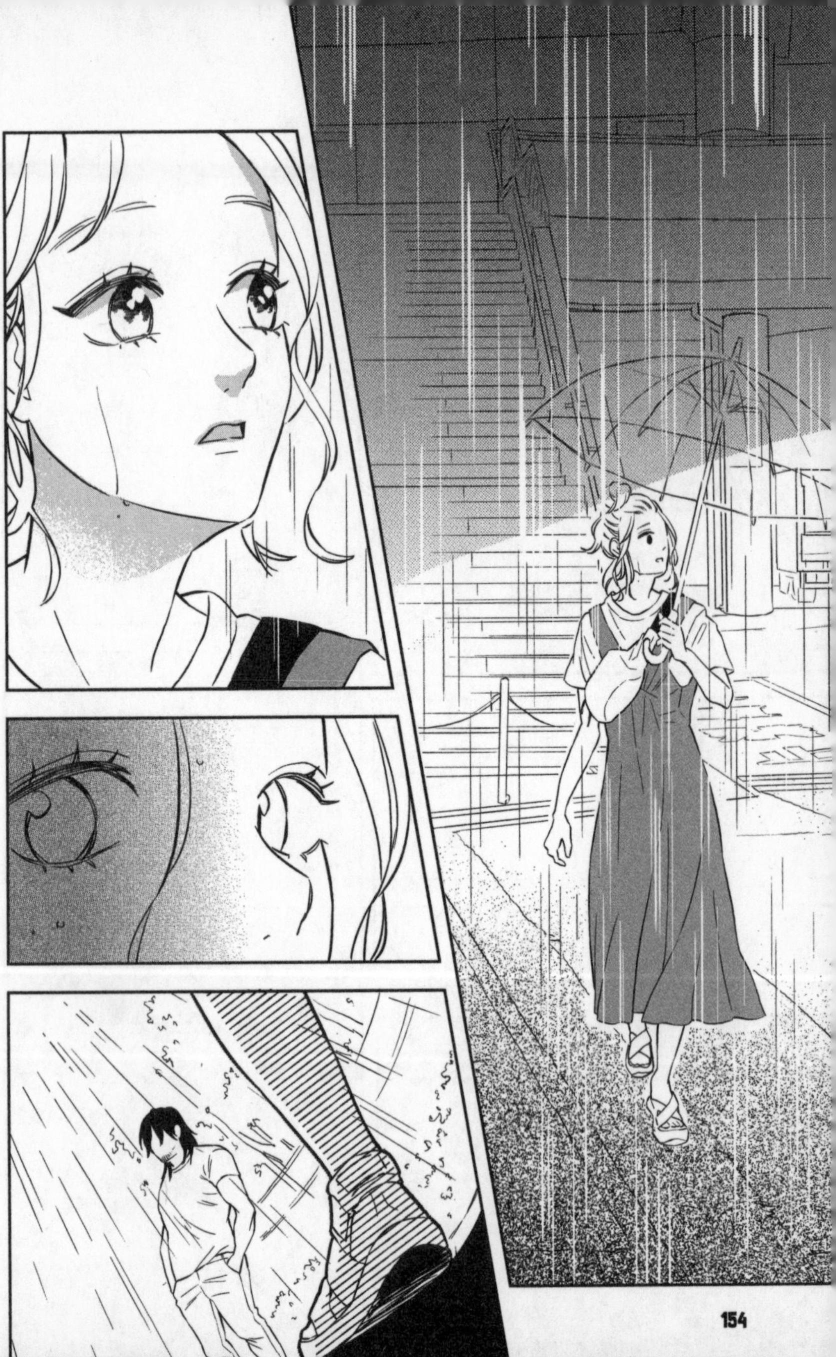

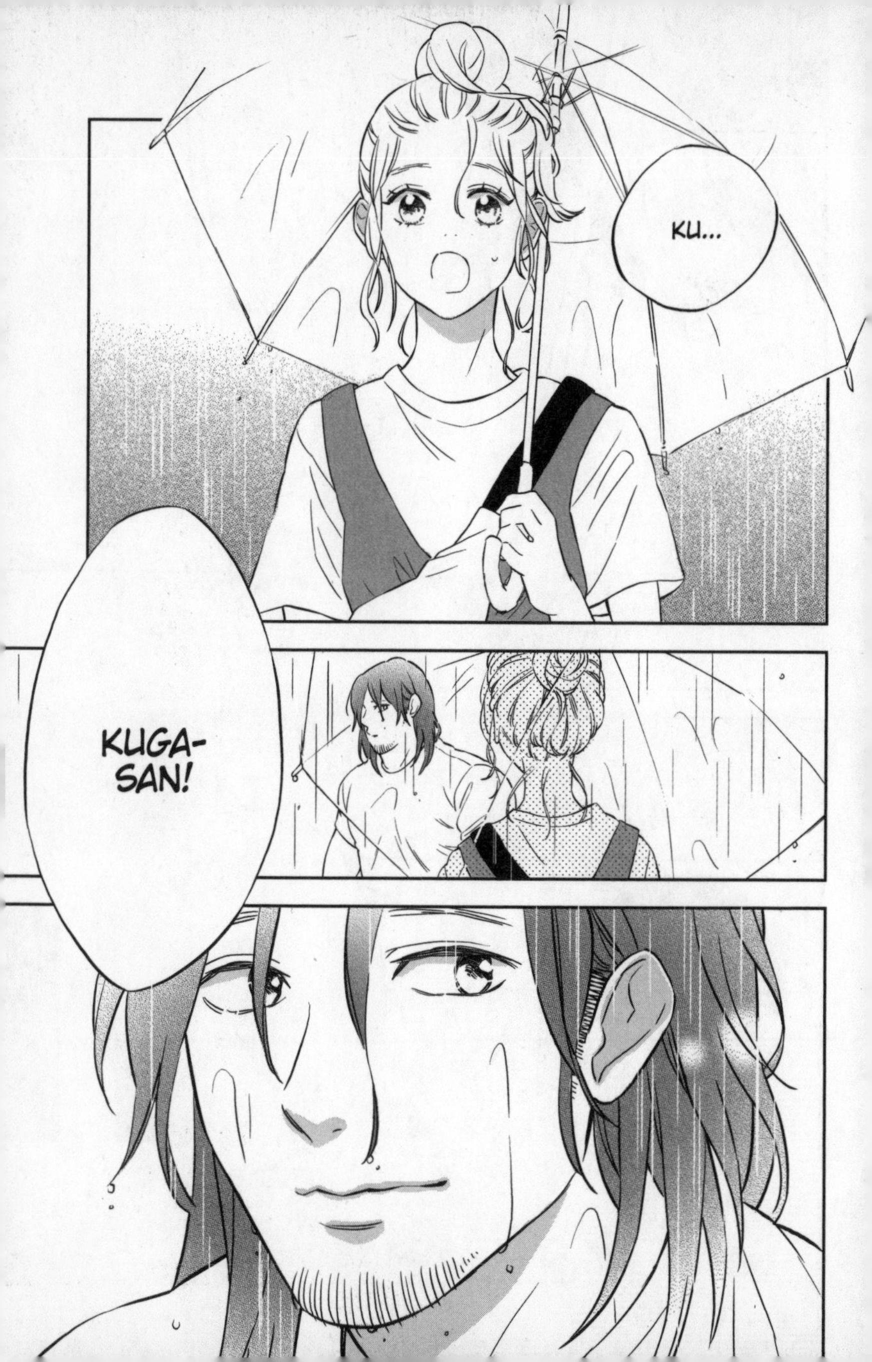
KU...
KUGA-SAN!

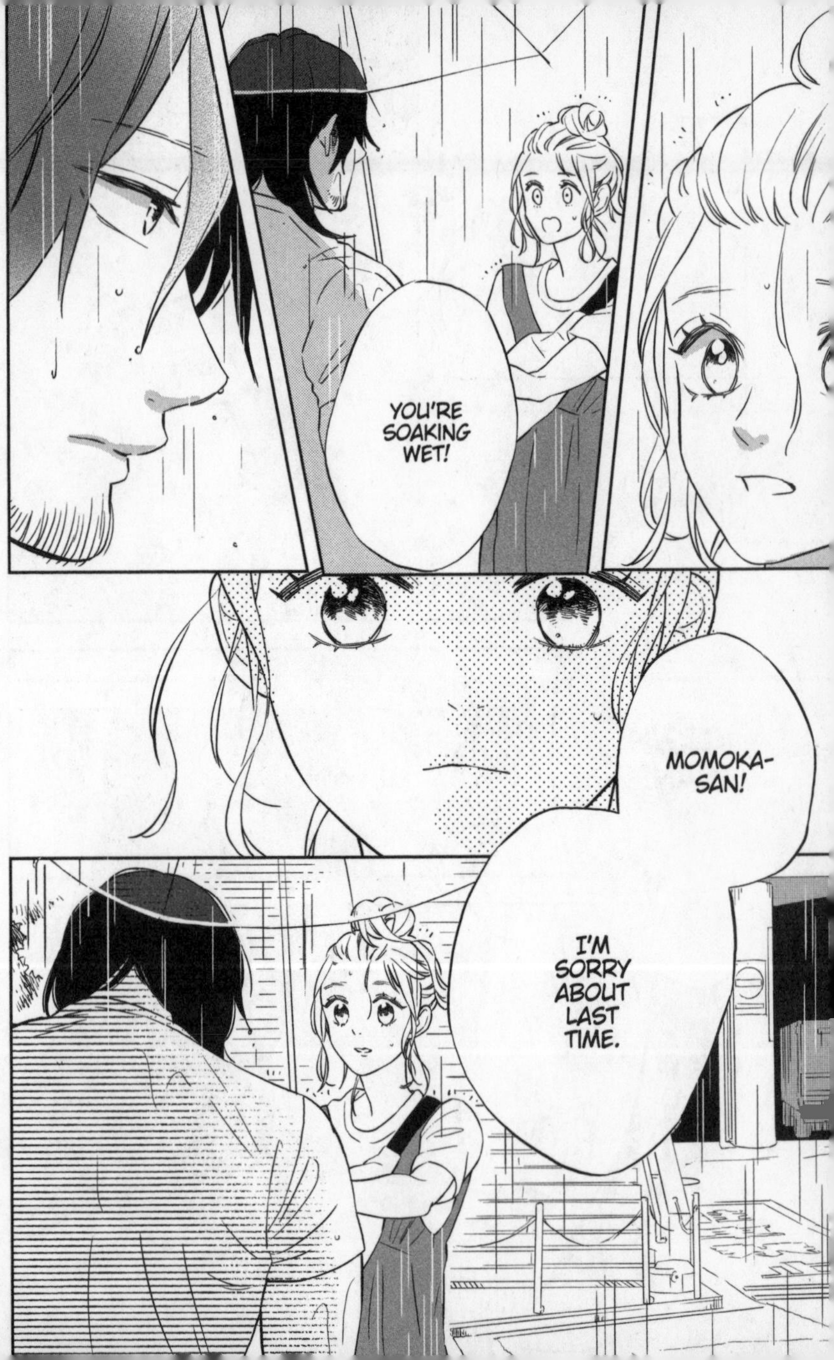
YOU'RE SOAKING WET!
MOMOKA-SAN!
I'M SORRY ABOUT LAST TIME.

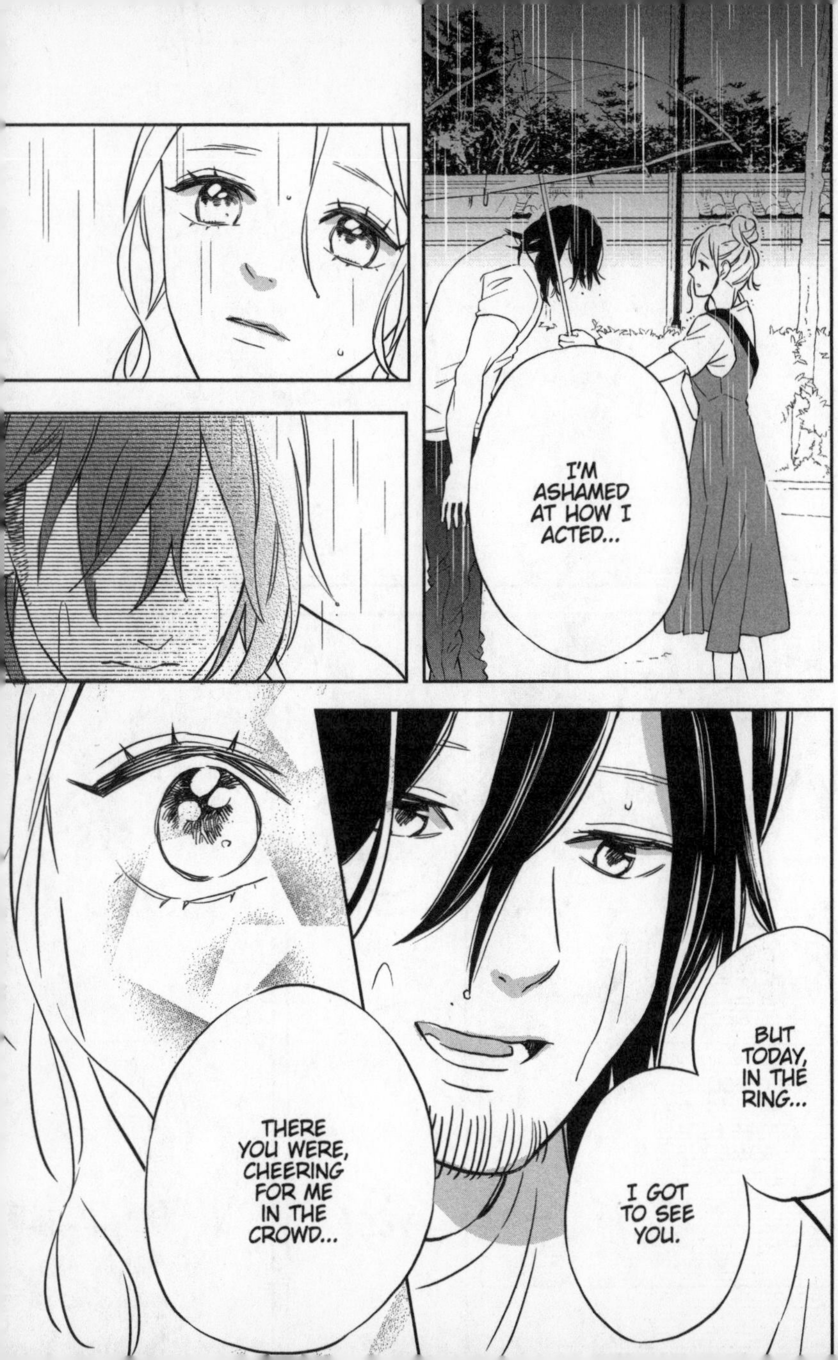
I'M ASHAMED AT HOW I ACTED...
BUT TODAY, IN THE RING...
THERE YOU WERE, CHEERING FOR ME IN THE CROWD...
I GOT TO SEE YOU.

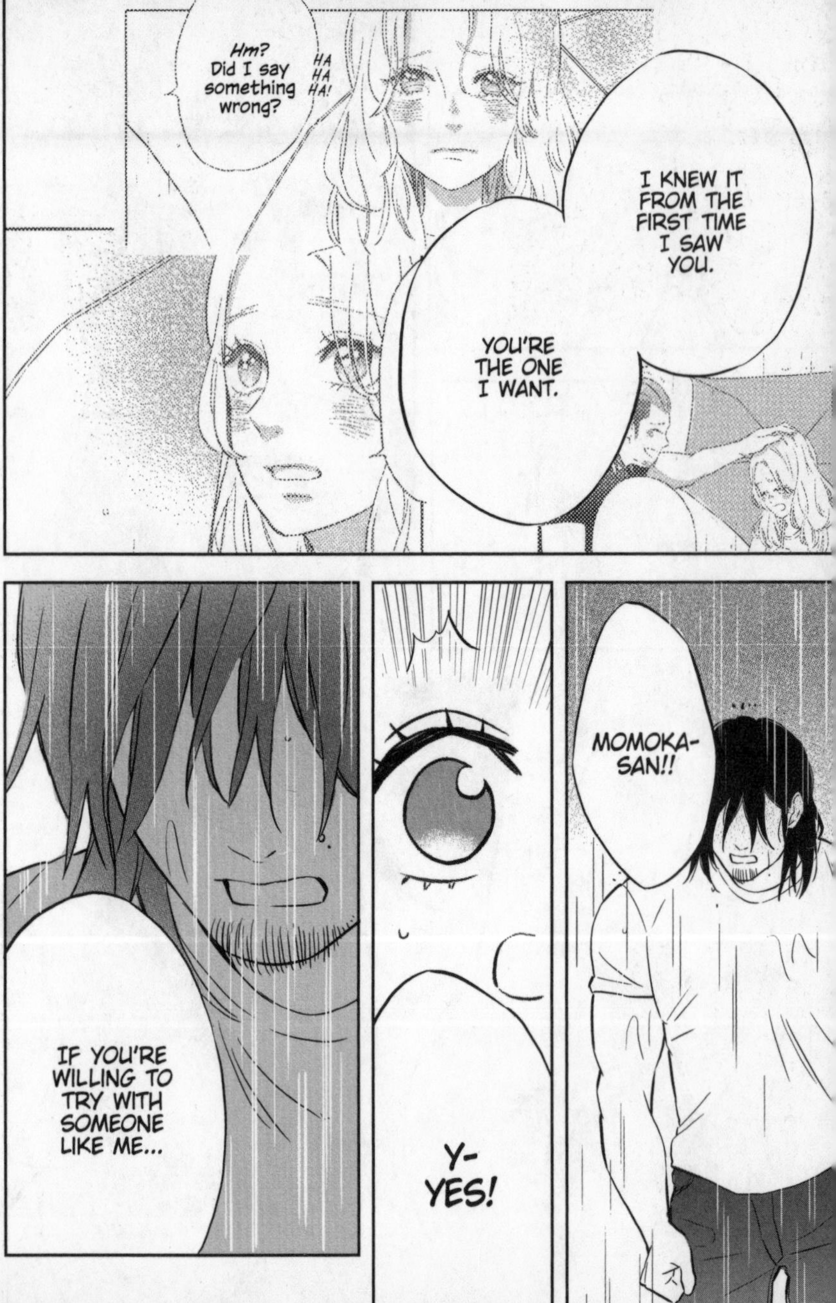
I KNEW IT FROM THE FIRST TIME I SAW YOU.
YOU'RE THE ONE I WANT.
Hm? Did I say something wrong?
HA HA HA!
MOMOKA-SAN!!
Y- YES!
IF YOU'RE WILLING TO TRY WITH SOMEONE LIKE ME...

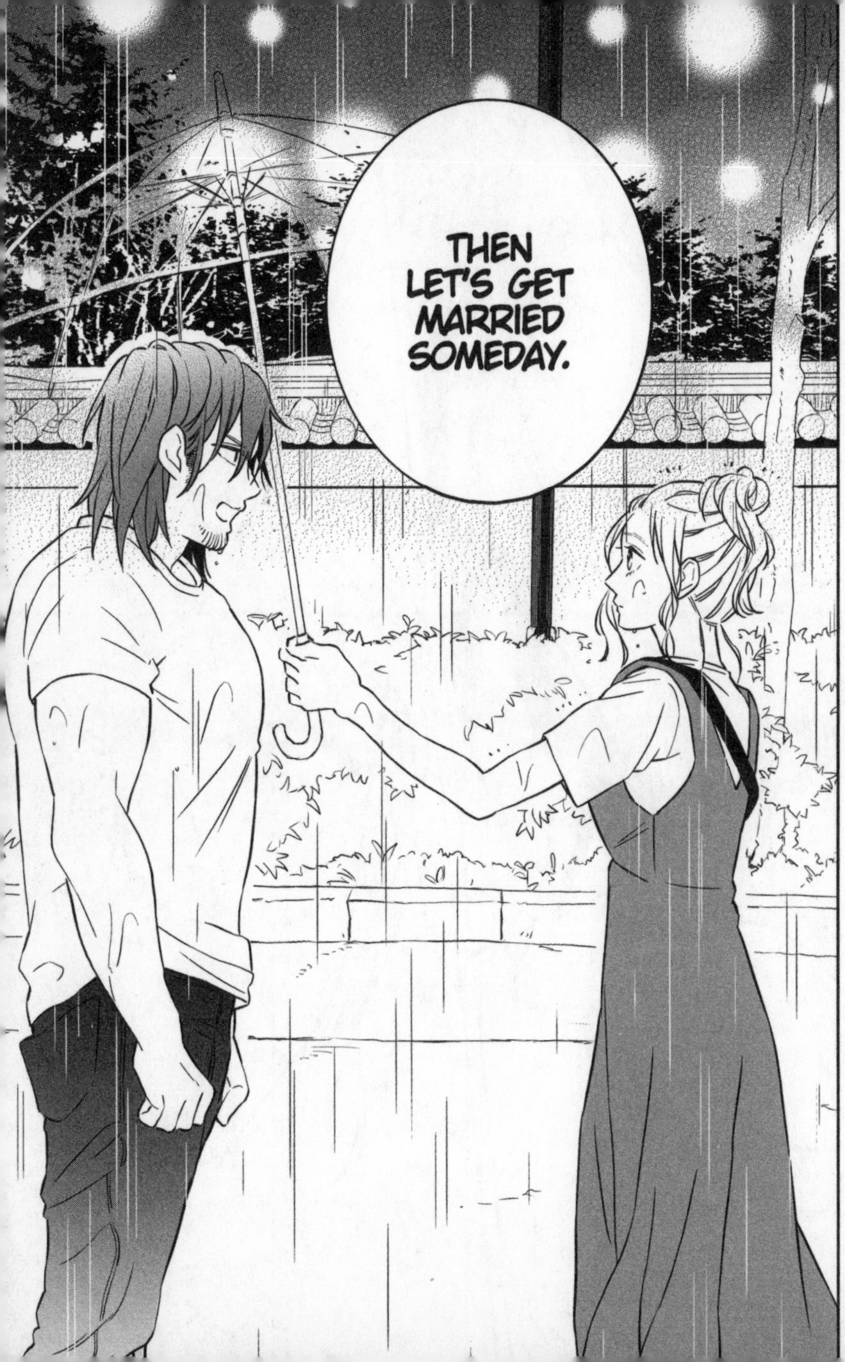
THEN LET'S GET MARRIED SOMEDAY.

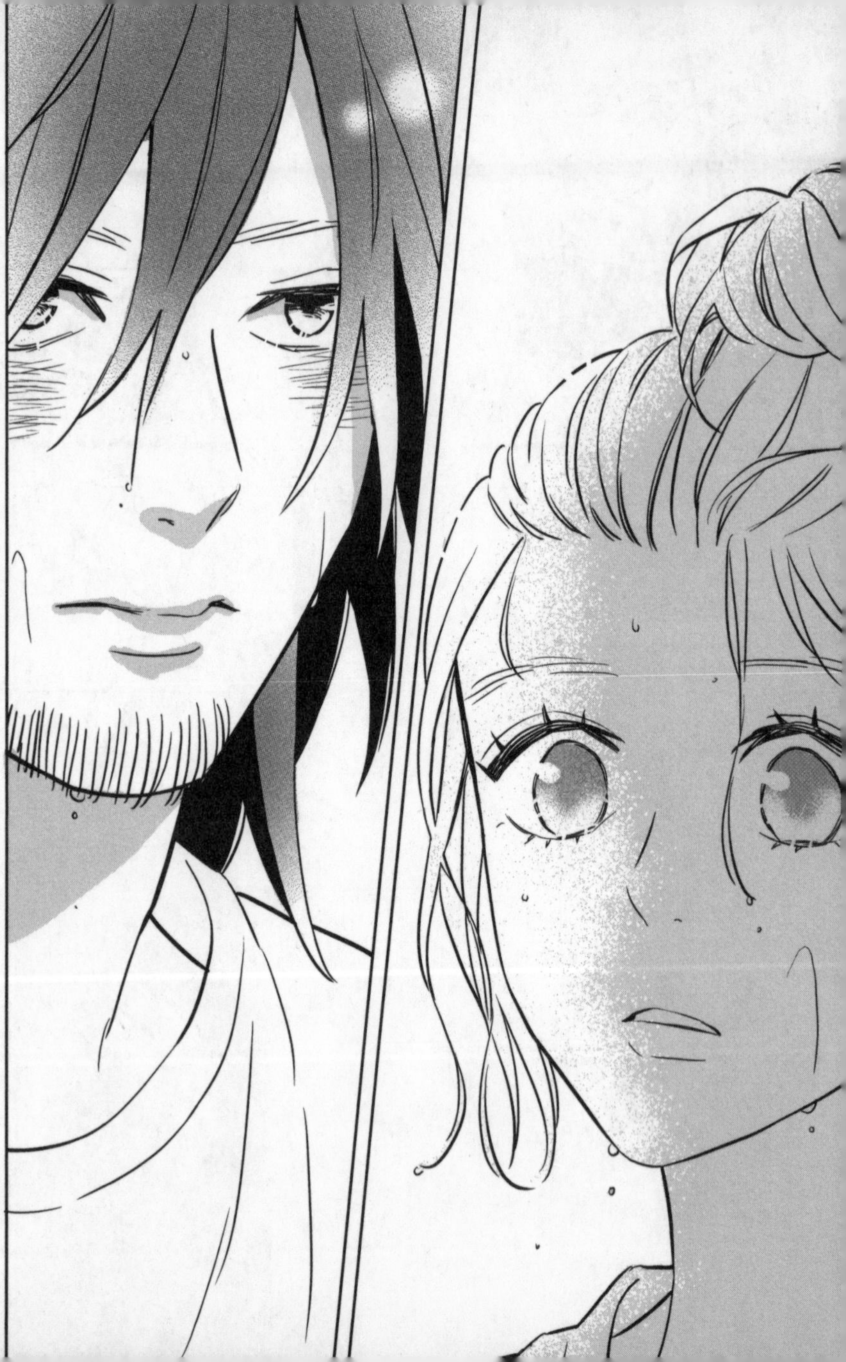

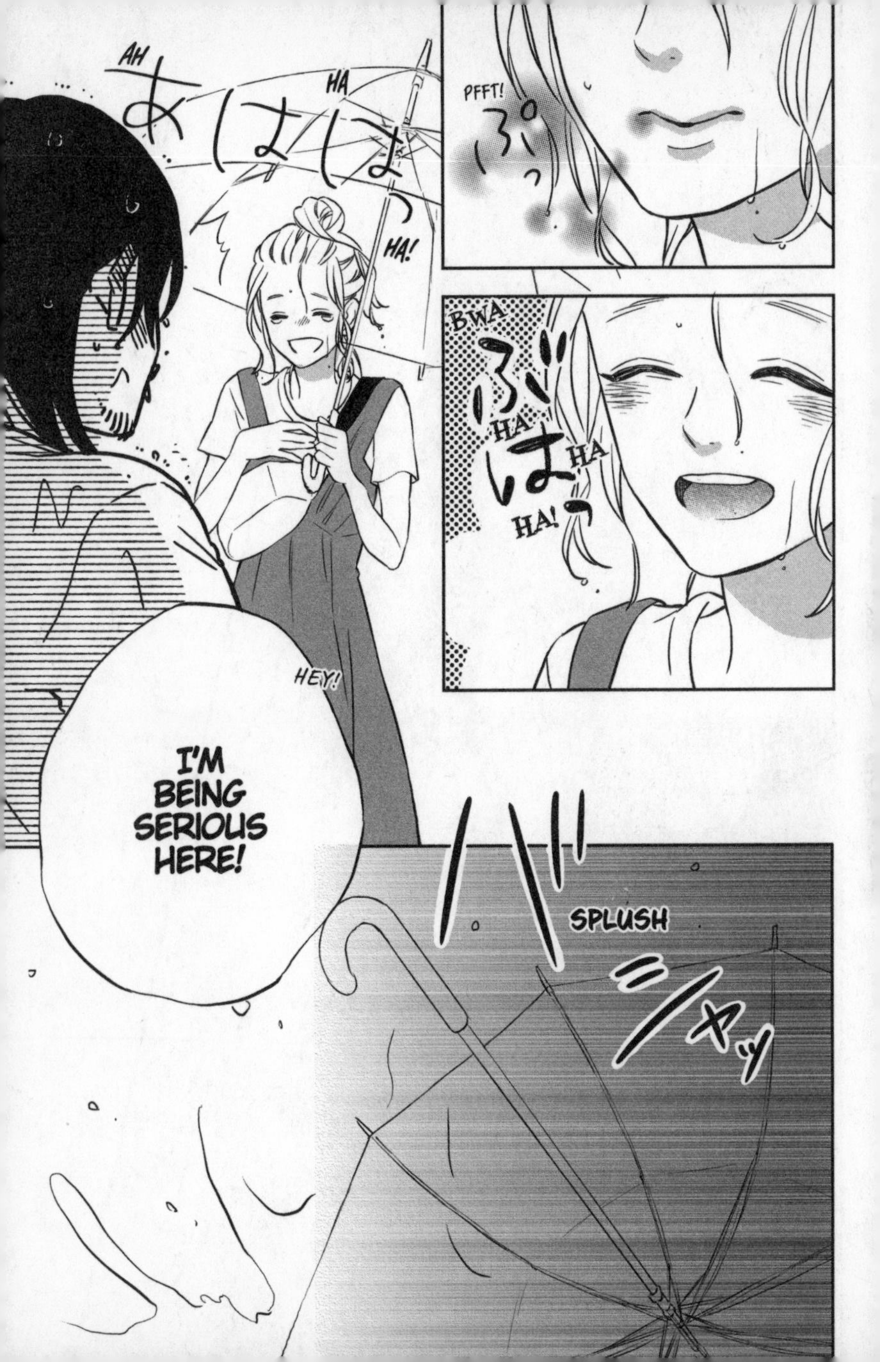
ぷっ
PFFT!
ぶはっ
BWA HA HA HA!
あははっ
AH HA HA!
HEY!
I'M BEING SERIOUS HERE!
バシャッ
SPLUSH

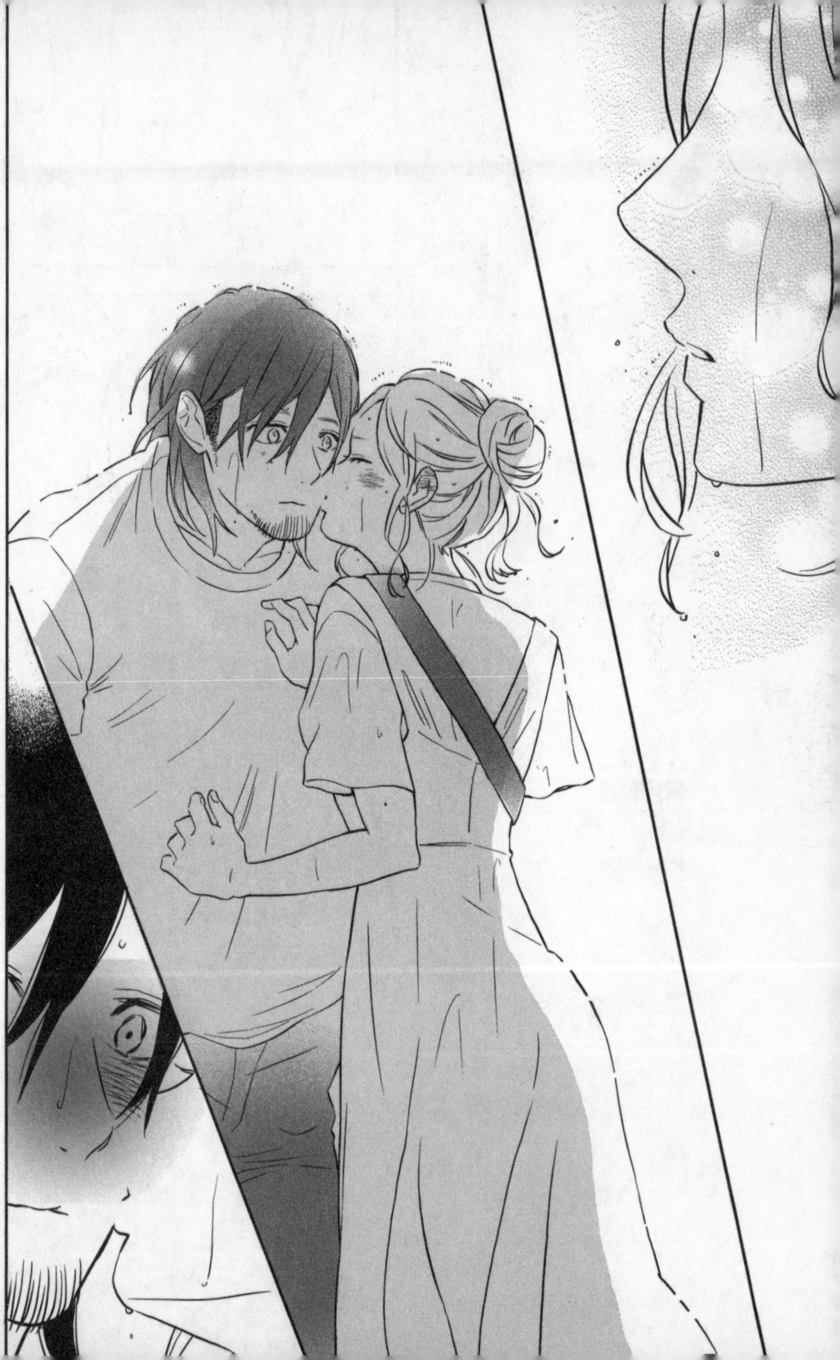

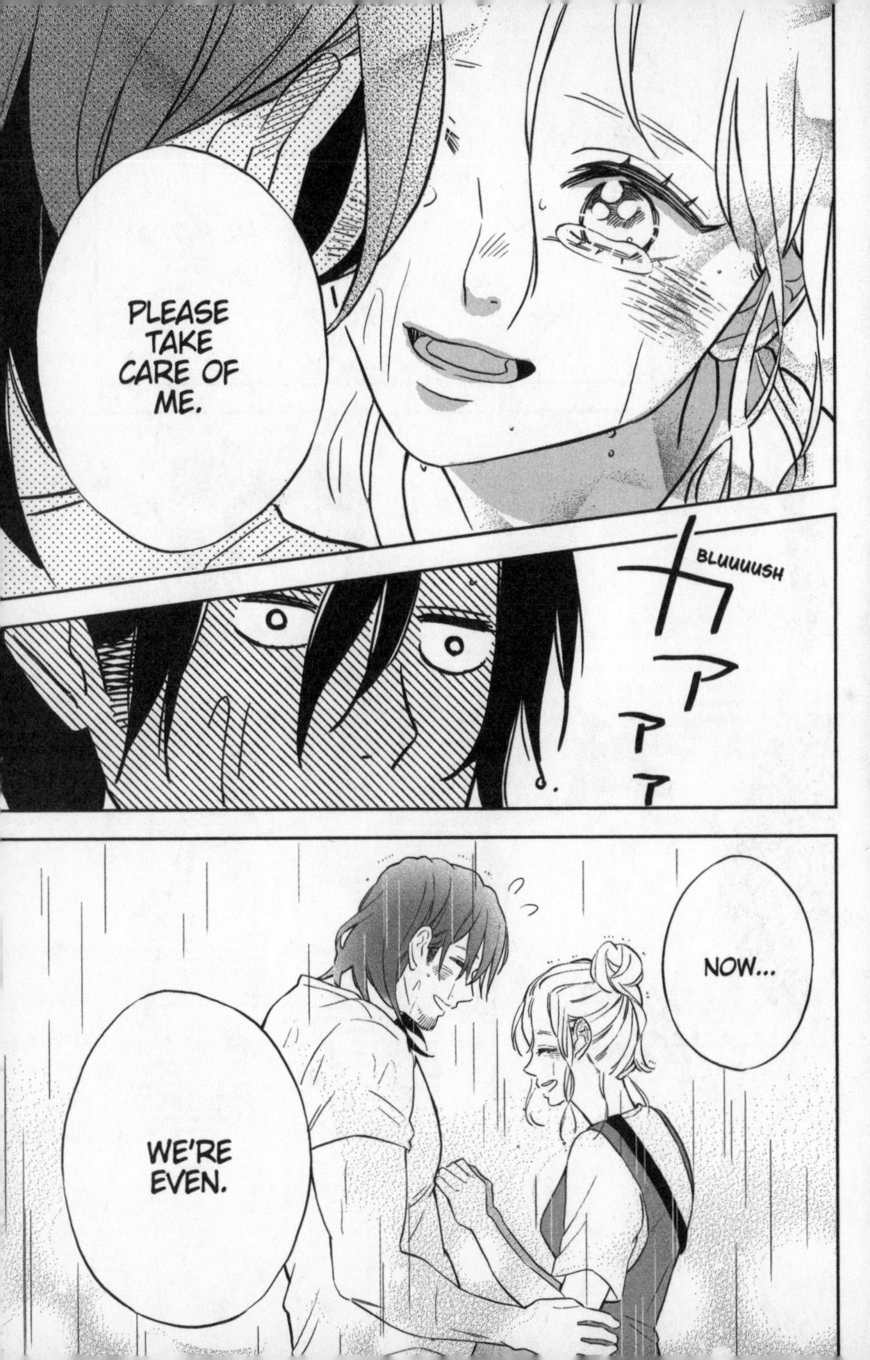
PLEASE TAKE CARE OF ME.
BLUUUUSH
カァァァ
NOW...
WE'RE EVEN.

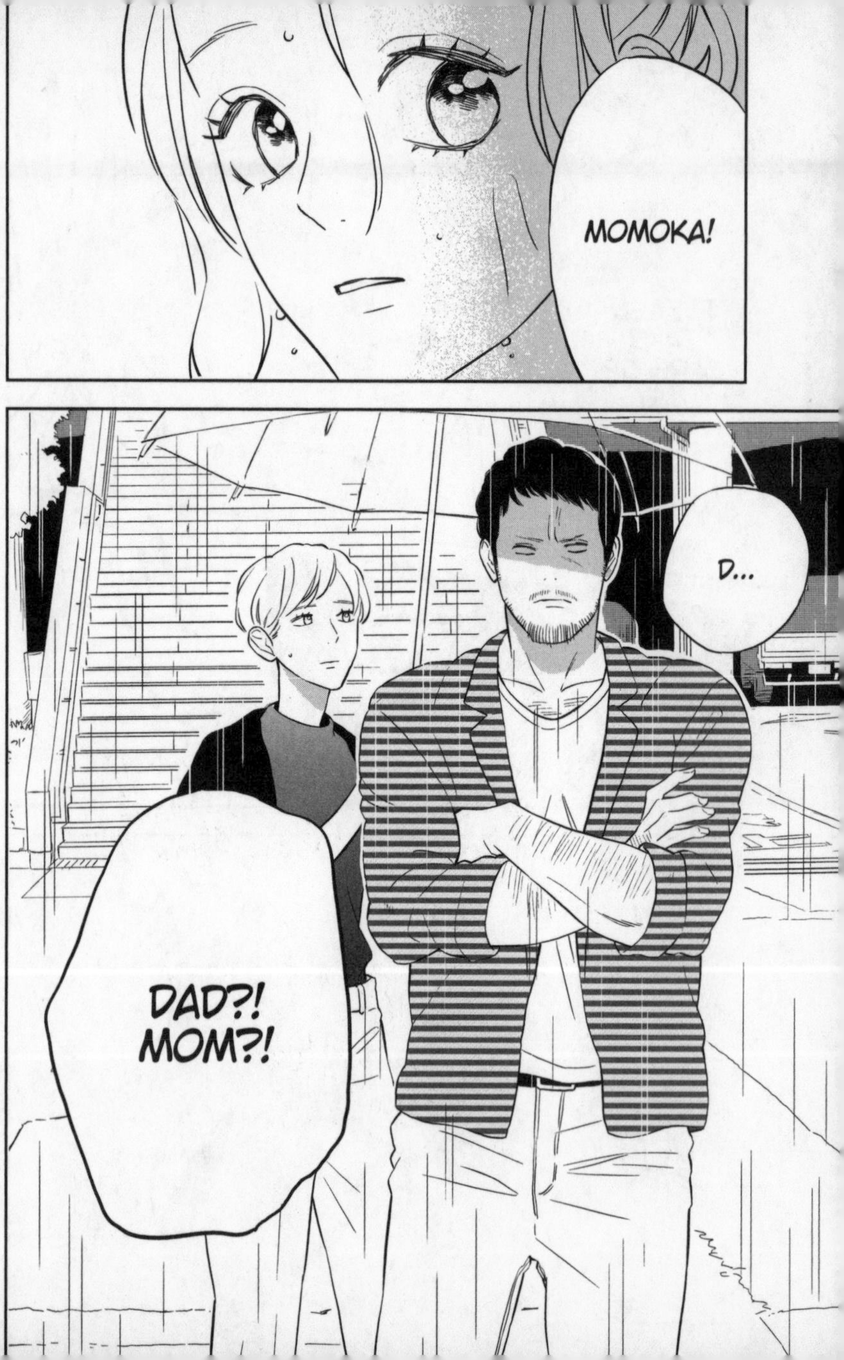
MOMOKA!
D...
DAD?! MOM?!

Cutie and the BEAST

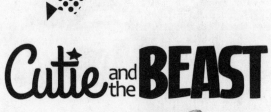

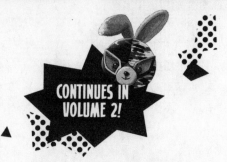

CONTINUES IN VOLUME 2!

GREETING

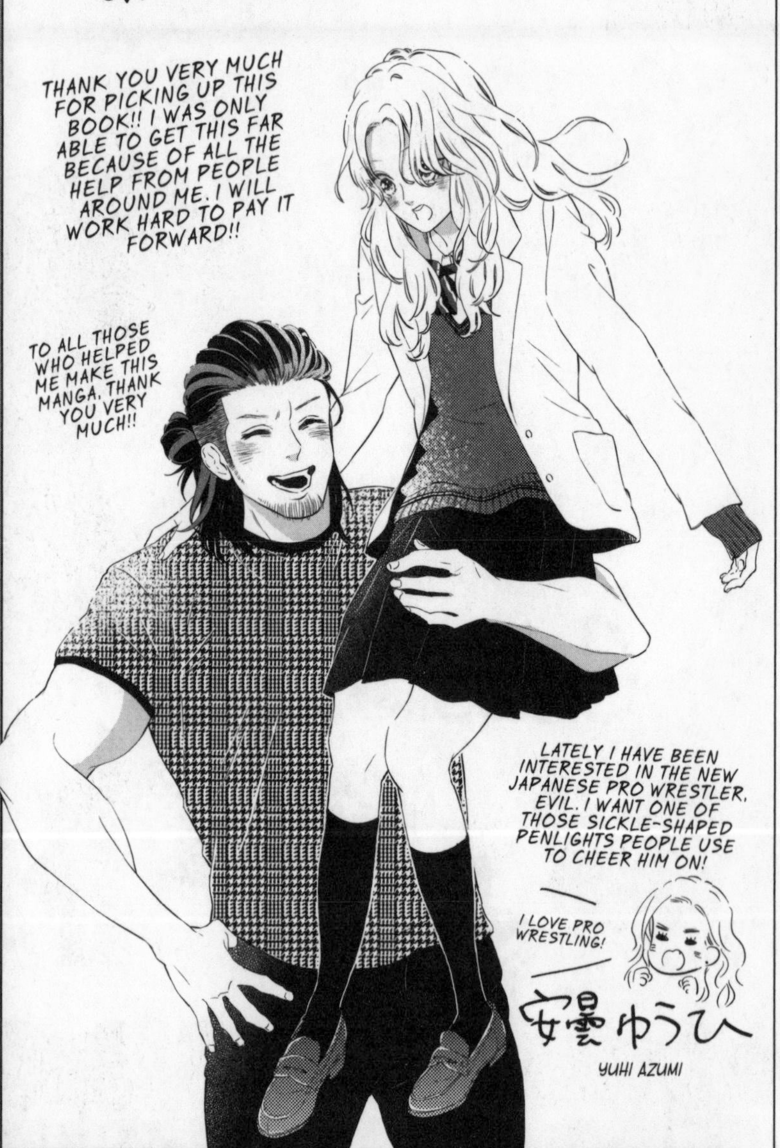
THANK YOU VERY MUCH FOR PICKING UP THIS BOOK!! I WAS ONLY ABLE TO GET THIS FAR BECAUSE OF ALL THE HELP FROM PEOPLE AROUND ME. I WILL WORK HARD TO PAY IT FORWARD!!
TO ALL THOSE WHO HELPED ME MAKE THIS MANGA, THANK YOU VERY MUCH!!
LATELY I HAVE BEEN INTERESTED IN THE NEW JAPANESE PRO WRESTLER, EVIL. I WANT ONE OF THOSE SICKLE-SHAPED PENLIGHTS PEOPLE USE TO CHEER HIM ON!
I LOVE PRO WRESTLING!
安曇ゆうひ
YUHI AZUMI

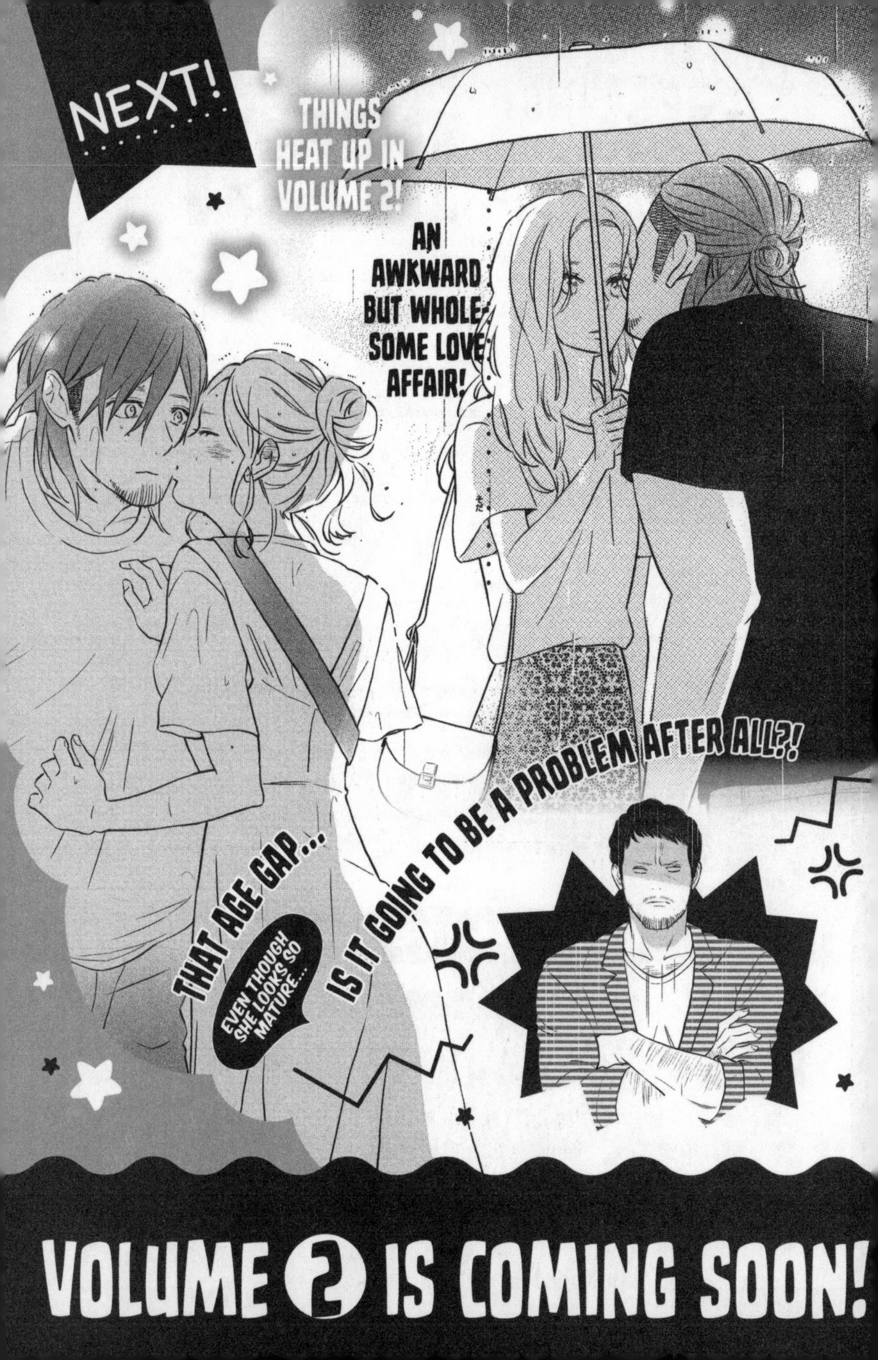
NEXT!
THINGS HEAT UP IN VOLUME 2!
AN AWKWARD BUT WHOLESOME LOVE AFFAIR!
THAT AGE GAP...
EVEN THOUGH SHE LOOKS SO MATURE...
IS IT GOING TO BE A PROBLEM AFTER ALL?!
VOLUME 2 IS COMING SOON!

SEVEN SEAS ENTERTAINMENT PRESENTS

Cutie and the BEAST

story and art by YUHI AZUMI

VOLUME 1

TRANSLATION
Angela Liu

ADAPTATION
Andrea Puckett

LETTERING AND RETOUCH
Erika Terriquez

COVER DESIGN
Nicky Lim
(LOGO) **George Panella**

PROOFREADER
Brett Hallahan

EDITOR
J.P. Sullivan

PREPRESS TECHNICIAN
Rhiannon Rasmussen-Silverstein

PRODUCTION MANAGER
Lissa Pattillo

MANAGING EDITOR
Julie Davis

ASSOCIATE PUBLISHER
Adam Arnold

PUBLISHER
Jason DeAngelis

PUJO TO YAJU VOL. 1
©2019 Yuhi Azumi. All rights reserved.
First published in Japan in 2019 by Kodansha Ltd., Tokyo.
Publication rights for this English edition arranged through Kodansha Ltd., Tokyo.

Seven Seas press and purchase enquiries can be sent to Marketing Manager Lianne Sentar at press@gomanga.com. Information regarding the distribution and purchase of digital editions is available from Digital Manager CK Russell at digital@gomanga.com.

Seven Seas and the Seven Seas logo are trademarks of Seven Seas Entertainment. All rights reserved.

ISBN: 978-1-64505-642-3

Printed in Canada

First Printing: October 2020

10 9 8 7 6 5 4 3 2 1

FOLLOW US ONLINE: *www.sevenseasentertainment.com*

READING DIRECTIONS

This book reads from ***right to left***, Japanese style. If this is your first time reading manga, you start reading from the top right panel on each page and take it from there. If you get lost, just follow the numbered diagram here. It may seem backwards at first, but you'll get the hang of it! Have fun!!

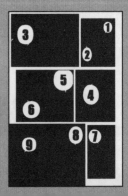